COLOR PLAY CROCHET

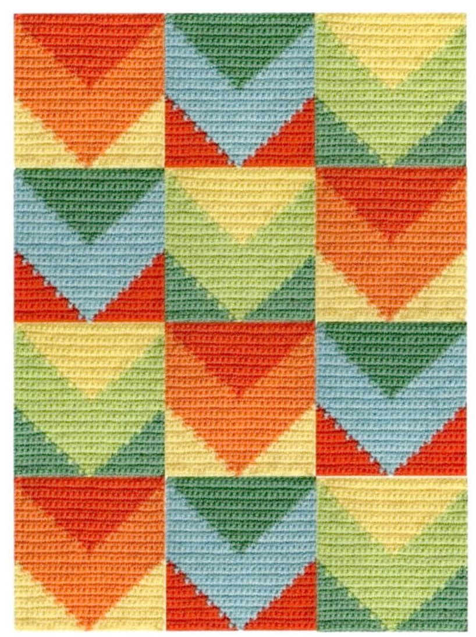

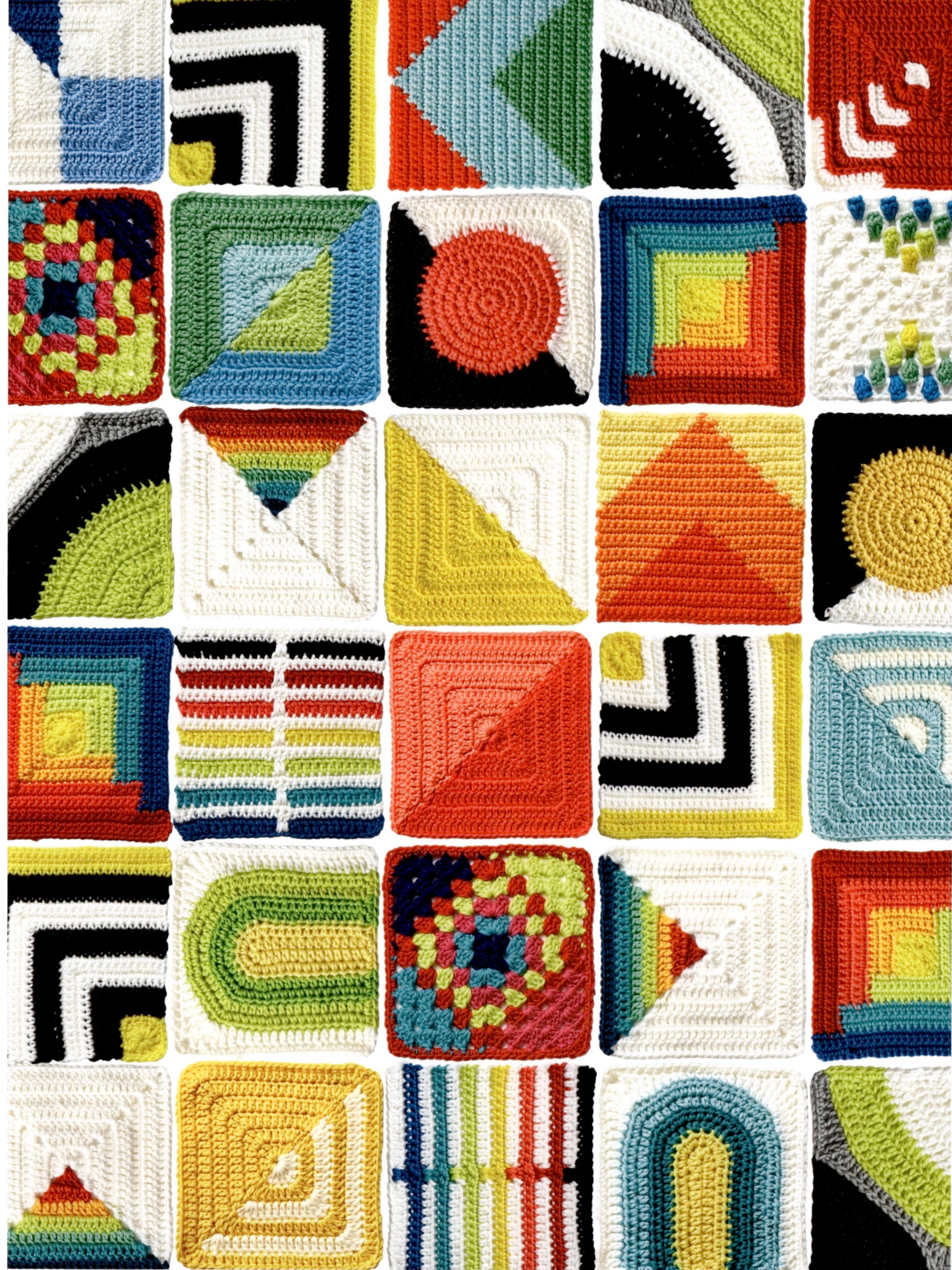

COLOR PLAY CROCHET

EXPLORING PATTERN, PALETTES & PLACEMENT WITH MIX-AND-MATCH GRANNY SQUARES & BLOCKS

Leonie Morgan

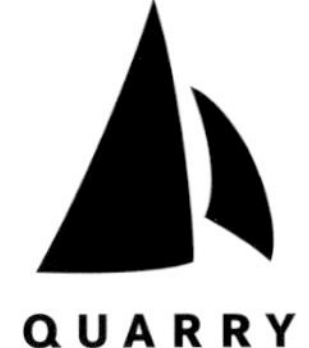

QUARRY

First published in 2026 by Quarry Books,
100 Cummings Center, Suite 265-D
Beverly, MA 01915, USA

EEA Representation, WTS Tax d.o.o.,
Žanova ulica 3, 4000 Kranj, Slovenia.
www.wts-tax.si

ISBN: 978-1-57715-716-8
Ebook ISBN: 978-1-57715-717-5

Conceived, edited, and designed by Quarto Publishing,
an imprint of The Quarto Group
1 Triptych Place
London SE1 9SH
www.quarto.com

QUAR.905438

Commissioning editor: Anna Galkina
Assistant editor: Ella Whiting
Copyeditor: Lindsay Kaubi
Tech editor: Nicole Hawkesford
Pattern checker: Sarah Hazell
Designer: Sally Bond
Art director: Martina Calvio
Illustrator: Kuo Kang Chen
Photography: Nicki Dowey
Production manager: David Hearn
Managing editor: Emma Harverson
Publisher: Lorraine Dickey

Printed in China

10 9 8 7 6 5 4 3 2 1

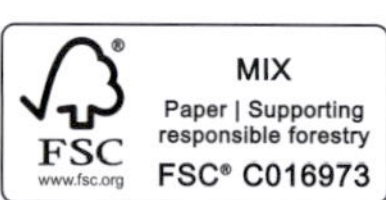

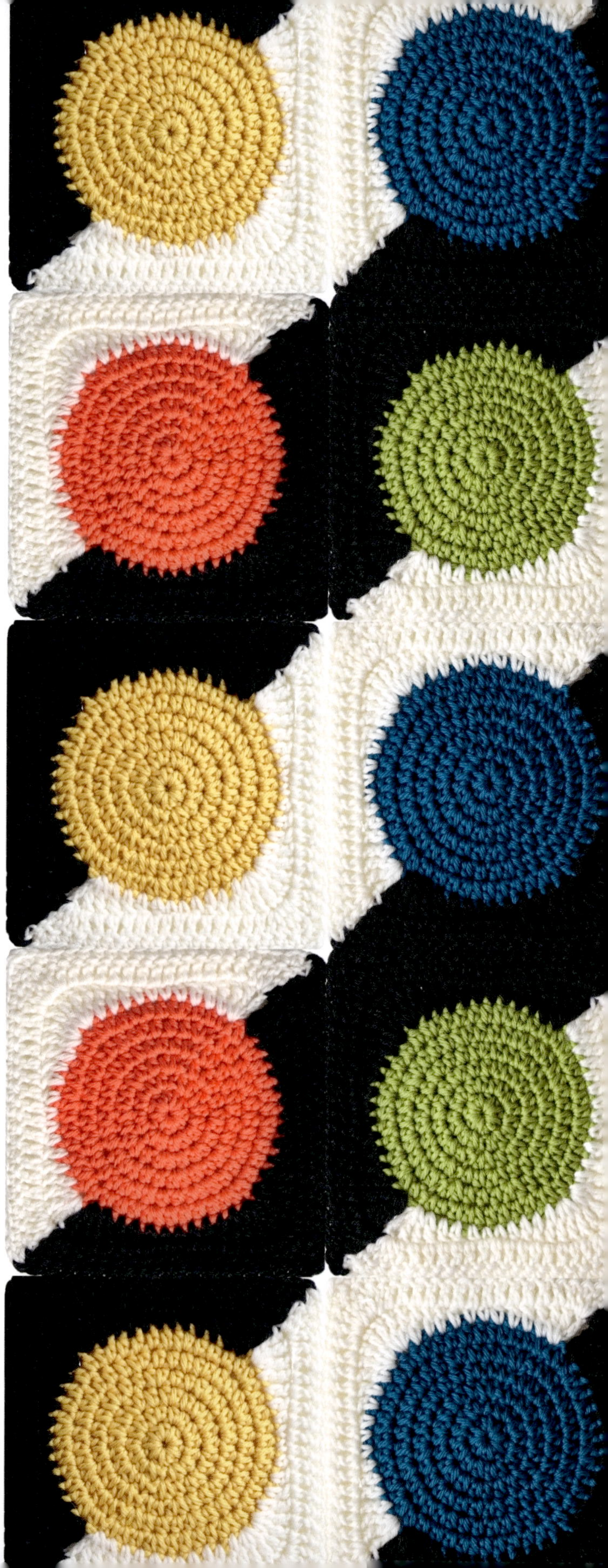

CONTENTS

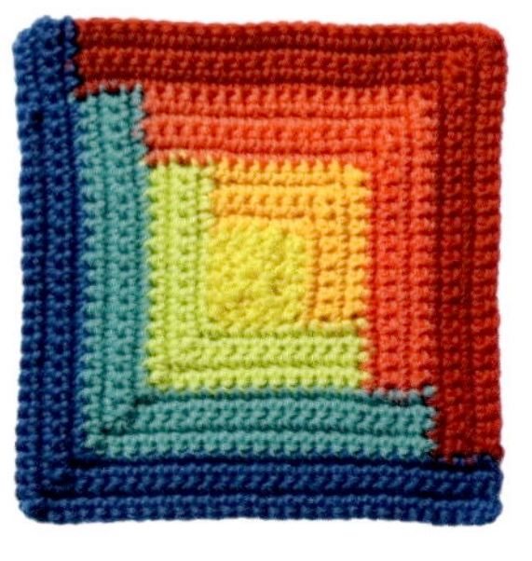
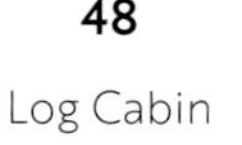

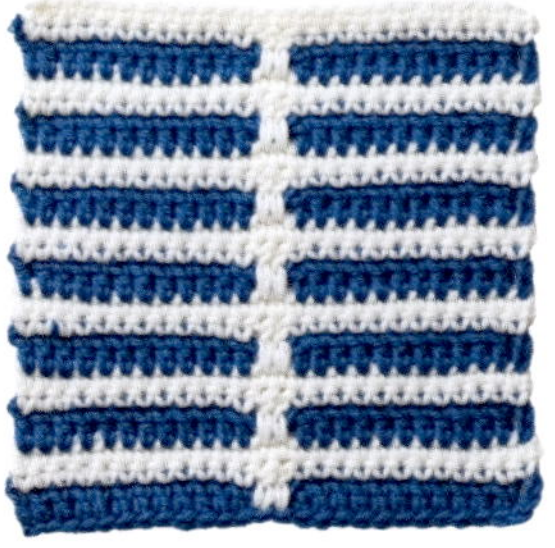

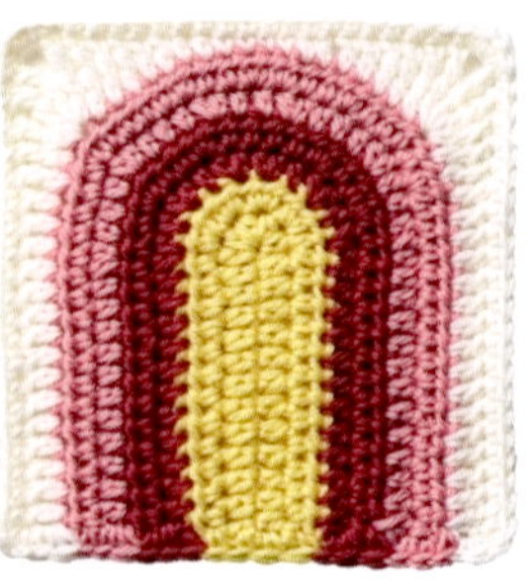

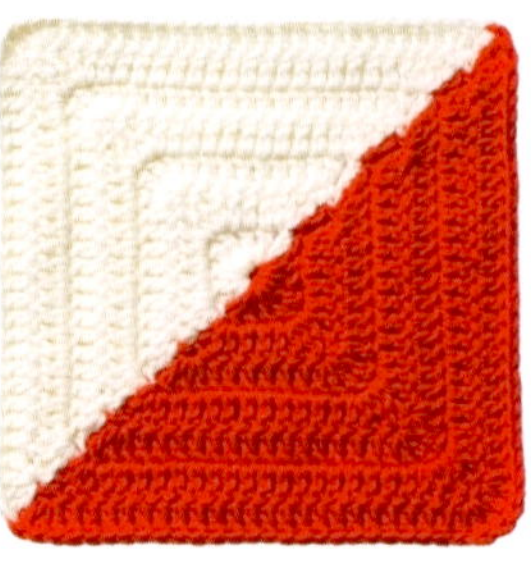

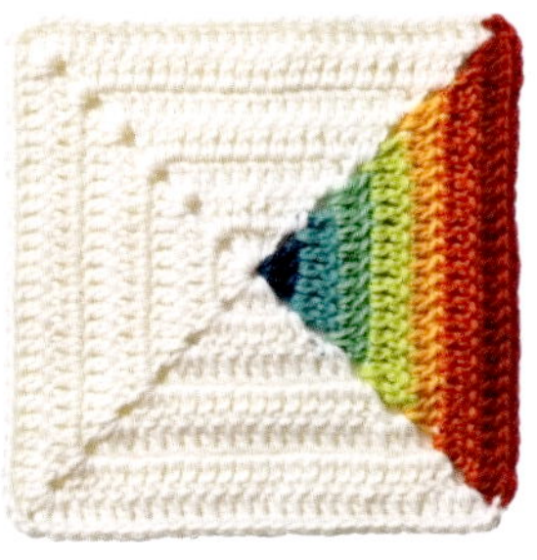

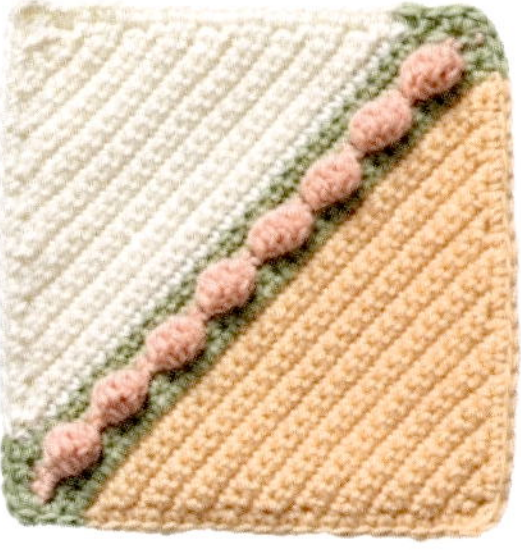

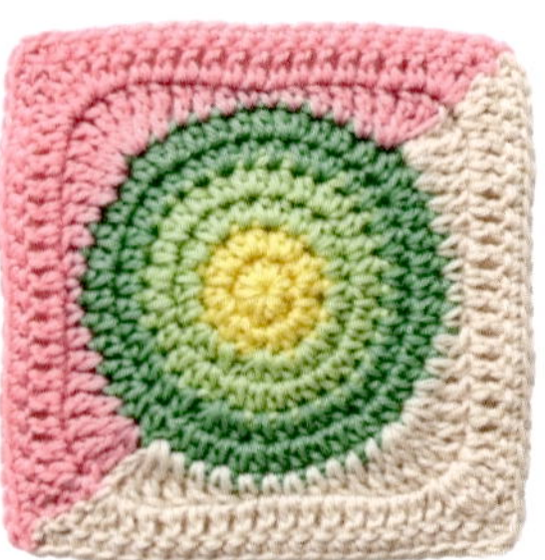

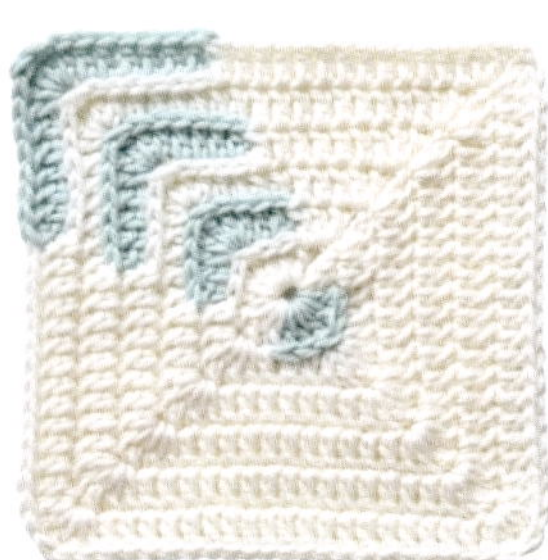

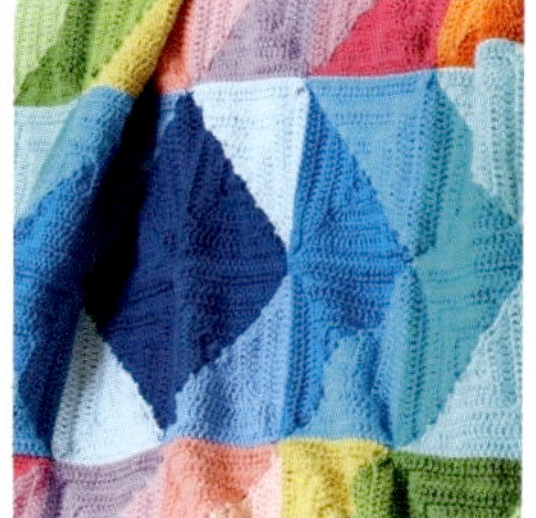

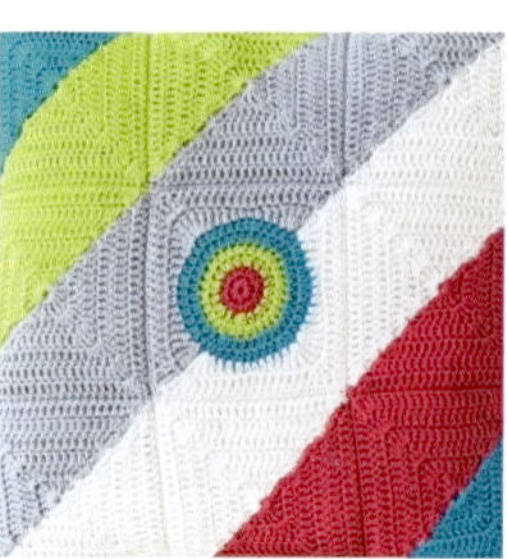

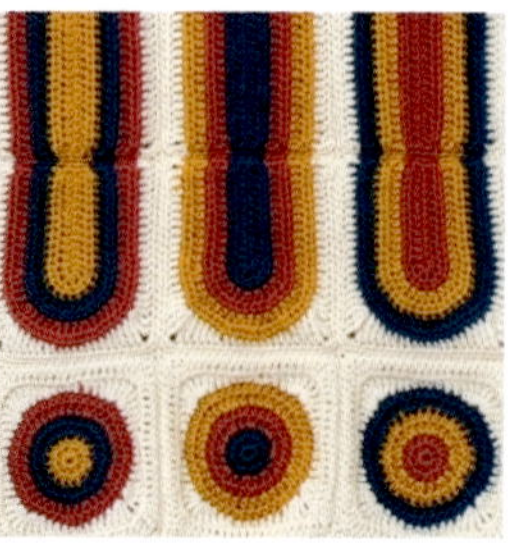

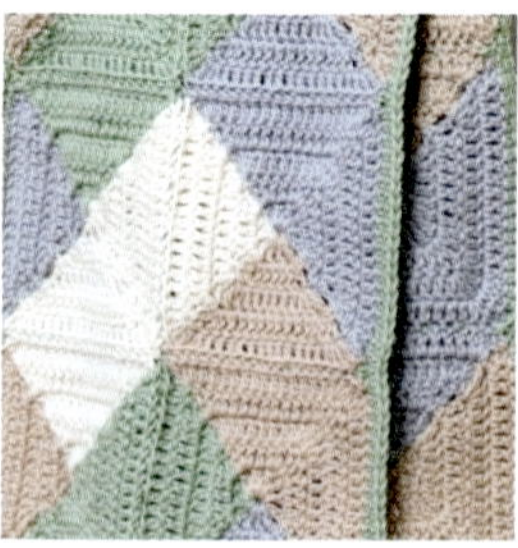

INTRODUCTION

My name is Leonie and I'm a crochet designer, knitter, cross-stitcher, photographer, and general crafty soul. I'm delighted to have been asked to write this book and hope it will inspire you to grab your hook and experiment with colors to your heart's content! There are so many options when it comes to color palettes and layouts, and I hope your own ideas and creativity will be sparked by what you read here.

This book begins with a general techniques section that will help you understand the basics of crochet, including pages dedicated specifically to color theory and how to translate that to crochet. As you move into the granny square blocks and projects that make up the heart of the book, the theories you've learned are explored in more detail. You'll also find lots of designs, layout ideas, and orientations to try. Many of the blocks would work well mixed together, so you'll be able to create unique layouts. I have worked each block in more than one colorway, to show you how a variation in colorway can change the whole look of a crochet piece. Use these examples to guide you in creating your own layouts.

When picking a colorway, I tend to begin with a favorite color or color pairing and gradually add more to it. Color preference is very personal, so I recommend you start with your favorite color and, using the color theory section as a guide, begin to add colors, trying to include light and dark shades for added contrast, until you have a colorway you love. There are four projects at the end of the book that you can make as described, or you could adapt them using your own palette. You could even switch up the blocks used in the projects to make your own unique projects.

With so many beautiful options to choose from, there is plenty of inspiration here to help you gain confidence in picking your own color palettes for crochet projects.

Happy hooking!

Leonie

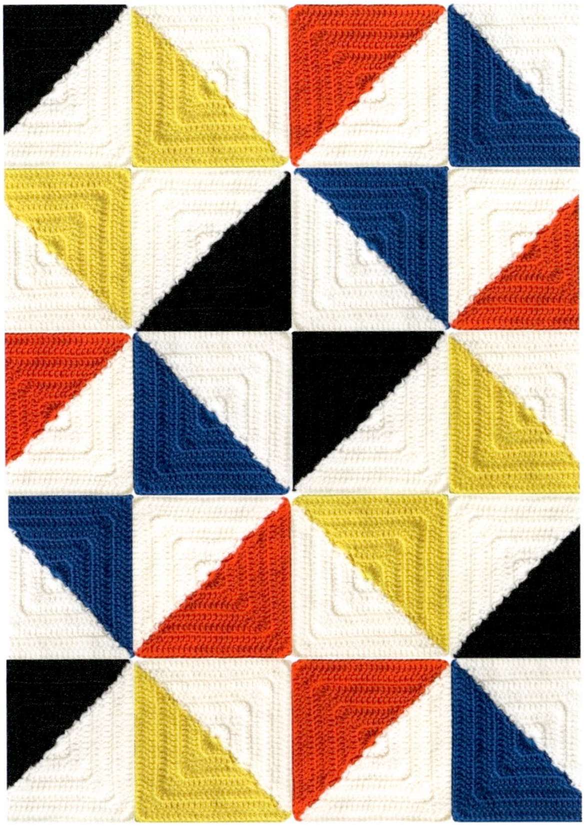

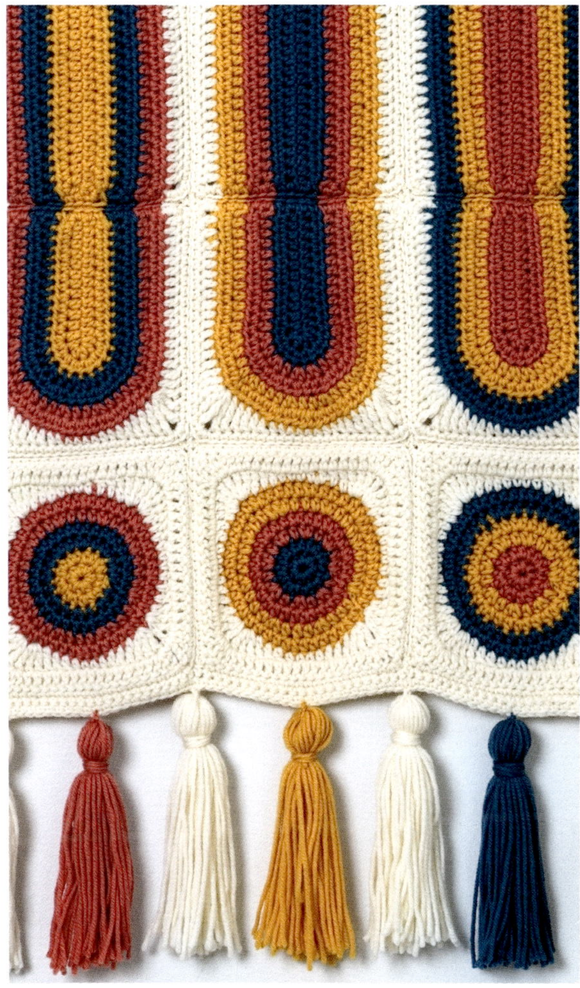

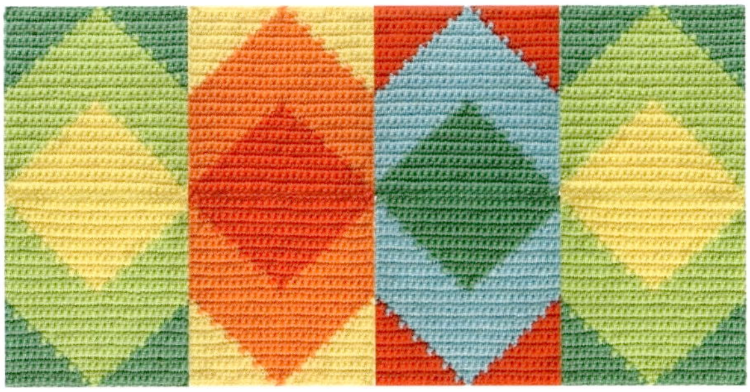

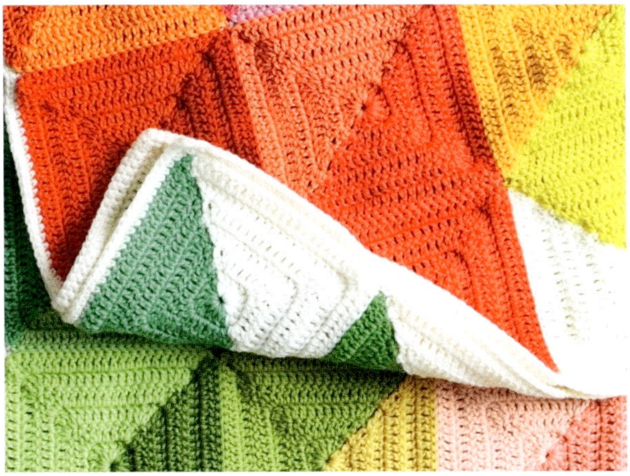

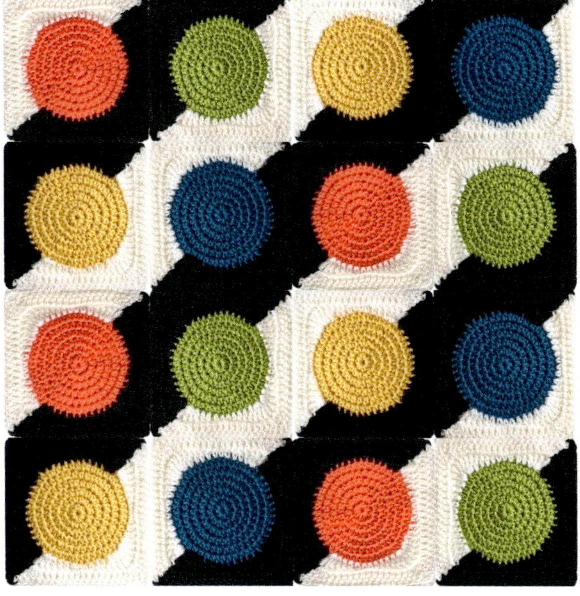

ABOUT THIS BOOK

This book is a colorful resource of 20 crochet granny square blocks that you can mix and match to create a wonderful array of layouts and designs. You can use the blocks to make anything from afghans to wall hangings; see pages 112–125 for four inspirational projects that will help you develop your ideas. Turn to the next section for information on materials and crochet techniques to help you get started.

The Blocks

Pages 30–111

At the heart of this book are the block designs. With written patterns, stitch diagrams, and photographs taking you through each design, you will want to start crocheting right away.

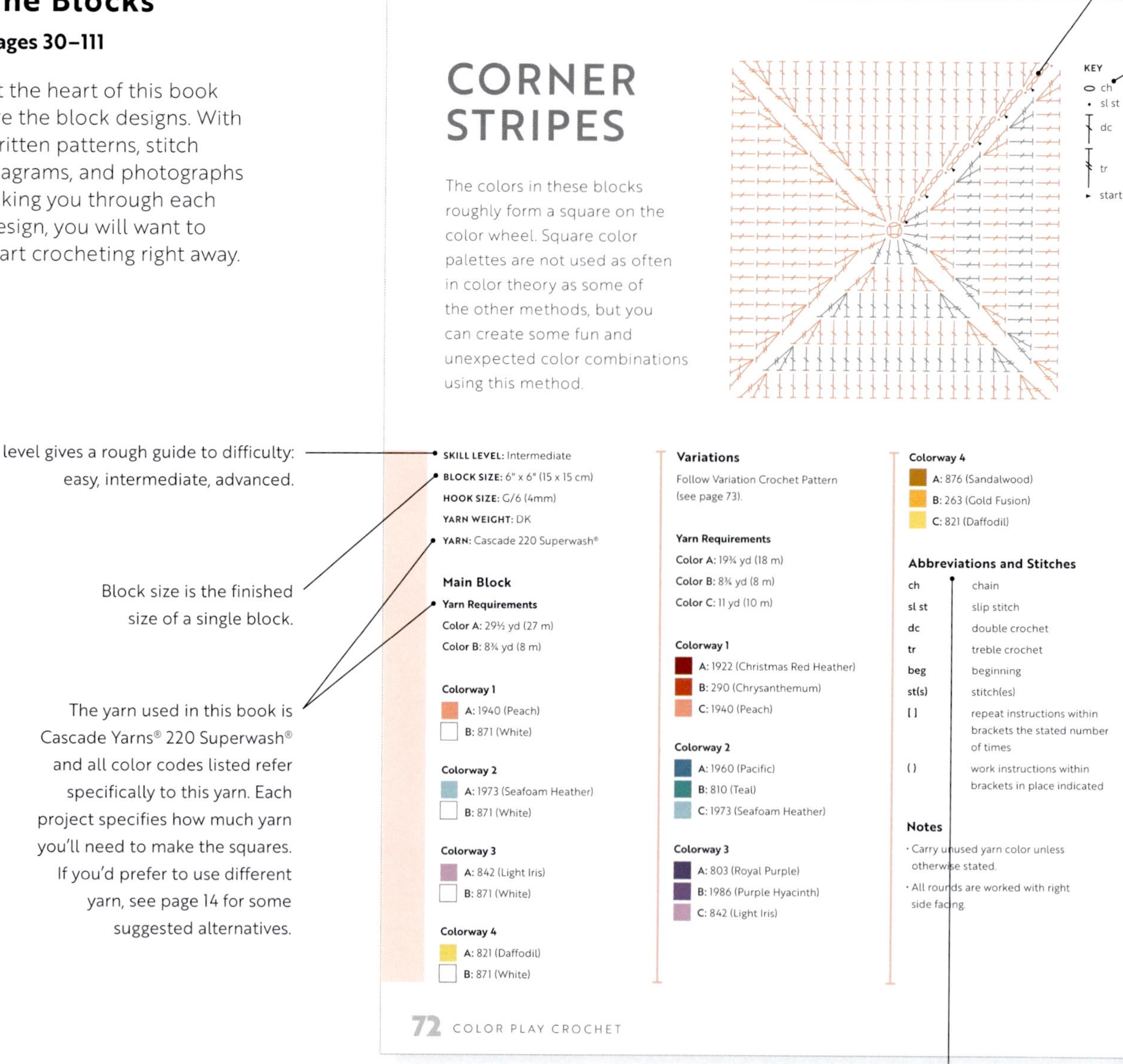

Each pattern includes a stitch diagram, with alternating colors indicating yarn color changes.

A key to the symbols used in the stitch diagram is provided for each block.

Main Block Crochet Pattern

Foundation Ring: Using A, ch 4, join with sl st to first ch made to form a ring.
Rnd 1: Ch 4 (counts as tr throughout), 2 dc, 2 tr, 2 dc, tr changing to B, tr, 2 dc, 2 tr, 2 dc, tr changing to A, join with sl st to top of beg ch-4, fasten off B—16 sts.
Rnd 2: Ch 4, 2 dc in same place, [dc in 2 sts, (2 dc, tr) in next st, (tr, 2 dc) in next st] three times, dc in next 2 sts, (2 dc, tr) in next st, join with sl st to top of beg ch-4—32 sts.
Rnd 3: Ch 4, 2 dc in same place, dc in next 6 sts, (2 dc, tr) in next st, (tr, 2 dc) in next st, dc in next 6 sts, (2 dc, tr) in next st changing to B, (tr, 2 dc) in next st, dc in next 6 sts, (2 dc, tr) in next st, (tr, 2 dc) in next st, dc in next 6 sts, (2 dc, tr) in next st changing to A, join with sl st to top of beg ch-4, fasten off B—48 sts.
Rnd 4: Ch 4, 2 dc in same place, [dc in next 10 sts, (2 dc, tr) in next st, (tr, 2 dc) in next st] three times, dc in next 10 sts, (2 dc, tr) in next st, join with sl st to top of beg ch-4—64 sts.
Rnd 5: Ch 4, 2 dc in same place, dc in next 14 sts, (2 dc, tr) in next st, (tr, 2 dc) in next st, dc in next 14 sts, (2 dc, tr) in next st changing to B, (tr, 2 dc) in next st, dc in next 14 sts, (2 dc, tr) in next st, (tr, 2 dc) in next st, dc in next 14 sts, (2 dc, tr) in next st changing to A, join with sl st to top of beg ch-4, fasten off B—80 sts.
Rnd 6: Ch 4, 2 dc in same place, [dc in next 18 sts, (2 dc, tr) in next st, (tr, 2 dc) in next st] three times, dc in next 18 sts, (2 dc, tr) in next st, join with sl st to top of beg ch-4, fasten off A—96 sts.

Weave in all ends and block to measure 6" x 6" (15 x 15 cm).

A written pattern takes you through the block round by round or row by row.

Variation Crochet Pattern

Work as for the main block making the following changes:
Rnd 2: Ch 4, 2 dc in same place, dc in next 2 sts, (2 dc, tr) in next st, (tr, 2 dc) in next st, dc in next 2 sts, (2 dc, tr) in next st changing to C, (tr, 2 dc) in next st, dc in next 2 sts, (2 dc, tr) in next st, (tr, 2 dc) in next st, dc in next 2 sts, (2 dc, tr) in next st changing to A, join with sl st to top of beg ch-4, fasten off C—32 sts.
Rnd 4: Ch 4, 2 dc in same place, dc in next 10 sts, (2 dc, tr) in next st, (tr, 2 dc) in next st, dc in next 10 sts, (2 dc, tr) in next st changing to C, (tr, 2 dc) in next st, dc in next 10 sts, (2 dc, tr) in next st, (tr, 2 dc) in next st, dc in next 10 sts, (2 dc, tr) in next st changing to A, join with sl st to top of beg ch-4, fasten off C—64 sts.
Rnd 6: Ch 4, 2 dc in same place, dc in next 18 sts, (2 dc, tr) in next st, (tr, 2 dc) in next st, dc in next 18 sts, (2 dc, tr) in next st changing to C, (tr, 2 dc) in next st, dc in next 18 sts, (2 dc, tr) in next st, (tr, 2 dc) in next st, dc in next 18 sts, (2 dc, tr) in next st changing to A, join with sl st to top of beg ch-4, fasten off C—96 sts. Fasten off A.

Weave in all ends and block to measure 6" x 6" (15 x 15 cm).

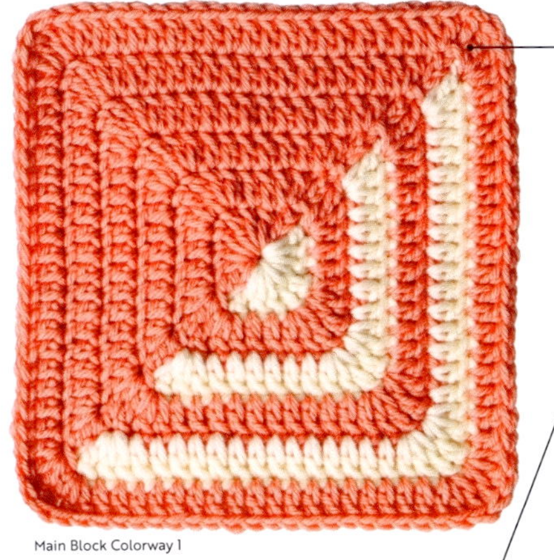

Main Block Colorway 1

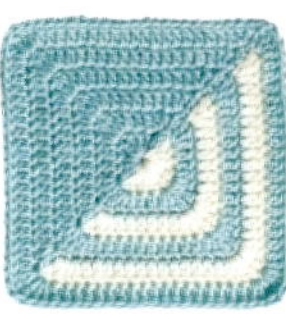

Main Block Colorway 2

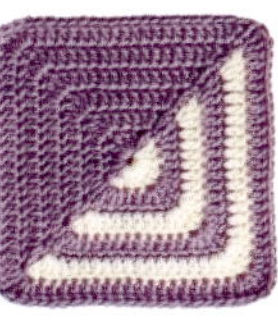

Main Block Colorway 3

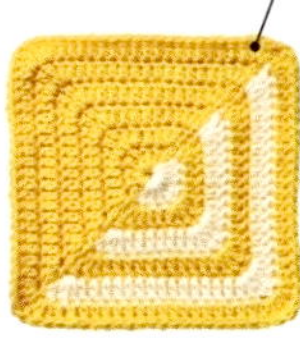

Main Block Colorway 4

CORNER STRIPES 73

Photographs of the finished block in multiple colorways will help you choose which to make at a glance.

THE PROJECTS
Pages 112–125

Once you're happy with your block collection, flip to these pages for inspiration on how to turn them into beautiful projects.

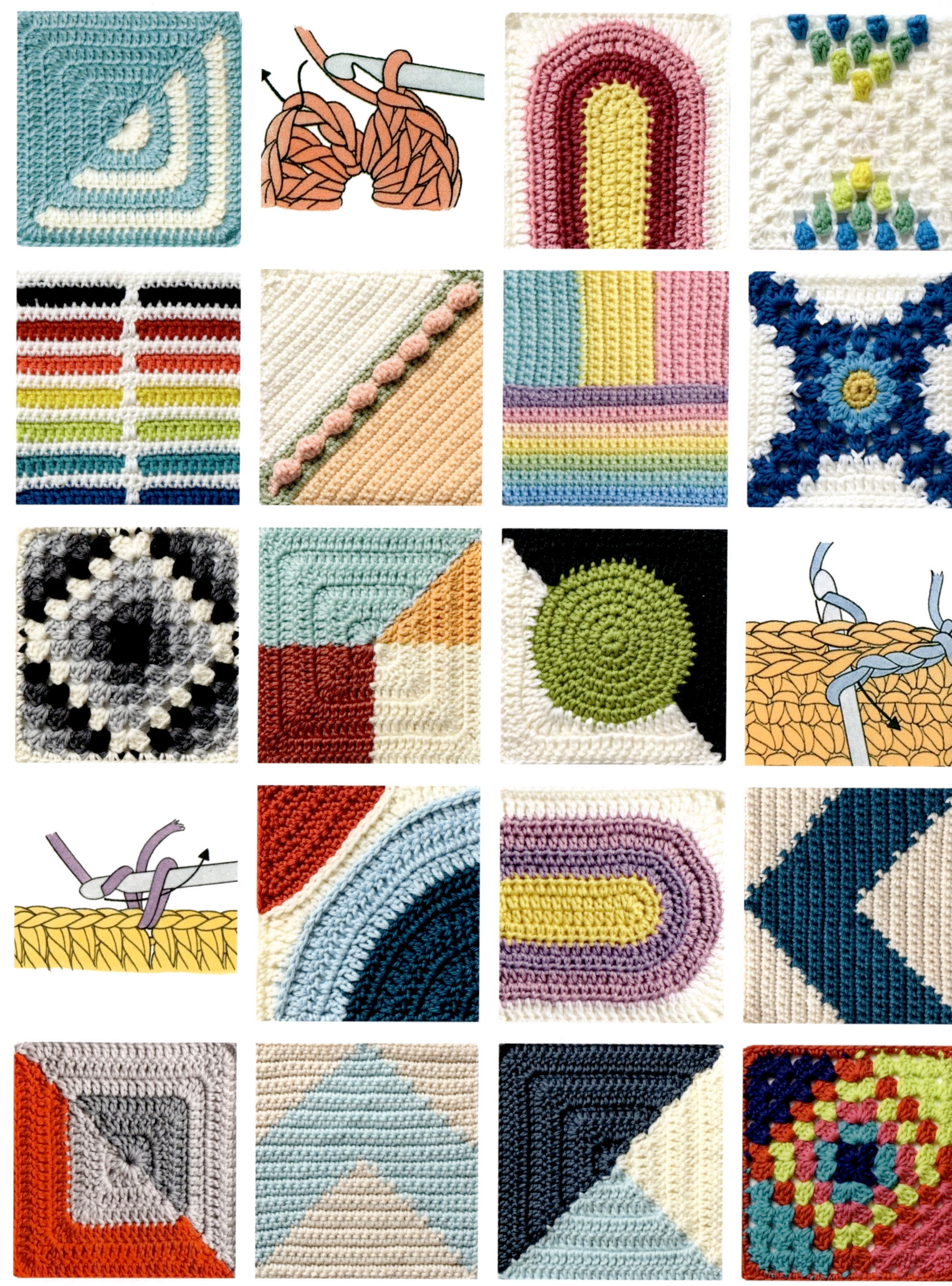

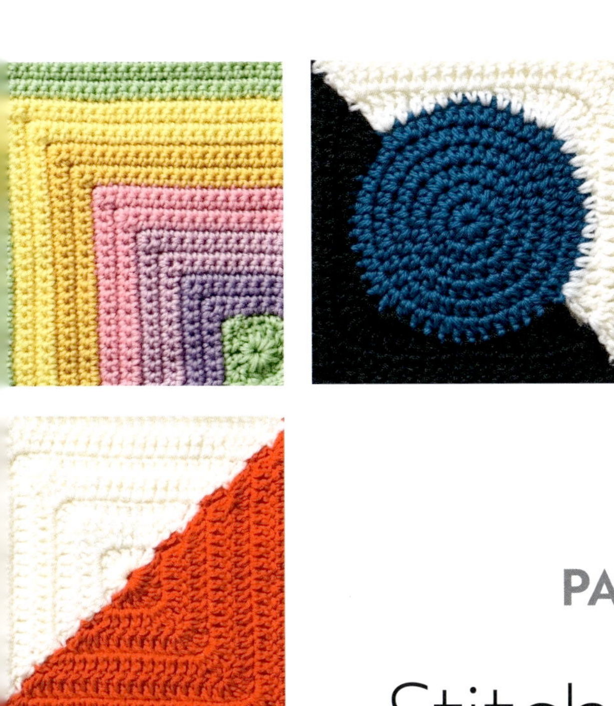
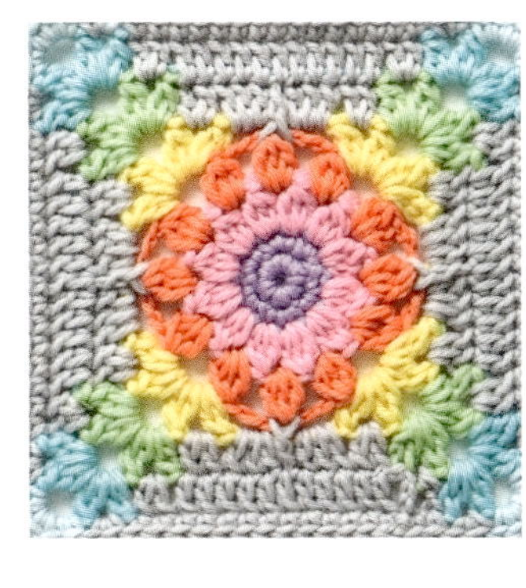
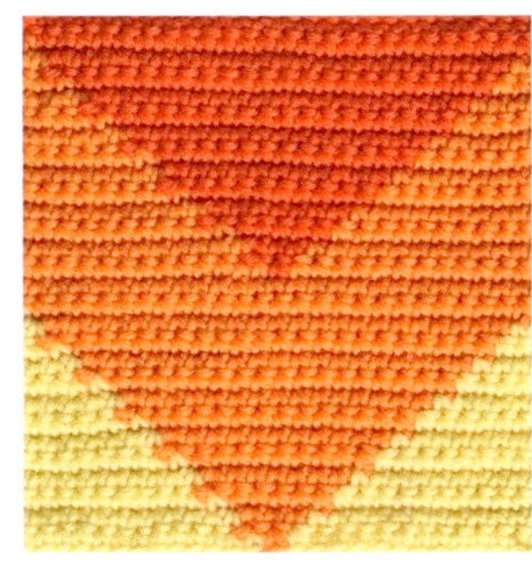
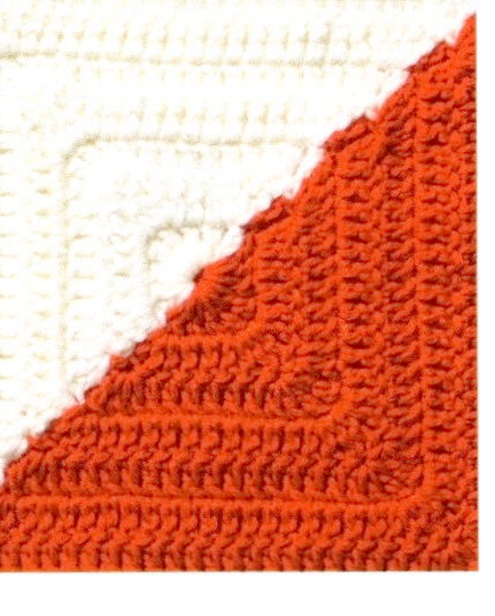

PART 1

Stitches and Techniques

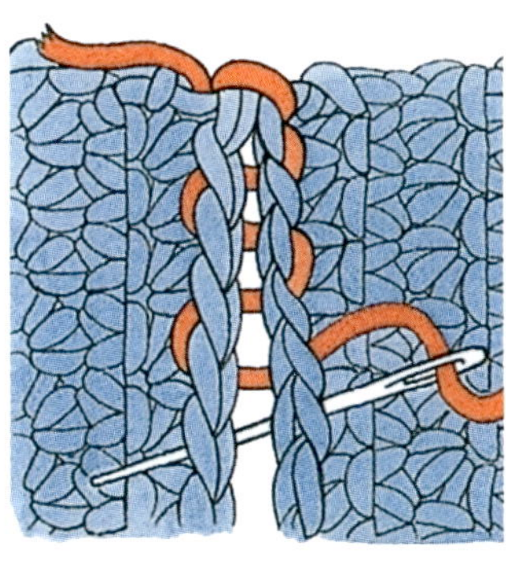
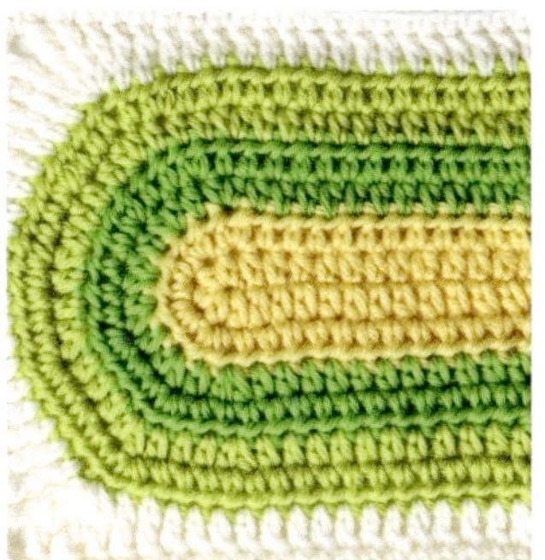
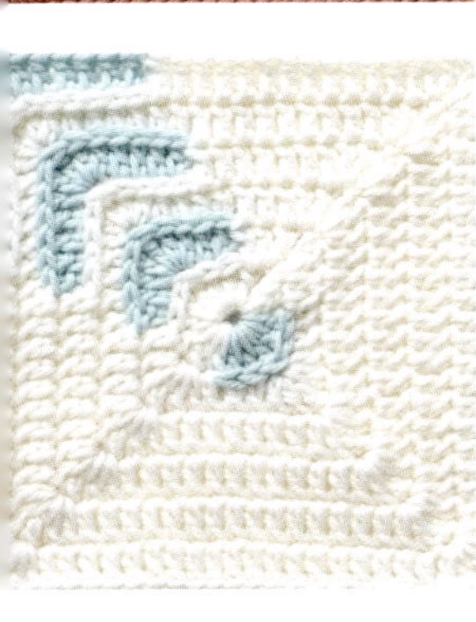
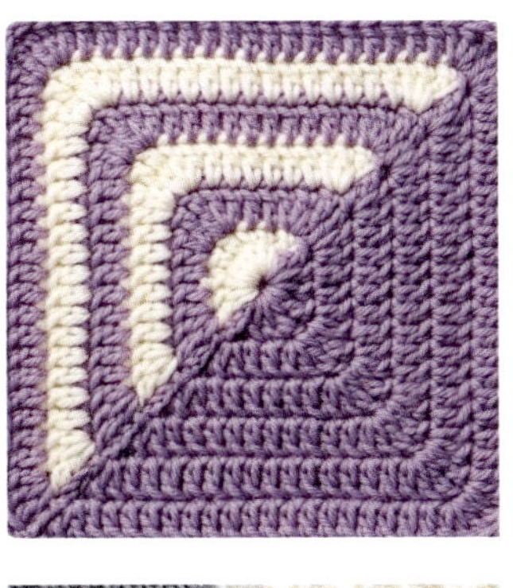
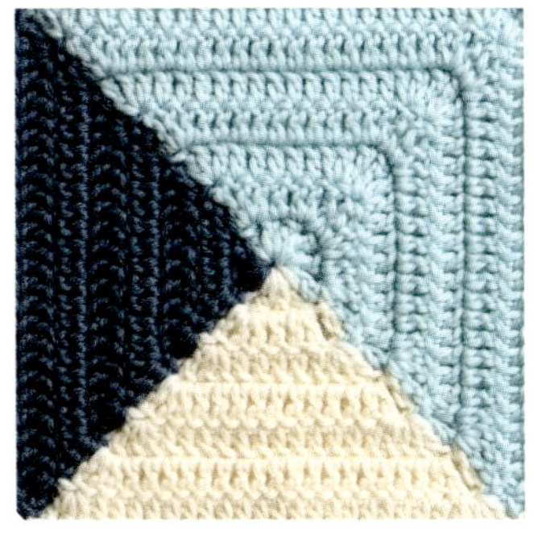
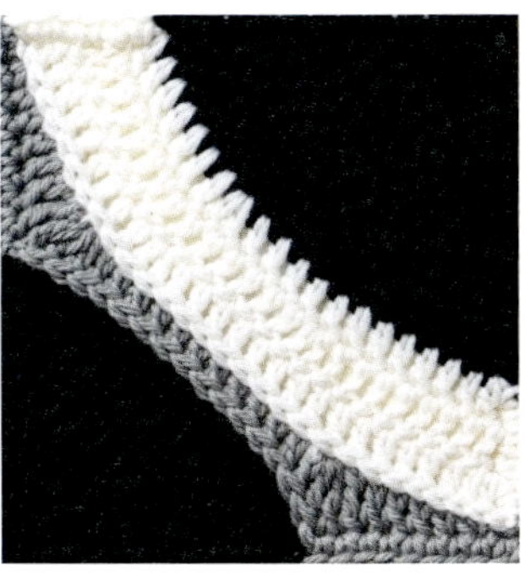
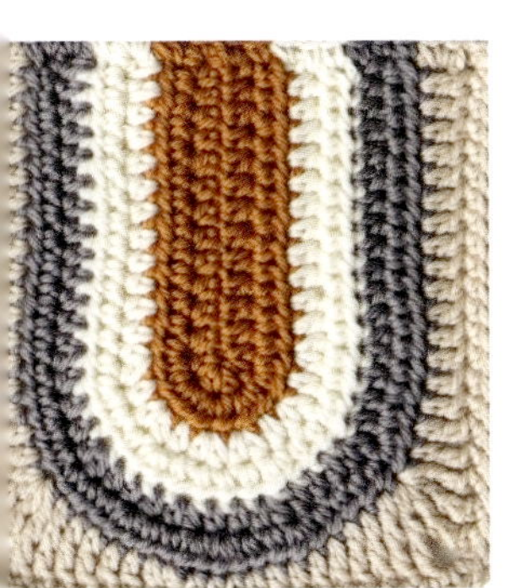
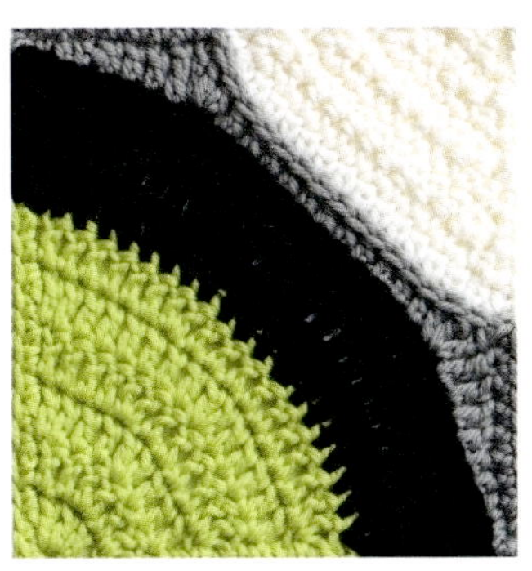
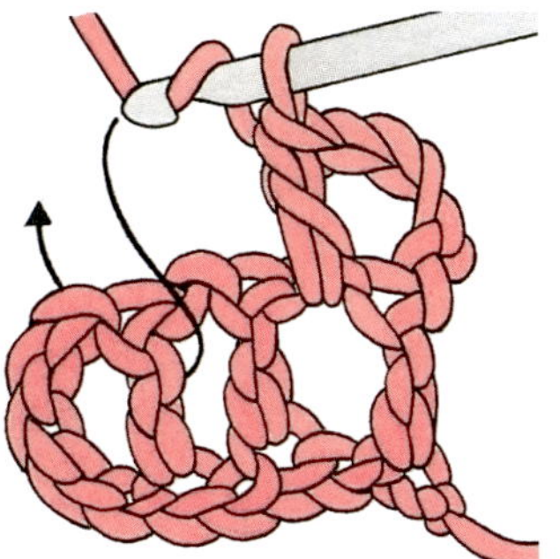
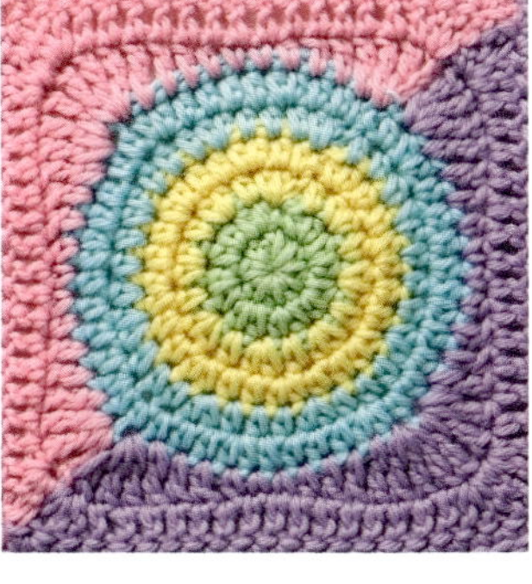

YARNS, HOOKS, AND NOTIONS

When you walk into a yarn store, you'll find yourself bombarded with gorgeous yarns in scrumptious colors, differing weights, and all types of textures. The choice is exciting but can be a little perplexing, and the same is true for hooks and notions. Use this guide to find out what you'll need to get started.

Yarn Choice

Suitable yarns for crochet range from very fine cotton to bulky wool. As a rule, yarns that have a smooth texture and a medium or high twist are the easiest to work with. For making blocks, a medium-weight yarn is best, as it works up quickly and has good drape and stitch definition.

For all the patterns in this book I chose to crochet with Cascade Yarns® 220 Superwash® yarn because it is available in a huge variety of colors, is easy to work with, and is machine washable.

The block sizes can vary if a different yarn weight or brand is used, so before you purchase enough yarn to complete a project, it's a good idea to buy just one ball, make a test swatch or block, wash it following the instructions on the ball band, pin to measurements, and allow to dry. Think about whether you are comfortable using the yarn and if it turned out how you intended.

Yarn comes in a range of different fibers and combinations.

Wool

Wool is an excellent choice for blocks. It is a resilient fiber that feels good to crochet with and has great stitch definition. Be sure to check whether the wool can be machine washed. Home decor items like blankets and throw pillows see a lot of wear. You'll want to be sure you can wash them without shrinking them. Otherwise, plan to handwash anything made with non-superwash wool.

Acrylic

Acrylic yarn is an affordable choice for beginners and popular with crochet enthusiasts. It's great for practicing stitches and techniques and testing color combinations. It has the benefit of being machine washable, making it a good choice for items that may require frequent washing. Also, acrylic is a great option for people with wool allergies, or who don't wish to use animal-based products.

Wool/Synthetic Blends

A yarn comprised of both wool and synthetic fiber is a dependable choice. Picking a yarn which contains a small percentage of synthetic fiber, such as nylon or acrylic, retains the advantages of wool and can add benefits like easier care and greater longevity.

Cotton and Cotton Blends

Cotton can present a challenge for beginners since it can be a little stiff to work with, but the stitches are crisp and neat. A cotton blend, such as cotton combined with wool, is usually softer to work with, yet still retains crisp, neat stitch definition.

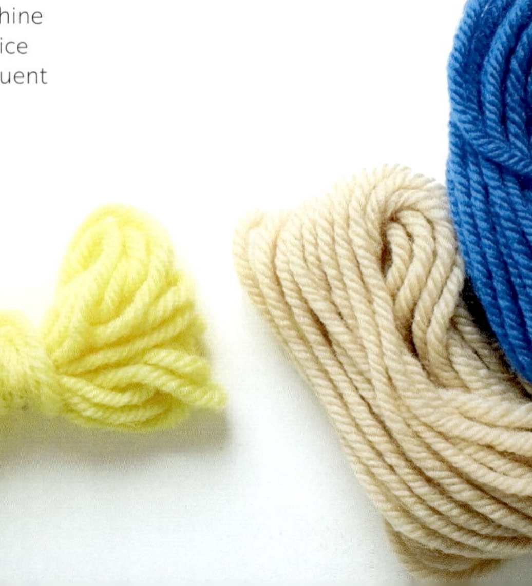

Crochet Hooks

Hooks come in different sizes and materials. The material a hook is made from can affect your gauge. To start out, it's best to use aluminum hooks, as they have a pointed head and well-defined throat and work well with most yarns. Bamboo hooks are also pleasing to work with but can be slippery with some yarns. Plastic hooks can be squeaky with synthetic yarns.

You can also purchase hooks with softgrip or wooden handles, which are more ergonomic to work with, particularly if crochet becomes an obsession.

What Size Hook?

You may find that using the hook size recommended for a particular yarn or pattern isn't right for you, and your work may be too tight or too loose. Try different hook sizes until you are happy with the completed block. Ultimately, you want to use a hook and yarn weight that you are comfortable with—yarn/hook recommendations are not set in stone. Be aware that not all yarn labels give a recommended hook size. Use the recommended knitting needle size as a guide, or a hook one or two sizes bigger.

Notions

Although all you need to get started is a hook and some yarn, it's handy to have the following items in your bag.

Scissors

Use a pair of small, sharp embroidery scissors.

Ruler and Measuring Tape

A rigid ruler is best for measuring gauge. A sturdy measuring tape is a useful tool for taking larger measurements.

Stitch Markers

Split-ring and locking stitch markers are handy for keeping track of the first stitch of a row or round, particularly when starting out. You can also use them to hold the working loop when you put your work down, or pop one on the wrong side of your work so you can tell at a glance which side is which.

Pins

Use rustproof, glass-headed pins for blocking.

Yarn Needles

Yarn or tapestry needles are used for sewing seams and weaving in yarn ends. Choose needles with blunt ends to avoid splitting stitches. Yarn needles have different-sized eyes, so choose one that will accommodate the weight of yarn you are using.

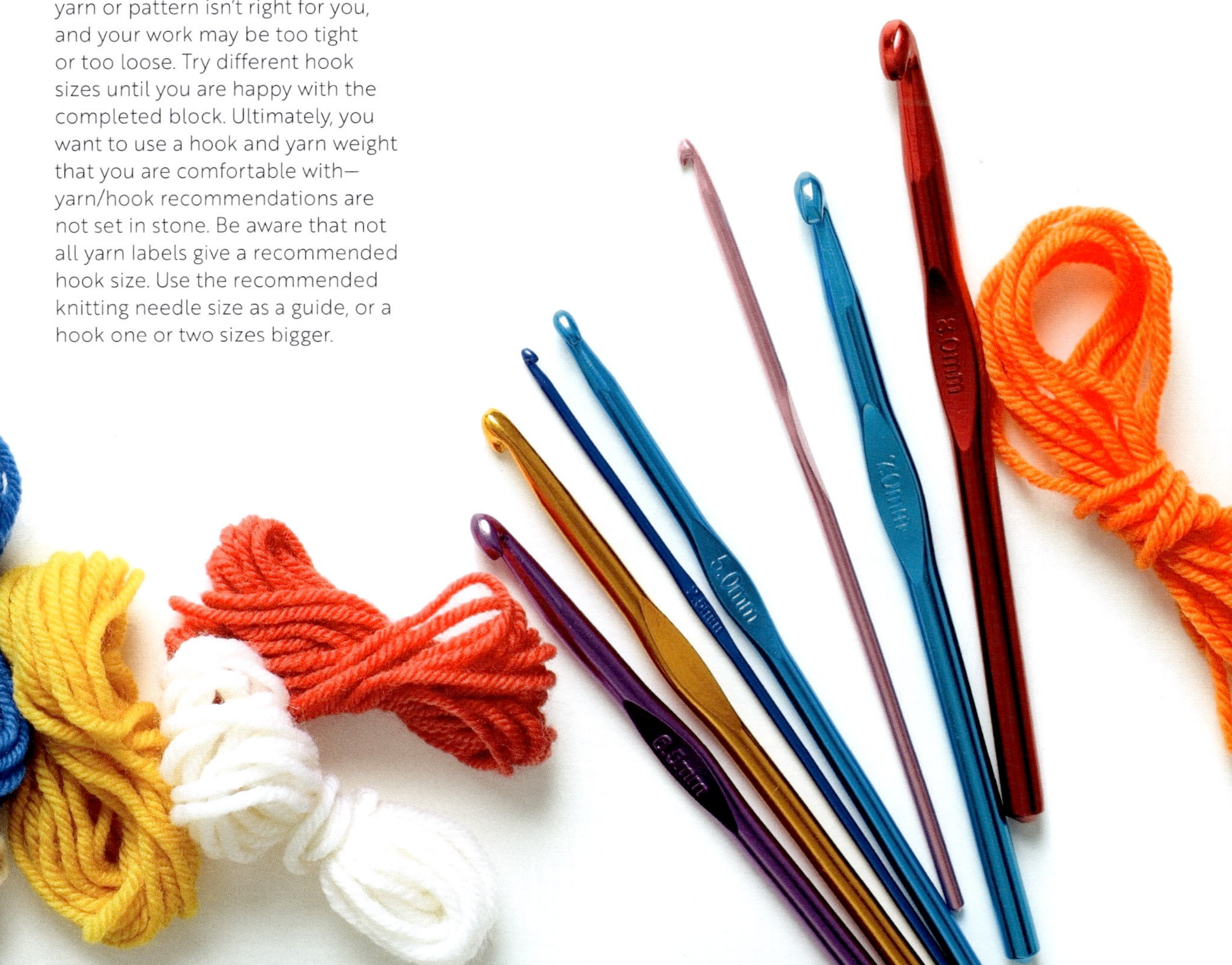

STARTING AND FINISHING

Crochet can be worked in rows, beginning with a foundation chain, or in rounds, working outward from a foundation ring of chain stitches. See page 18 for a reminder of how to work the basic crochet stitches.

1. Holding the Hook and Yarn

There are two common ways to hold the hook: "knife" and "pencil". In both cases, grip the hook on the flat section with the tips of your thumb and forefinger. In knife hold, the handle of the hook is held inside your hand, whereas pencil hold has the handle emerging on top of your hand. Try both and see which one feels most comfortable to you.

To control the working yarn and keep an even tension, loop the working yarn over your left forefinger and take the yarn coming from the ball loosely around the little finger on the same hand. Use the middle finger on the same hand to help hold the work. If you are left-handed, hold the hook in your left hand and the yarn in your right.

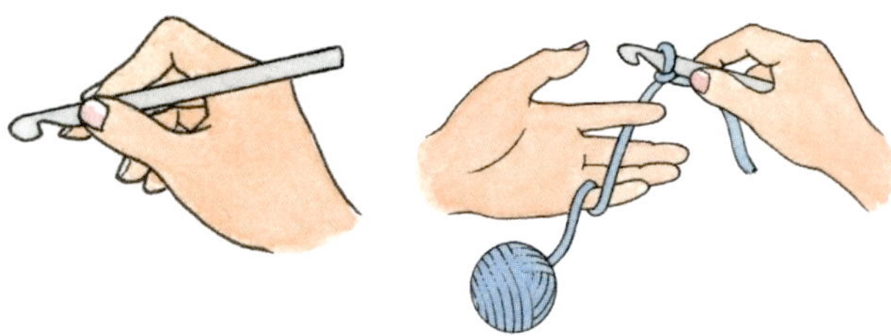

2. Making a Slip Knot

Loop the yarn as shown, insert the hook into the loop, catch the yarn with the hook, and pull it through to make a loop over the hook.

Gently pull the yarn to tighten the loop around the hook and complete the slip knot.

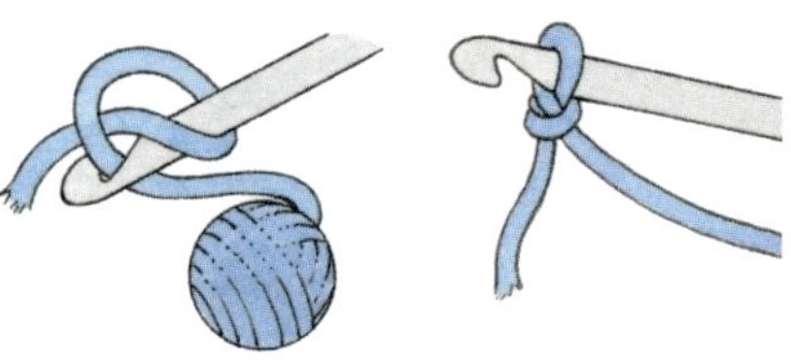

3. Foundation Chain

The pattern will tell you how many chains to make. This may be a specific number or a multiple. If a pattern tells you to make a multiple of 3 + 2, this does not mean make a multiple of 5. It means that you should make a multiple of 3 and then add 2 chains—e.g., 3 + 2, 6 + 2, 9 + 2 and so on. You may also be instructed to add a turning chain for the first row.

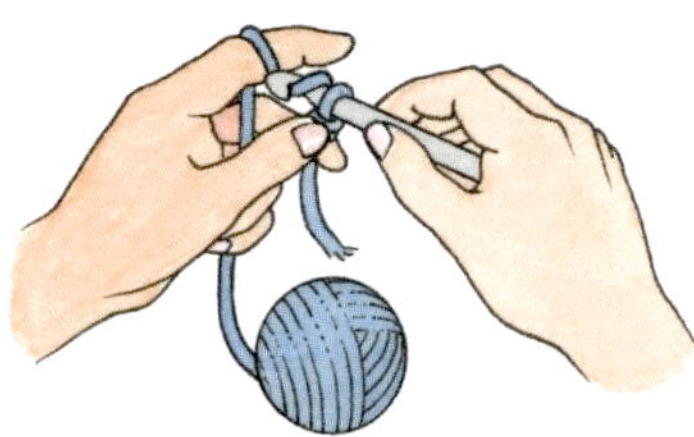

1 Holding the hook with the slip knot in your right hand and the yarn in your left hand, wrap the yarn over the hook. Draw the yarn through to make a new loop. This completes the first chain stitch.

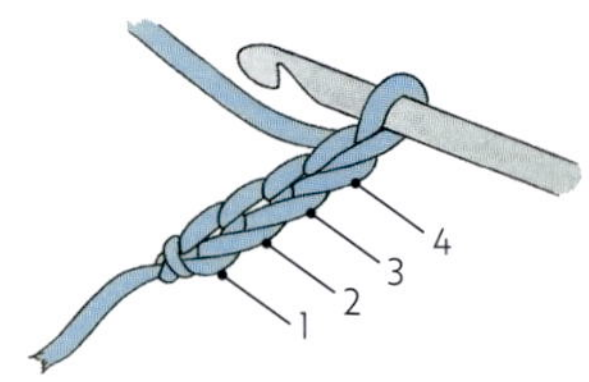

2 Repeat this process, drawing a new loop of yarn through the loop already on the hook until the foundation chain is the required length. Count each V-shaped loop on the front of the chain as one chain stitch, except for the loop on the hook, which is not counted. After every few stitches, move up the thumb and finger that are grasping the chain to keep the chain stitches even.

4. Foundation Ring

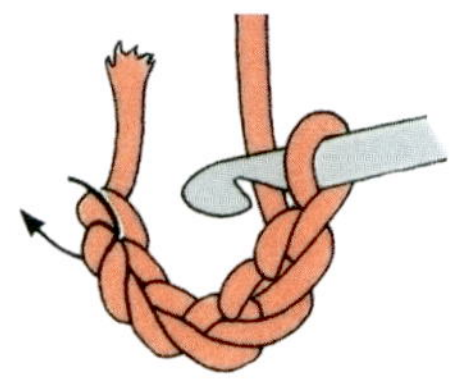

1 Work a short length of foundation chain as specified in the pattern. Join the chains into a ring by working a slip stitch into the first chain of the foundation chain.

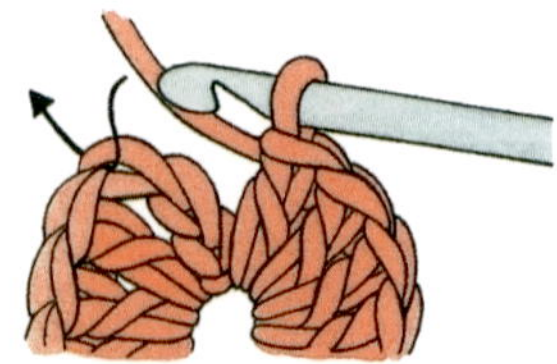

2 Work the first round of stitches into the center of the ring unless specified otherwise. At the end of the round, the final stitch is usually joined to the first stitch with a slip stitch.

Turning and Starting Chains

When working crochet, you will need to work a specific number of extra chains at the beginning of each row or round. When the work is turned at the end of a straight row, the extra chains are called a turning chain, and when they are worked at the beginning of a round, they are called a starting chain. You'll see these both called "beg ch" in the patterns in this book.

The extra chains bring the hook up to the correct height for the stitch you will be working next. The turning or starting chain is counted as the first stitch of the row or round, except when working single crochet where the single turning chain is ignored. A chain may be longer than the number required for the stitch, and in that case counts as one stitch plus a number of chains.

At the end of the row, the final stitch is usually worked into the turning chain at the beginning of the previous row. The final stitch may be worked into the top chain of the turning chain or into another specified stitch of the chain. At the end of a round, the final stitch is usually joined to the starting chain with a slip stitch.

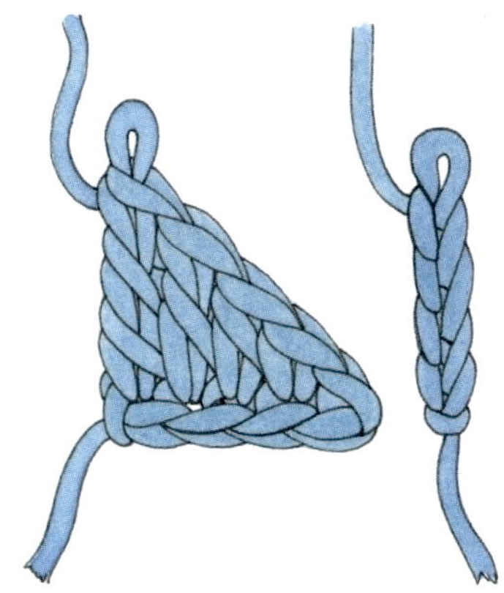

Number of Turning/ Starting Chains

- *Single crochet (sc): 1 turning chain*
- *Half-double crochet (hdc): 2 turning chains*
- *Double crochet (dc): 3 turning chains*
- *Treble crochet (tr): 4 turning chains*
- *Double treble crochet (dtr): 5 turning chains*

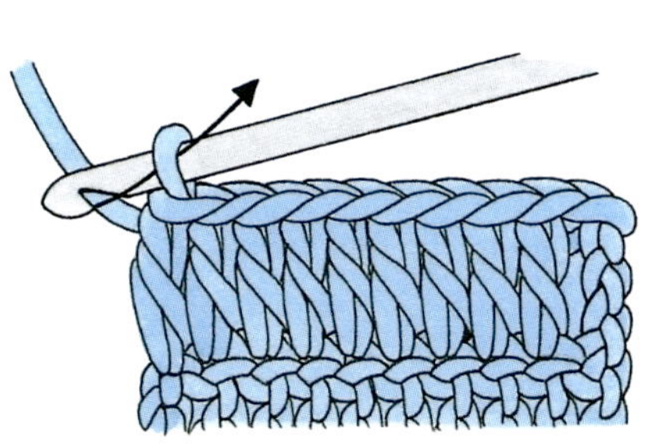

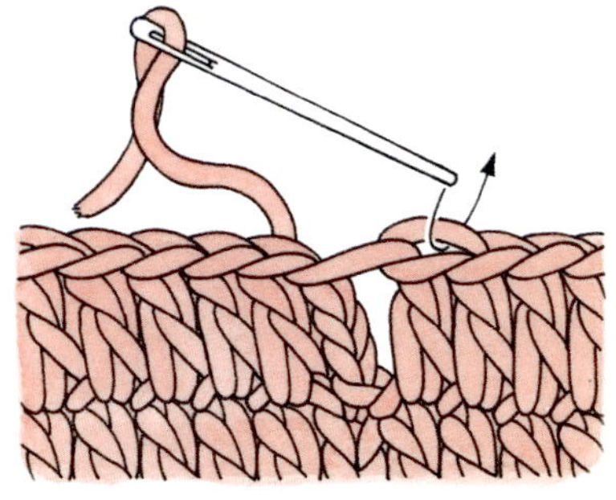

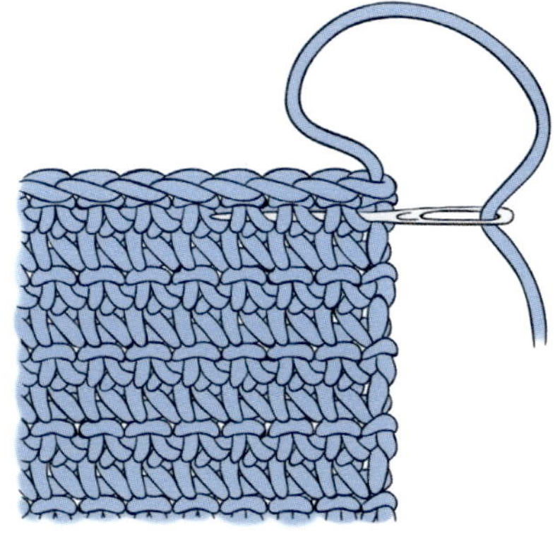

Fastening Off

Once the crochet is complete, cut the yarn about 6" (15 cm) from the last stitch. Wrap the yarn over the hook and draw the yarn end through the loop on the hook. Gently pull the yarn to tighten the last stitch and weave in the yarn end.

Finishing the Last Round

For a neater finish, don't use a slip stitch to join the last stitch of the final round to the first stitch of the round. Instead, cut the yarn and pull it through the top of the final stitch of the round. Thread a yarn needle with this end, and pass it under the top loops of the first stitch of the round and back through the center of the last stitch.

Weaving In Ends

For crochet worked in rows, use a yarn needle to weave in ends diagonally on the wrong side. For crochet worked in rounds, weave in ends under stitches for an inch or two. If the pattern doesn't allow this, weave under a few stitches, then up through the back of a stitch and under a few more stitches on the next row.

BASIC STITCHES

All crochet stitches are based on a loop pulled through another loop by the hook. There are only a few stitches to master, each of a different length. Here is a concise guide to the basic stitches used to make the blocks in this book.

Note On Abbreviations

The patterns in this book use US crochet terms. Crochet stitches are worked in the same way in both the US and UK, but the stitch names are not the same, and identical names are used for different stitches. See below for US terms and the UK equivalents:

US	UK
Single crochet (sc)	Double crochet (dc)
Double crochet (dc)	Treble (tr)
Half-double crochet (hdc)	Half treble (htr)
Treble crochet (tr)	Double treble (dtr)
Double treble crochet (dtr)	Triple treble crochet (ttr)

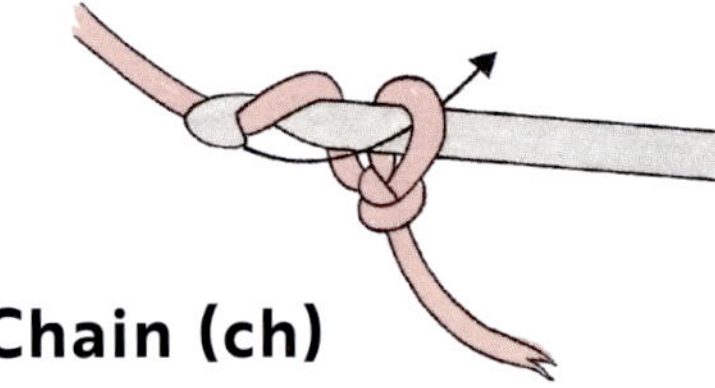

Chain (ch)

Wrap the yarn over the hook and pull it through the loop already on the hook to form a new loop on the hook.

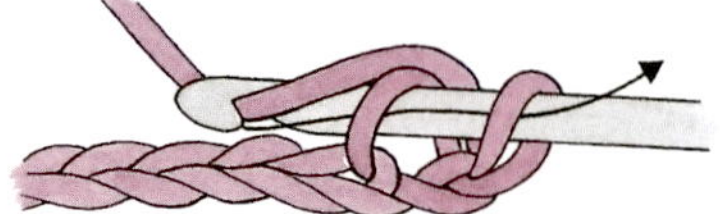

Slip Stitch (sl st)

Insert the hook into the specified stitch, yarn over and pull it through the stitch and the loop on the hook.

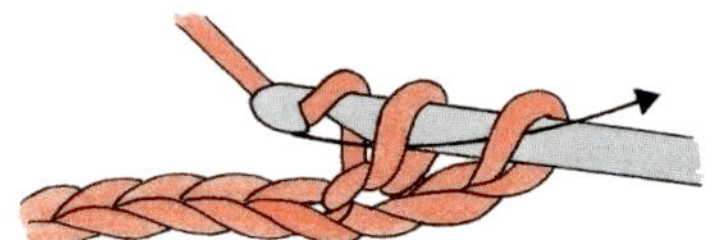

Single Crochet (sc)

Insert the hook into the specified stitch, wrap the yarn over the hook and pull it through the stitch (2 loops on hook). Yarn over and pull it through both loops.

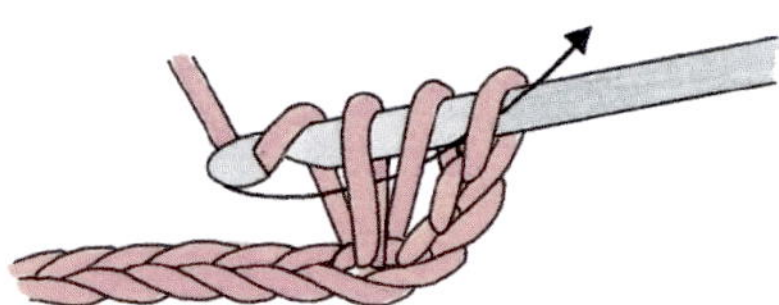

Half-Double Crochet (hdc)

Yarn over, insert the hook into the specified stitch, yarn over and pull it through the stitch (3 loops on hook). Yarn over and pull it through all three loops.

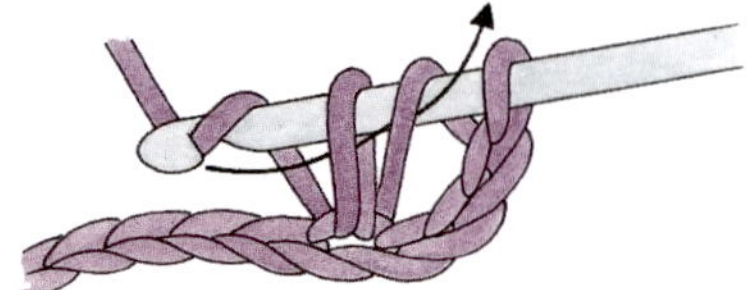

Double Crochet (dc)

Yarn over, insert the hook into the specified stitch, yarn over and pull it through the stitch (3 loops on hook). [Yarn over, pull through two loops] twice.

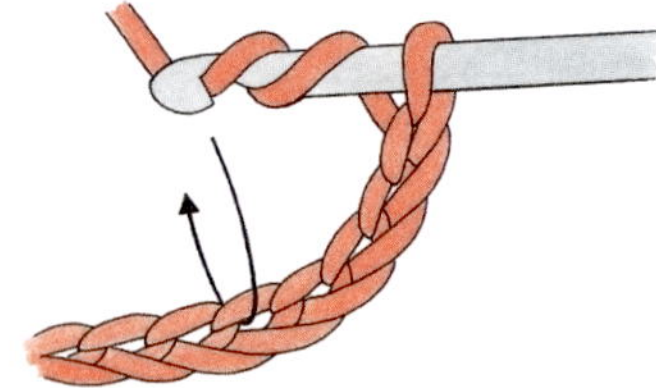

Treble Crochet (tr)

Yarn over twice, insert the hook into the specified stitch, yarn over and pull it through the stitch (4 loops on hook). [Yarn over, pull through two loops] three times.

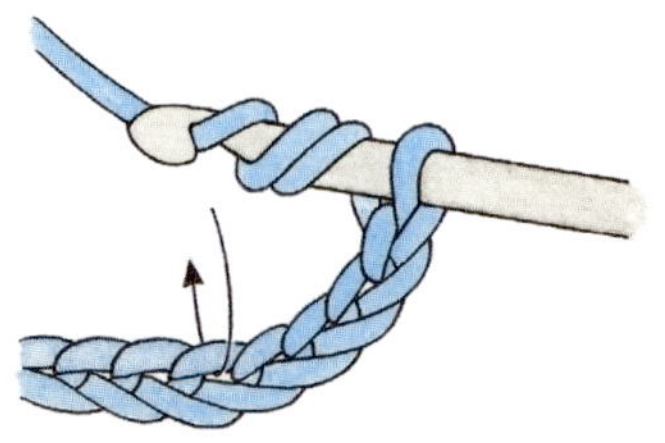

Double Treble Crochet (dtr)

Yarn over three times, insert the hook into the specified stitch, yarn over and pull it through the stitch (5 loops on hook). [Yarn over, pull through two loops] three times.

SIMPLE STITCH VARIATIONS

Basic stitches may be varied in many ways to achieve different effects. These simple variations are all made by inserting the hook in different places in the crochet to work the stitches.

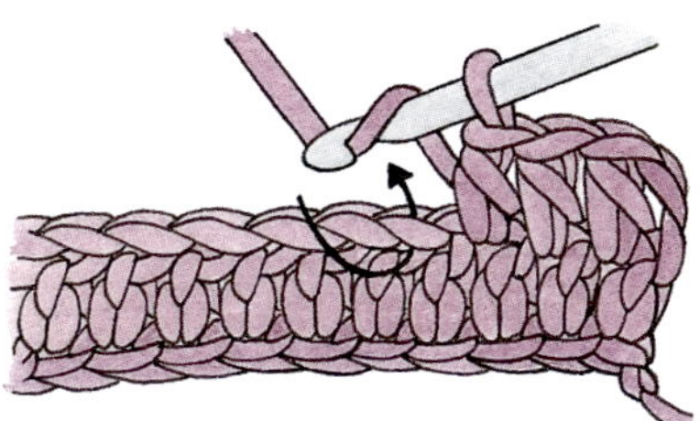

Through Front Loop Only (FLO)

Rather than inserting the hook under both top loops to work the next stitch in the usual way, insert it only under the front loop.

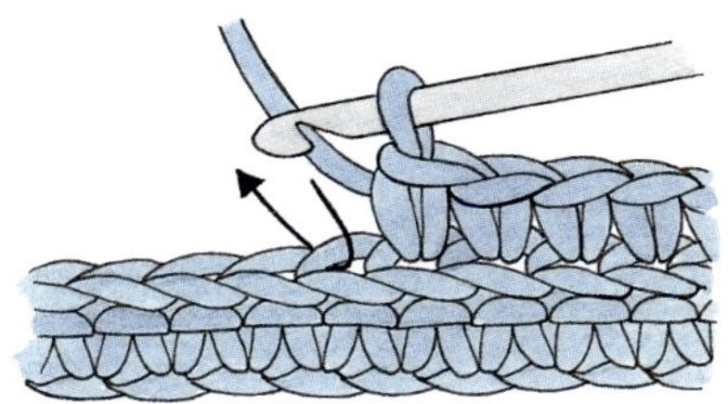

Through Back Loop Only (BLO)

Rather than inserting the hook under both top loops to work the next stitch in the usual way, insert it only under the back loop.

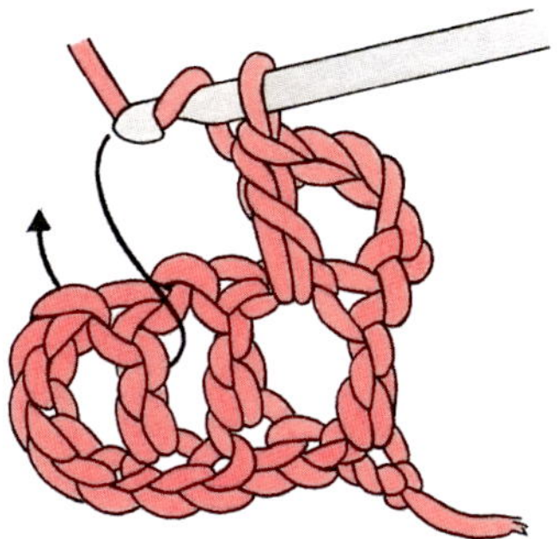

Into a Chain Space (ch sp)

Insert the hook into the space below a chain or chains. Here, a treble crochet is being worked into a chain space.

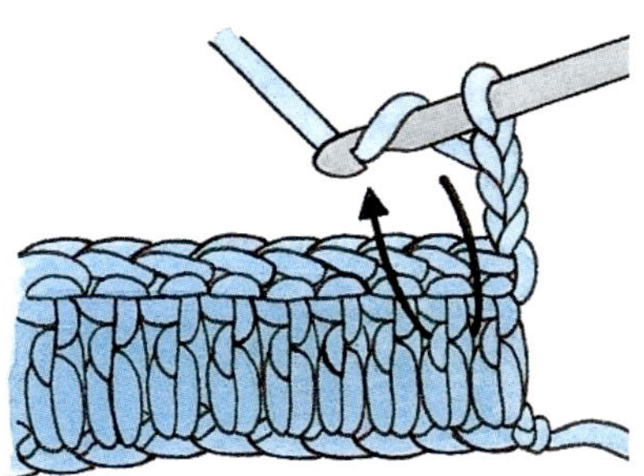

Around the Front Post (FP)

Work around the stem of the stitch, inserting the hook from front to back, around the post and to the front again, as shown above.

Working Through the Horizontal Bar (THB)

The technique below is similar to working into the front or back loop only. Working into the bar at the back of each stitch raises the front and back loops to add some textural interest.

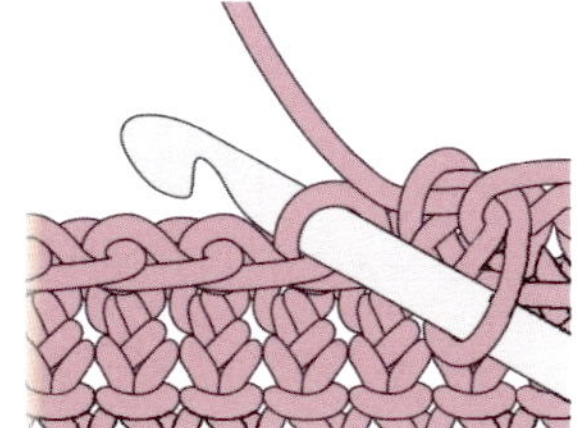

1 Tilt the stitches forward and insert the hook from top to bottom through the horizontal bar or "bump" at the back of the specified stitch.

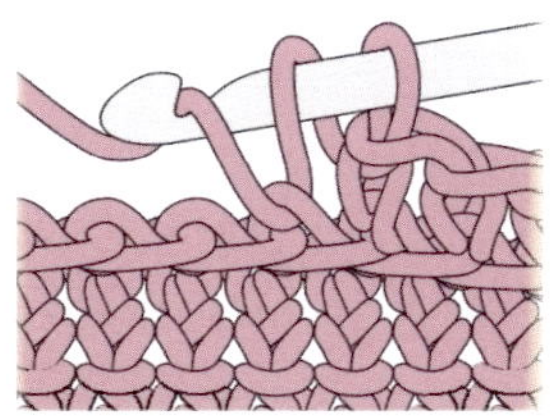

2 Continue working the stitch as usual.

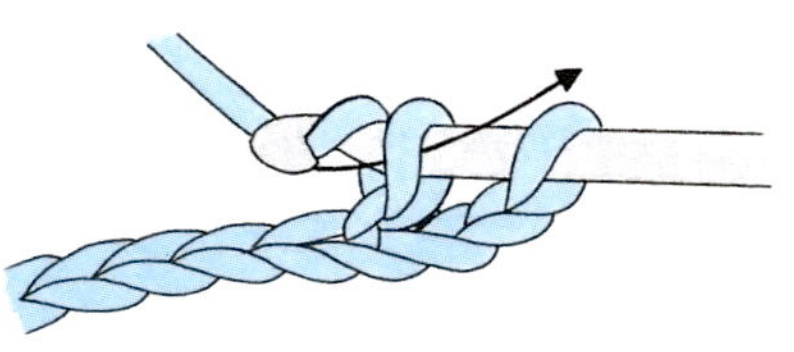

Extended Single Crochet (exsc)

The extended single crochet stitch is a variation of the single crochet that creates a taller and more flexible stitch. Begin by inserting your hook into the place indicated, yarn over and pull up a loop, yarn over and pull through one loop, then yarn over and pull through the remaining two loops on your hook.

SPECIAL STITCHES

By working multiple stitches in the same place, joining several stitches together at the top, or a combination of both, you can create interesting shapes, patterns, and textures. The turning or starting chain may be counted as the first stitch of a special stitch.

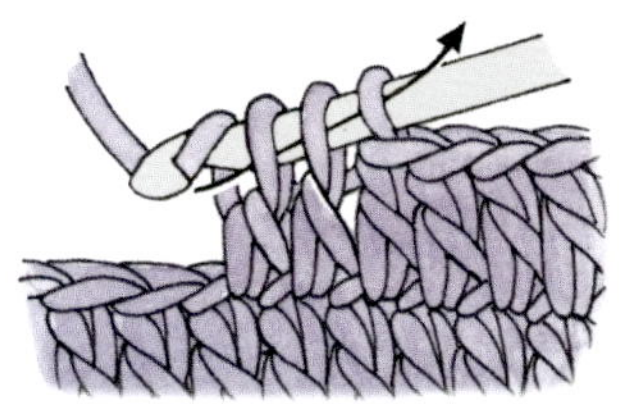

Decrease (e.g. sc2tog, dc3tog)

One or two stitches can be decreased by working two or three incomplete stitches together. Work the specified number of stitches, omitting the final stage (the last yarn over) of each stitch so that the last loop of each stitch remains on the hook. Yarn over and draw it through all the loops on the hook.

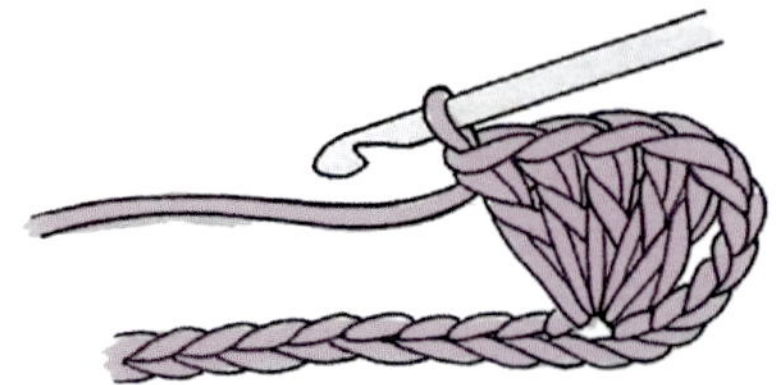

Increase (e.g. 5 dc in next ch)

This technique is used to increase the total number of stitches when shaping an item, or to create a decorative effect such as a shell. Simply work the required number of stitches in the same place. Increases may be worked at the edges of flat pieces, or at any point along a row or round.

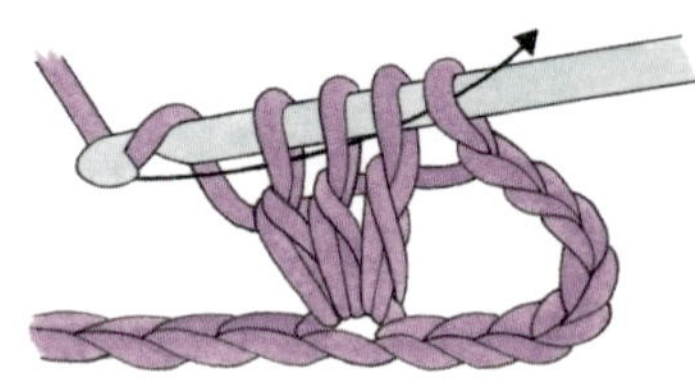

Bobble

A bobble is a group of between three and six double crochet or longer stitches worked in the same place and closed at the top. Work the specified number of stitches, omitting the final stage of each stitch so that the last loop of each stitch remains on the hook. Yarn over and draw it through all the loops on the hook.

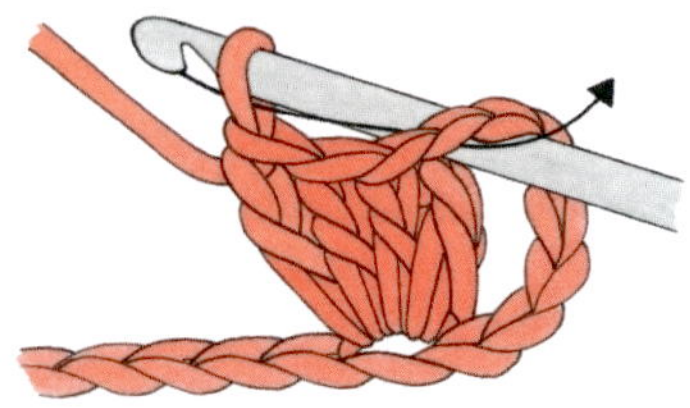

Popcorn

A popcorn is a group of double crochet or longer stitches worked in the same place, and then folded and closed at the top so that the popcorn is raised from the background stitches. Work the specified number of stitches in the same place. Take the hook out of the working loop and insert it under both top loops of the first stitch of the popcorn. Pick up the working loop with the hook and draw it through to fold the group of stitches and close the popcorn at the top. Chain 1 to secure.

COLORWORK

Most of the block patterns use a single color for each row or round, with the new color being joined at the end of a row or round. Tapestry (or jacquard) and intarsia designs involve using multiple colors across the row.

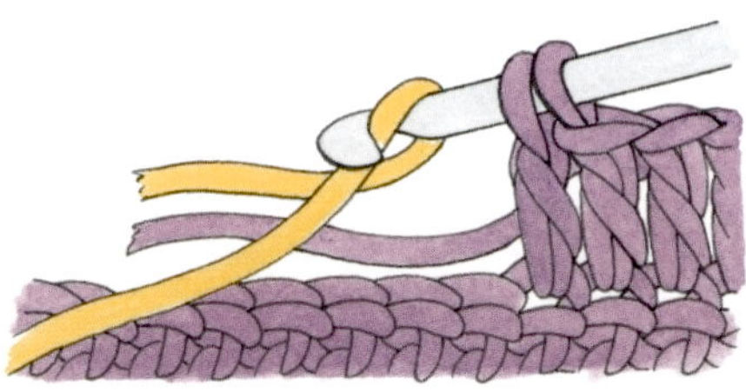

Changing Color Mid-stitch

When working the last stitch of the old color, omit the final stage (the last yarn over) to leave the stitch incomplete. Yarn over with the new color and draw it through all of the loops on the hook to complete the stitch. The new yarn will form the top loops of the next stitch in the new color.

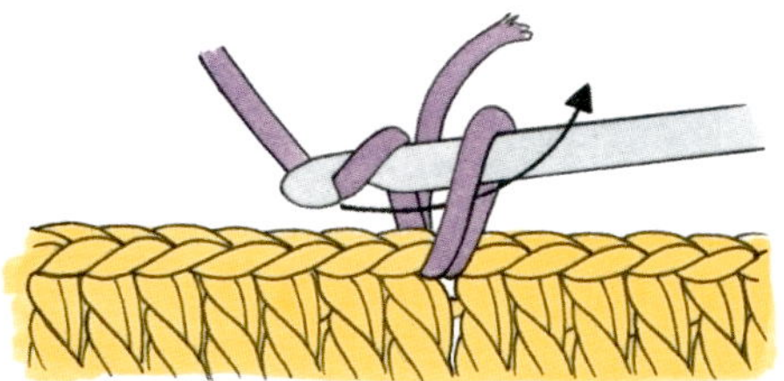

Joining a New Color

Insert the hook where required and draw up a loop of the new color, leaving a 4" (10 cm) tail. Work the specified number of turning or starting chains. Continue with the new yarn.

Intarsia Crochet

Use a separate ball of yarn for each area of color. If the same color is used twice across the row, you will need two balls.

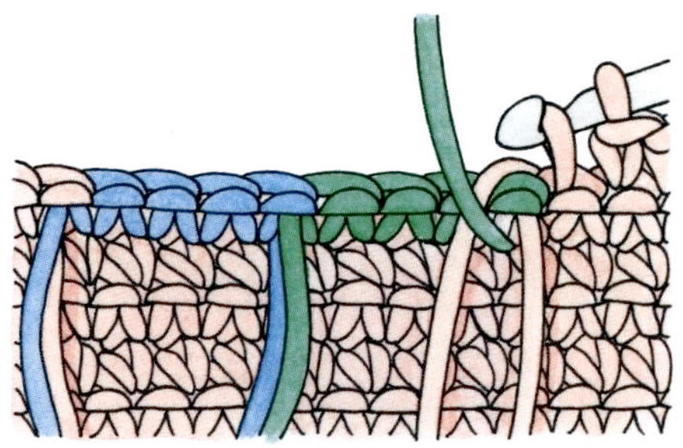

1 Follow the pattern, changing colors in the usual way where indicated and dropping the unused yarns to the wrong side of the work. At each color change on subsequent rows, loop the new yarn around the old one on the wrong side of the work to prevent holes.

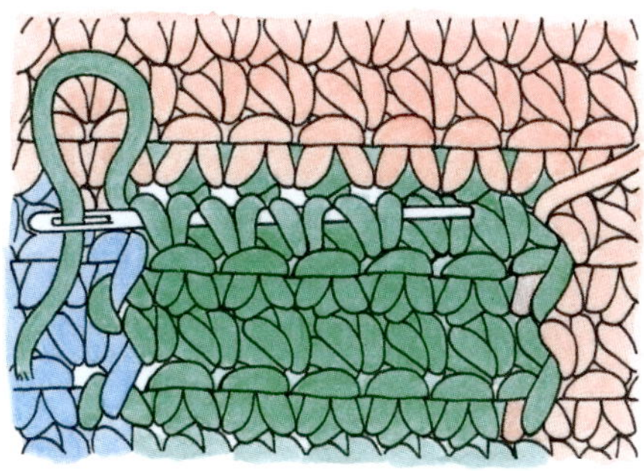

2 Take extra care when dealing with all the yarn ends on a piece of intarsia. Carefully weave each end into an area of crochet worked in the same color so that it is not visible on the right side.

Tapestry Crochet

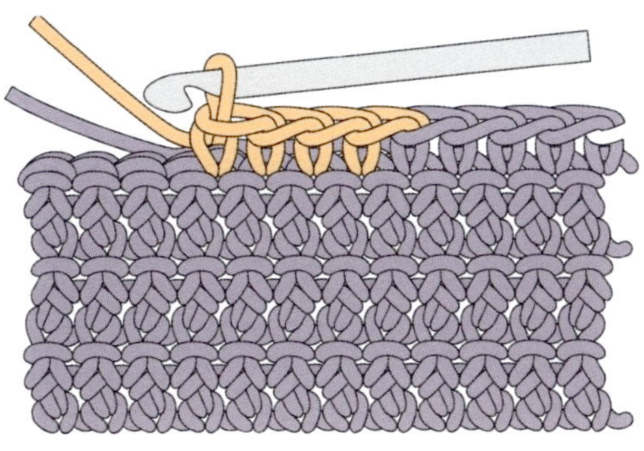

1 Change to the new color in the usual way. Continue following the pattern, carrying the unused yarn along the top of the previous row at the back of the work and crocheting over it. After the next color change, continue to carry and work over the unused yarn in the same way.

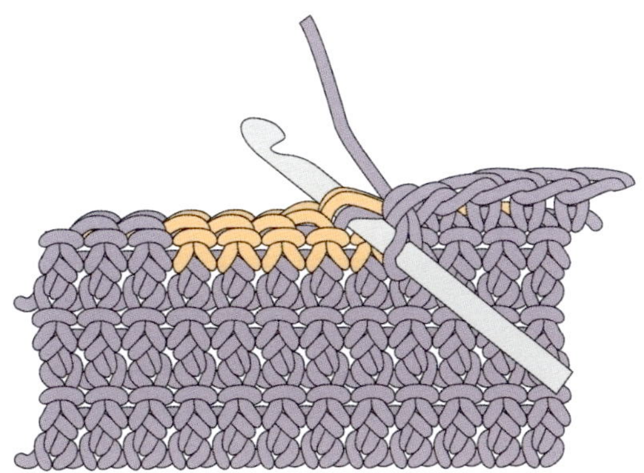

2 On the next and all other rows, insert the hook under the carried yarn and into the stitch to lock the carried yarn in place.

Working Over Unused Colors

When working over an unused color, hold the carried thread to the back of the work and crochet over it. When carrying more than one color, hold the color with the most contrast to the working yarn at the back and the yarn with the least contrast toward the front while keeping both strands at the back of the work.

READING PATTERNS AND STITCH DIAGRAMS

Abbreviations are used to make crochet patterns quicker and easier to follow. Abbreviations and symbols may vary from one pattern publisher to another, so always check that you understand the system in use before starting work.

Understanding Symbols

SYMBOL	MEANING
[ ]	repeat the instructions within the brackets the stated number of times
( )	can either be explanatory (counts as tr) or can be read as a group of stitches worked in the same place (tr, ch 2, tr)
►	an arrowhead indicates the beginning of a row or round

SYMBOLS JOINED AT TOP

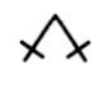 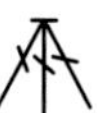

A group of symbols joined at the top should be worked together at the top, as in decreasing (e.g. sc2tog, dc3tog)

SYMBOLS JOINED AT BASE

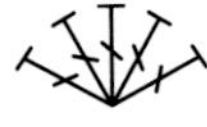

Symbols joined at the base should all be worked into the same stitch below

SYMBOLS JOINED AT TOP AND BASE

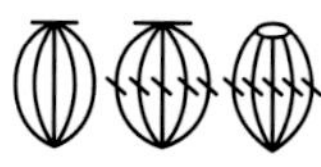

Sometimes a group of stitches is joined at both top and bottom, making a puff, bobble, or popcorn

SYMBOLS JOINED AT TOP ON A CURVE

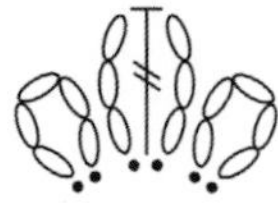

Sometimes symbols are drawn at an angle, depending on the construction of the stitch pattern

Symbols and Abbreviations

SYMBOL	MEANING	ABBREVIATION
o	chain	ch
•	slip stitch	sl st
+	single crochet	sc
T	half double crochet	hdc
	double crochet	dc
	treble crochet	tr
	double treble crochet	dtr
	decrease (e.g. dc3tog)	dec
	bobble (e.g. bobble of 5 dc)	BO
	popcorn (e.g. popcorn of 5 dc)	pc
	through back loop only	BLO
	through front loop only	FLO
	front post	FP
	through horizontal bar	THB
	beginning	beg
	space	sp
	right side/wrong side	RS/WS
	stitch(es)	st(s)
	together	tog
	yarn over	yo

Reading Stitch Diagrams

Each design in this book is accompanied by a stitch diagram, which should be read together with the written instructions. Once you are used to the symbols, they are quick and easy to follow. All stitch diagrams show the block from the right side (front) of the work.

Stitch Diagrams in Rows

Right-side rows start at the right and are read from right to left. Wrong-side rows start at the left and are read from left to right.

Stitch Diagrams in Rounds

These stitch diagrams begin at the center and each round is read counterclockwise, in the same direction as working. Occasionally a block worked in the round may require you to turn the work, indicated by an arrow on the stitch diagram, in which case the round should be read in the direction of the arrow.

GAUGE AND BLOCKING

It's important to crochet a test swatch before you start your project to establish gauge. To finish your work neatly, you will need to block it. You can use the gauge swatch to test blocking and cleaning methods.

Measuring Gauge

No two people will crochet to the exact same gauge, even when working with identical yarn and hooks. Always make a test swatch before starting a project so that you can compare your gauge with the pattern gauge and get an idea of how the finished project will feel and drape. It's also useful for testing out different color combinations.

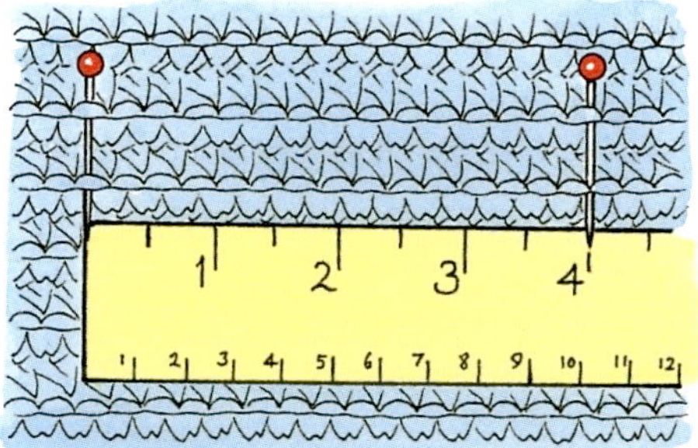

To test your gauge, make a sample swatch in the yarn you intend to use following the pattern directions. Measure, then block the sample (see below) and measure again. If your swatch is larger, try making another using a smaller hook. If your swatch is smaller, try making another using a bigger hook. Also do this if the fabric feels too loose and floppy or too dense and rigid. Keep trying until you find a hook size that will give you the required gauge, or until you are happy with the drape and feel of your work. Ultimately, it's more important that you use a hook and yarn you are comfortable with than that you rigidly follow the pattern instructions.

Blocking

Blocking is crucial to set the stitches and even out the piece. Choose a method based on the care label of the yarn. When in doubt, use the wet method. You'll need an ironing board, foam blocking mats, or an old quilt or towels to pin the work on. Alternatively, you could make a blocking board by securing one or two layers of quilter's batting, covered with a sheet of cotton fabric, over a flat board.

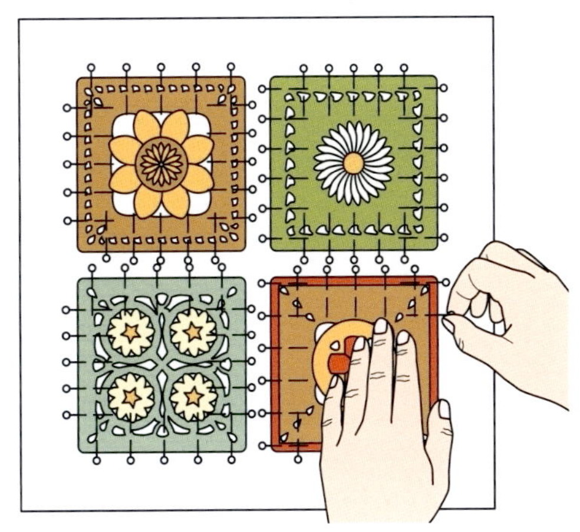

Wet Method—Acrylic and Wool/Acrylic Blend

Using rustproof pins, pin the crochet fabric to the correct measurements on a flat surface and dampen using a spray bottle of cold water. Pat the fabric to help the moisture penetrate. Ease stitches into position, keeping rows and stitches straight. Allow to dry before removing the pins.

Steam Method—Wools and Cottons

Pin out the fabric as above. For this method pin fabric with raised stitches right side up, to avoid squashing the stitches; otherwise, pin it wrong side up. Steam lightly, holding the iron 1" (2.5 cm) above the fabric. Allow the steam to penetrate for several seconds. It is safer to avoid pressing, but if you choose to do so, cover with a clean towel or cloth first.

JOINING AND EDGING

If you are making your project from a block pattern, you will need to sew or crochet the blocks together before adding an edging. A crochet edging not only finishes off a project with style, but it also helps the block to hold its shape and keeps the edges from stretching.

Joining Blocks

Blocks can be joined by sewing or by crochet. Pin seams together to help match up the blocks and give a neat finish. Use the same yarn that you used for the blocks, or a finer yarn, preferably with the same fiber content.

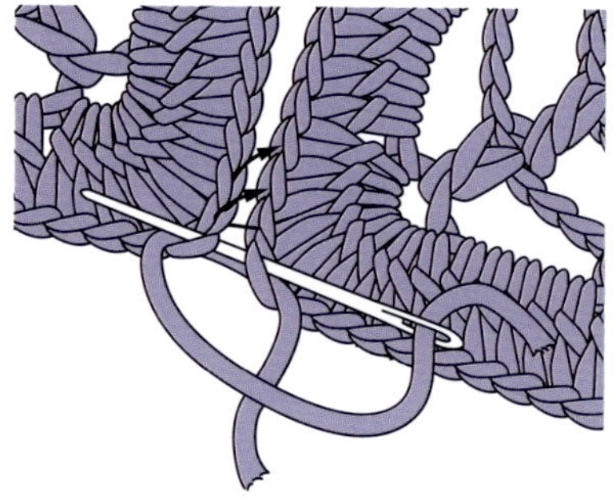

Oversewing

Using a yarn needle, sew through the back or front loops of corresponding stitches. For extra strength, work two stitches into the end loops.

Backstitch

Hold the blocks with right sides together. Using a yarn needle, work a line of backstitches along the edge. Take the needle under a pair of corresponding stitches, then go back into the space at the end of your previous backstitch.

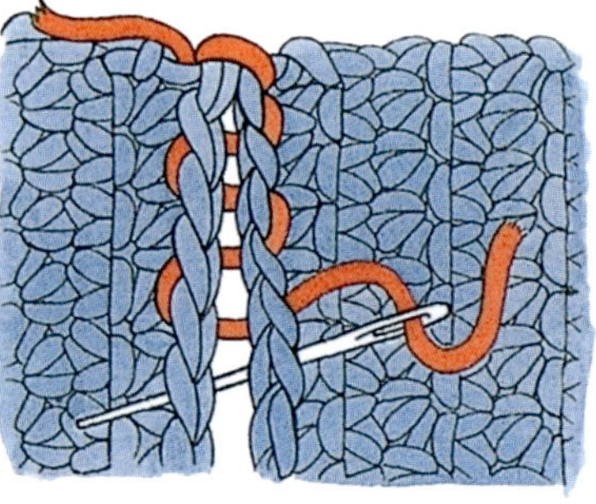

Mattress Stitch

Lay the blocks wrong side up and with edges touching. Using a yarn needle, weave back and forth around the centers of the stitches, without pulling the stitches too tight. Gently pull on the yarn every 1–2" (2.5–5 cm) to close up the seam.

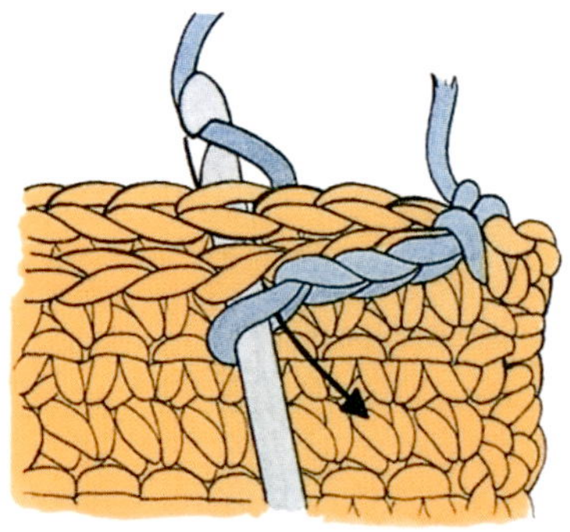

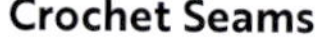

Crochet Seams

Join the blocks with wrong sides together for a visible seam, or with right sides together for an invisible one. Work a row of slip stitch or single crochet through both top loops of each block. When using this method along the side edges of blocks worked in rows, work enough evenly spaced stitches so that the seam is not too tight.

Simple Edging

Working a simple round of single crochet stitches helps to even out untidy edges at row ends and any uneven stitches. Make a simple edging by crocheting one round of single crochet around the block, working three stitches in each corner.

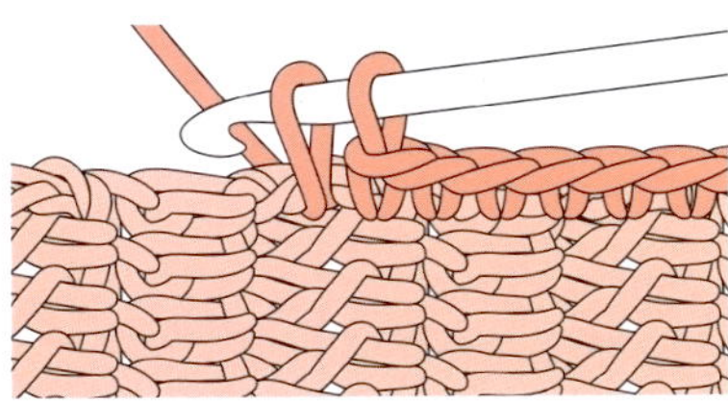

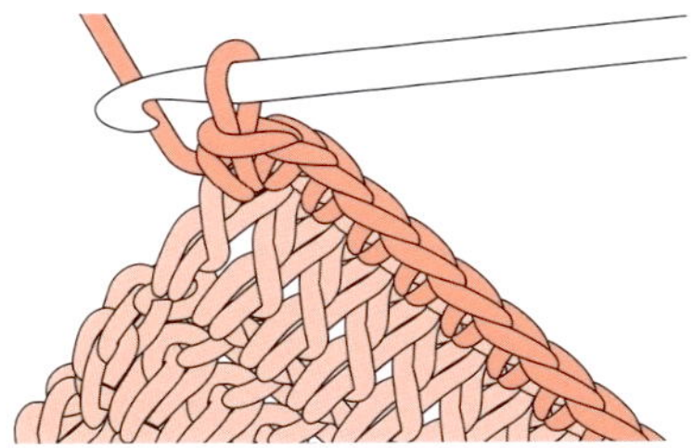

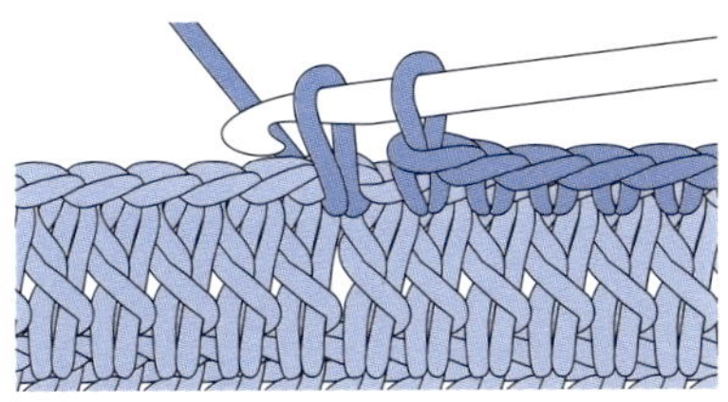

Along Sides of Row Ends

When working on the side edge of a block worked in rows, insert the hook under two threads of the first (or last) stitch of each row. Place the stitches an even distance apart along the edge. Try a short length to test the number of stitches required for a flat result. As a guide:

- Rows of sc: sc in side edge of each row.
- Rows of hdc: 2 sc in first row, sc in next (3 sc over 2 rows).
- Rows of dc: 2 sc in side edge of each row.
- Rows of tr: 3 sc in side edge of each row.

Around Corners

You will need to add a couple of stitches at each corner to allow the edging to turn the corner without distorting the block. As a guide, corners are normally turned by working 3 sc (or sc, hdc, sc) into the corner. If you want to add a larger or more complex edging and find that the base round is too wavy or too taut after it has been completed, it will probably get worse once the rest of the edging has been worked. Take time at this point to pull out the base round and redo it using fewer stitches if the edge is too wavy, or using more stitches if the edge is too taut.

Across The Top or Bottom Edge

When working across the top of a row, work sc into each stitch as you would if working another row. When working across the bottom edge of chain stitches, work sc in the remaining loop of each foundation chain.

Making Tassels

1 Cut a piece of cardboard slightly longer than you need the finished tassel to be. Wrap the yarn around the card until the tassel is the thickness needed, or the number of times stated in the pattern. With a long strand of yarn threaded onto a needle, bring it through all the yarn strands at the top.

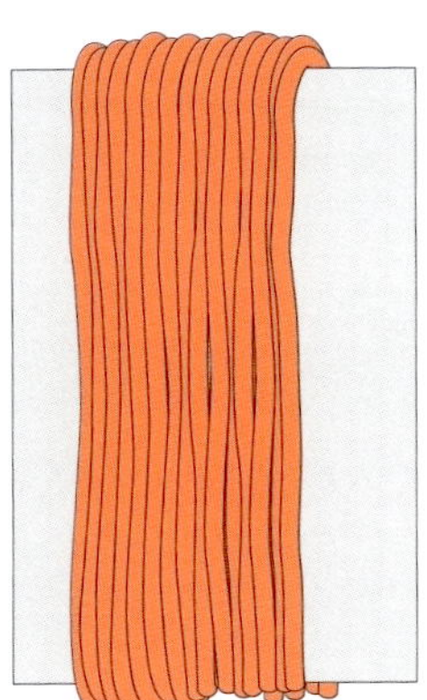

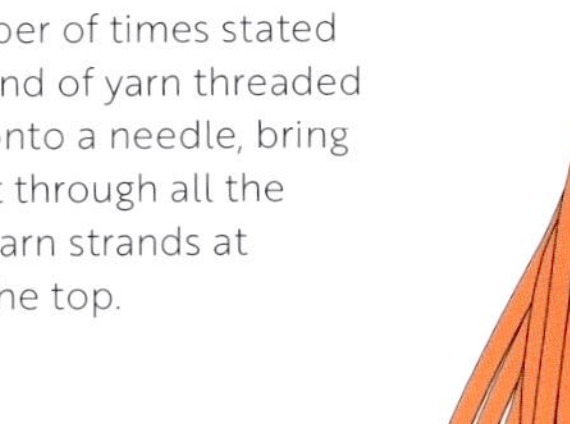

2 Wrap the yarn around the strands a few times and tie. With sharp scissors, cut the tassel ends at the bottom of the cardboard, leaving long yarn tails.

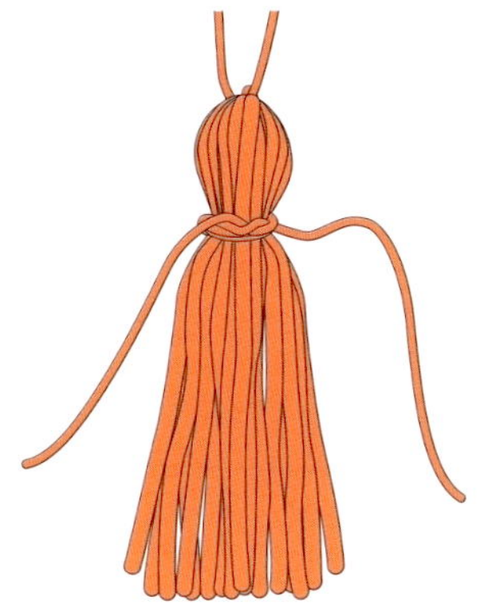

3 Tighten the knot at the top. Wrap the tassel with a strand of yarn a few times about ½" (1 cm) from the top and tie a tight knot.

COLOR THEORY

Making a simple granny square a few times and playing with color schemes is the best way to build your confidence in finding fun and creative color combinations. Here I show you ten different schemes that will allow you to explore color to the max.

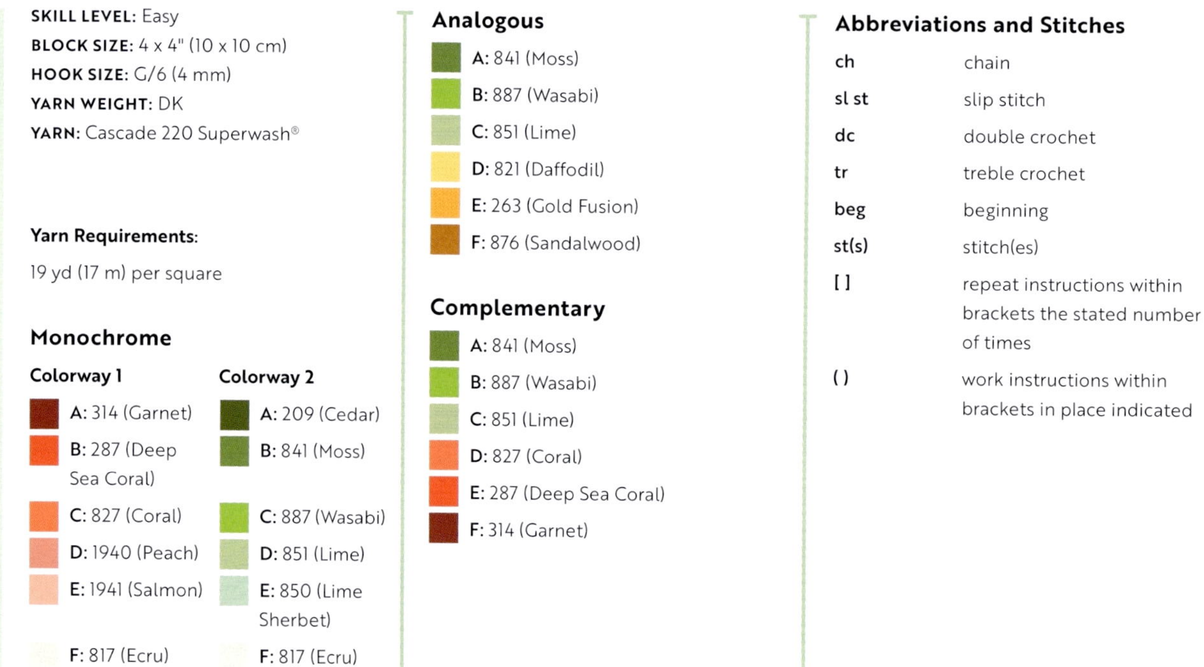

SKILL LEVEL: Easy
BLOCK SIZE: 4 x 4" (10 x 10 cm)
HOOK SIZE: G/6 (4 mm)
YARN WEIGHT: DK
YARN: Cascade 220 Superwash®

Yarn Requirements:

19 yd (17 m) per square

Monochrome

Colorway 1

- **A:** 314 (Garnet)
- **B:** 287 (Deep Sea Coral)
- **C:** 827 (Coral)
- **D:** 1940 (Peach)
- **E:** 1941 (Salmon)
- **F:** 817 (Ecru)

Colorway 2

- **A:** 209 (Cedar)
- **B:** 841 (Moss)
- **C:** 887 (Wasabi)
- **D:** 851 (Lime)
- **E:** 850 (Lime Sherbet)
- **F:** 817 (Ecru)

Analogous

- **A:** 841 (Moss)
- **B:** 887 (Wasabi)
- **C:** 851 (Lime)
- **D:** 821 (Daffodil)
- **E:** 263 (Gold Fusion)
- **F:** 876 (Sandalwood)

Complementary

- **A:** 841 (Moss)
- **B:** 887 (Wasabi)
- **C:** 851 (Lime)
- **D:** 827 (Coral)
- **E:** 287 (Deep Sea Coral)
- **F:** 314 (Garnet)

Abbreviations and Stitches

ch	chain
sl st	slip stitch
dc	double crochet
tr	treble crochet
beg	beginning
st(s)	stitch(es)
[ ]	repeat instructions within brackets the stated number of times
( )	work instructions within brackets in place indicated

Crochet Pattern

Foundation Ring: Ch 4, join with sl st to first ch made to form a ring.

Rnd 1: Ch 4 (counts as tr throughout), [3 dc into ring, tr into ring] three times, 3 dc into ring, join with sl st into the top of beg ch-4—16 sts.

Rnd 2: Ch 4, 2 dc in same place, [dc in 3 sts, (2 dc, tr, 2 dc) in next st] three times, dc in 3 sts, 2 dc in same place as beg st, join with sl st into the top of beg ch-4—32 sts.

Rnd 3: Ch 4, 2 dc in same place, [dc in 7 sts, (2 dc, tr, 2 dc) in next st] three times, dc in 7 sts, 2 dc in same place as beg st, join with sl st into the top of beg ch-4—48 sts.

Rnd 4: Ch 4, 2 dc in same place, [dc in 11 sts, (2 dc, tr, 2 dc) in next st] three times, dc in 11 sts, 2 dc in same place as beg st, join with sl st into the top of beg ch-4, end color—64 sts.

Weave in ends and block to measure 4" x 4" (10 x 10 cm).

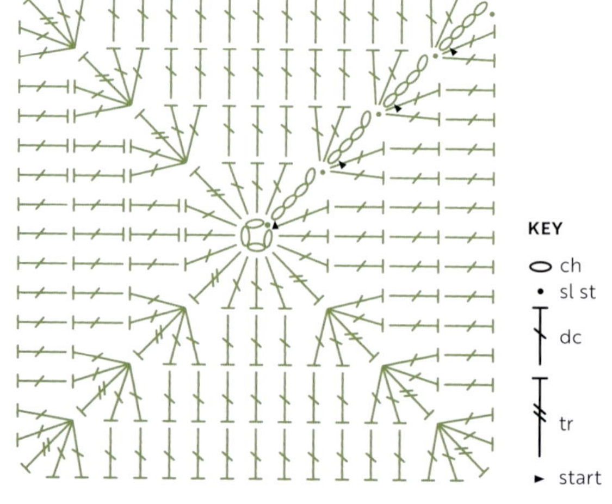

Types of Color Schemes

Monochrome

Monochrome color palettes consist of shades of one color. Here, I've shown two examples of a monochromatic palette—one using shades of red and one using shades of green. Monochromatic palettes will always work nicely for crochet projects.

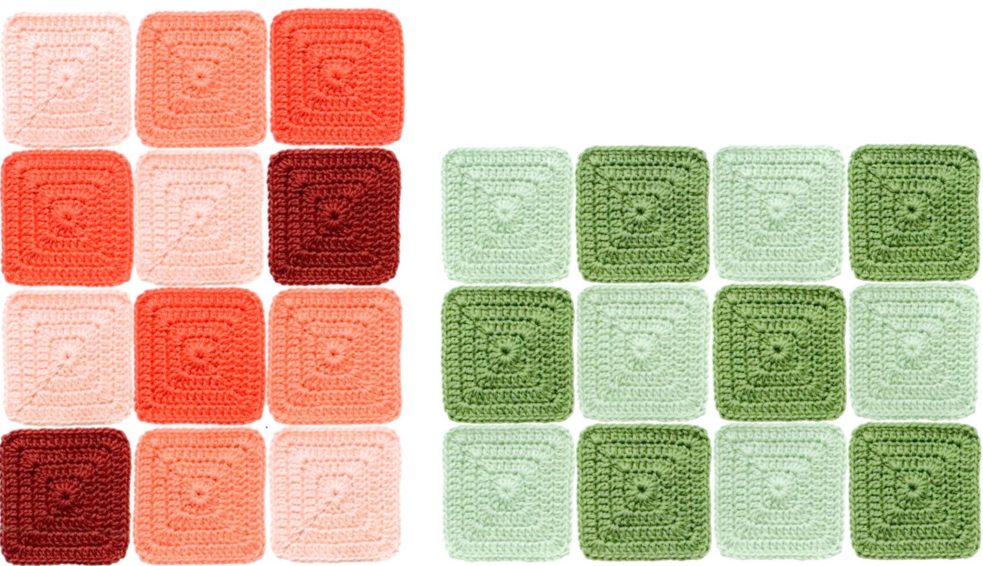

Analogous

Colors that sit next to each other on the color wheel coordinate well together. Here, I've used greens through to yellows. You could also add in some other shades of each of the colors for more contrast.

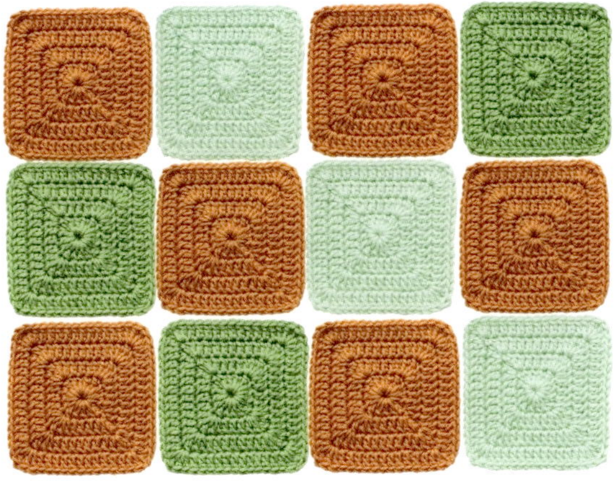

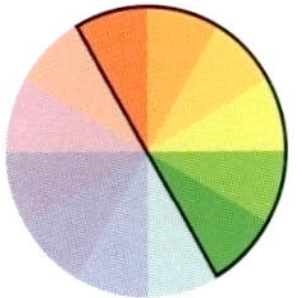

Complementary

Complementary colors sit directly opposite one another on the color wheel and have a vibrant look when combined. Adding a few shades of each color creates a lovely palette.

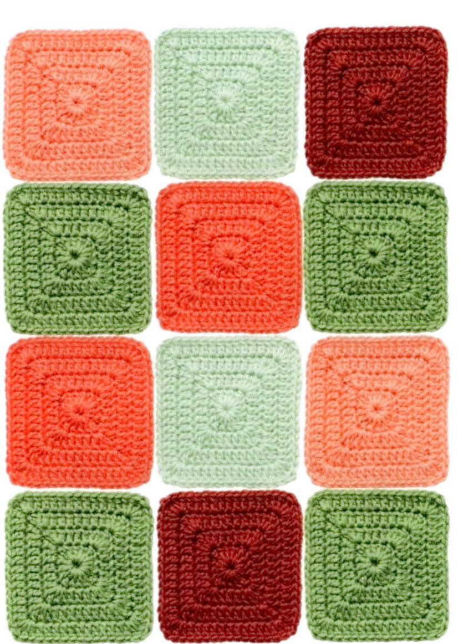

Triadic

Triadic color schemes use three colors that are evenly spaced around the color wheel. This creates a balanced and vibrant palette. For instance, choosing red, blue, and yellow as the primary colors of a triadic scheme creates a dynamic and visually engaging look. When paired with a neutral, such as white, you create a high contrast.

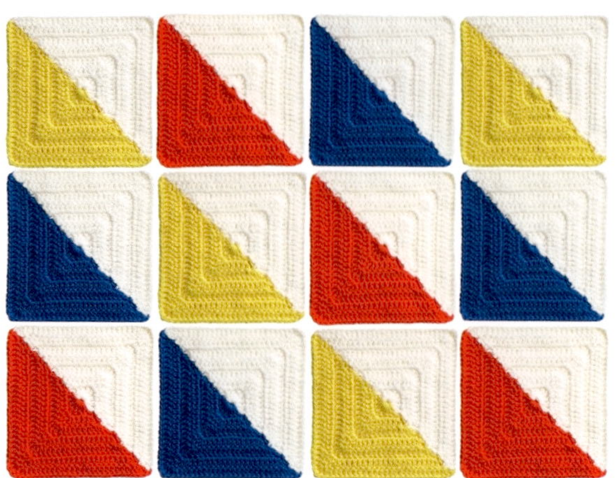

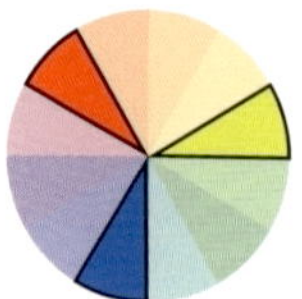

Split Complementary

Split-complementary color schemes are a variation on complementary color schemes. Instead of using a single complementary color, this scheme uses the color on either side of the direct complementary color. Split-complementary colors create softer contrasts, unlike the bold contrast in complementary color combinations. Here, I've roughly used three split-complementary colors for the squares but have added a few more colors in the stripes.

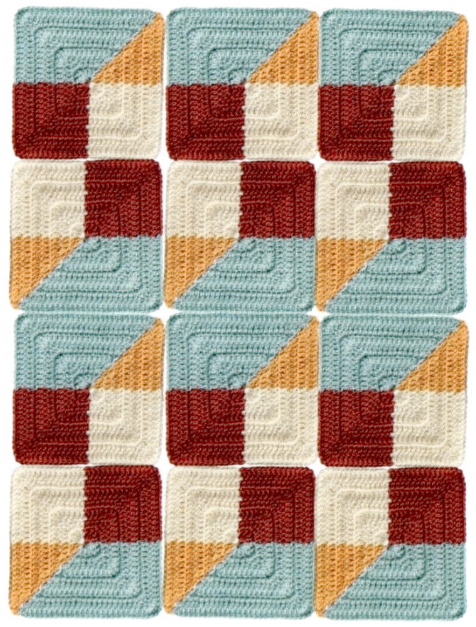

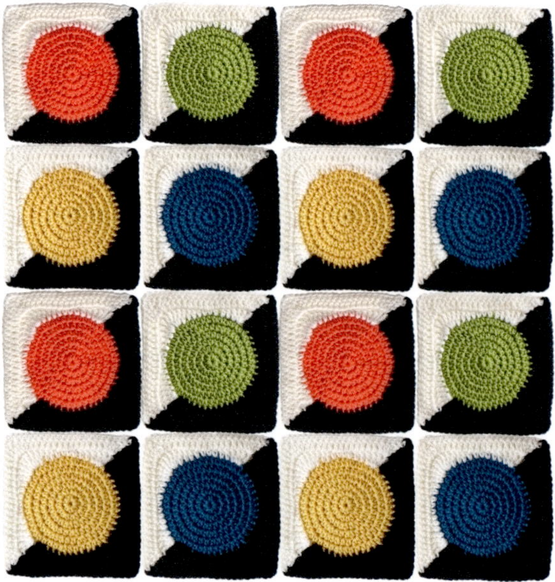

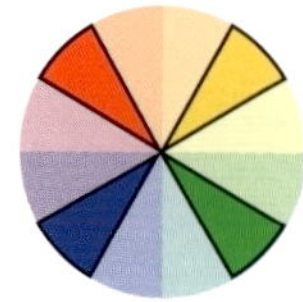

Square

Four colors equidistant from one another on the color wheel can be used to create square color schemes. Unlike the tetradic scheme, these colors create a softer contrast.

Tetradic

This color scheme uses four colors comprised of two complementary pairs that sit opposite each other on the color wheel. This color scheme uses both warm and cool colors in a pleasing way.

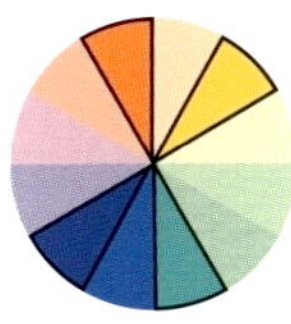

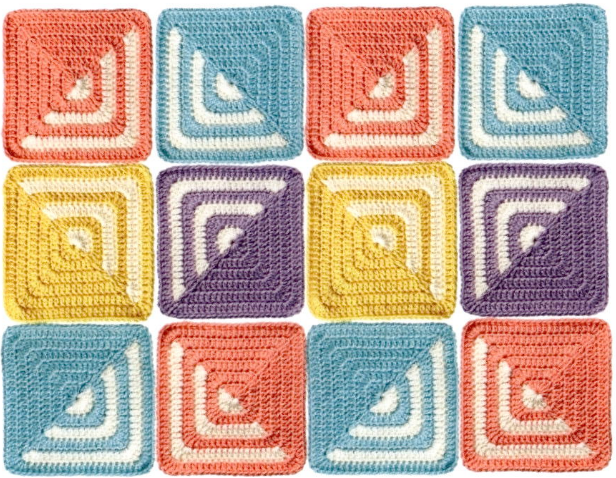

Neutrals

Neutrals are essential in crochet projects. Gray, black, white, and cream are brilliant at bringing color schemes togetherwhen used for joining blocks and edging projects, but they also have impact when used for the blocks themselves.

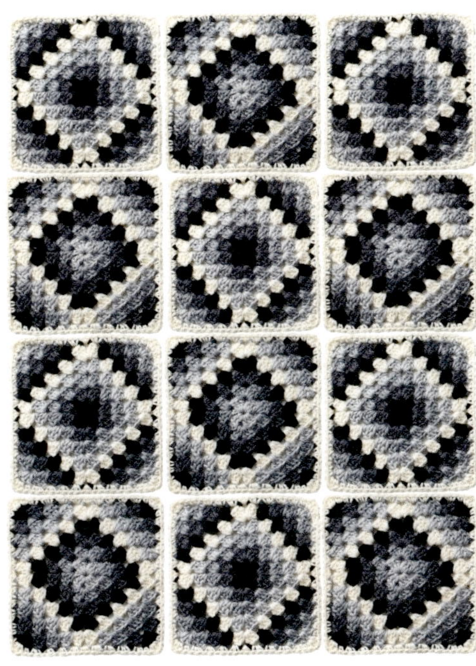

Contrast

By picking two colors that are drastically different in saturation you instantly create a strong contrast; black and white are a prime example of this. You can soften that contrast by selecting colors that are more closely matched in tone.

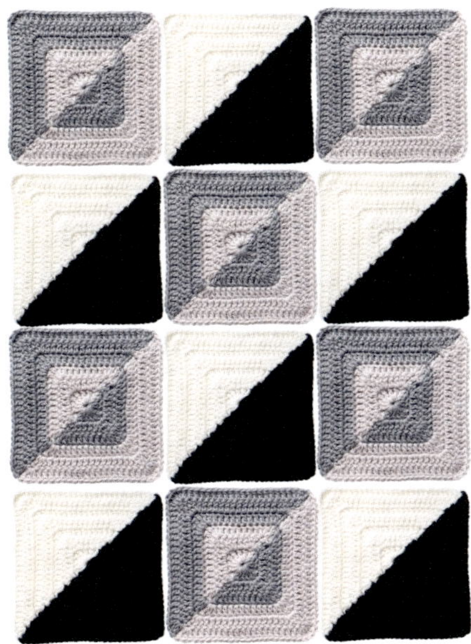

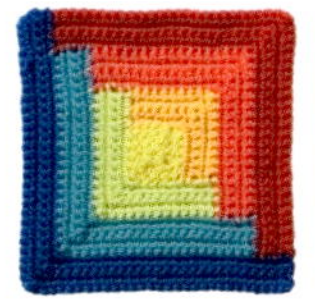

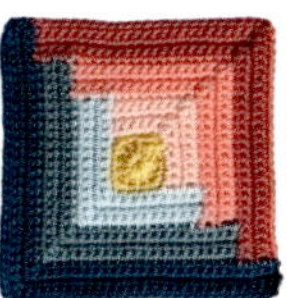

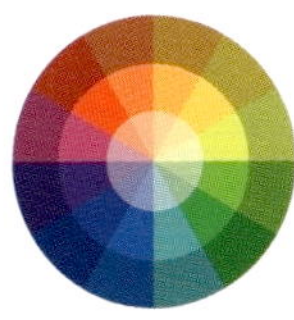

Tone

Tone refers to the amount of gray in a color. The amount of gray will affect the saturation. Saturated colors like hot pink, red, or lime green are vibrant tones, while pale pinks, corals, and soft greens have a more muted tone. For your projects, you can mix different tones together or just stick to vibrant or soft tones. To understand the tone of colors, take a photograph of them and convert the photograph to black and white to see how they work together. This is really handy when you are choosing colors for your projects.

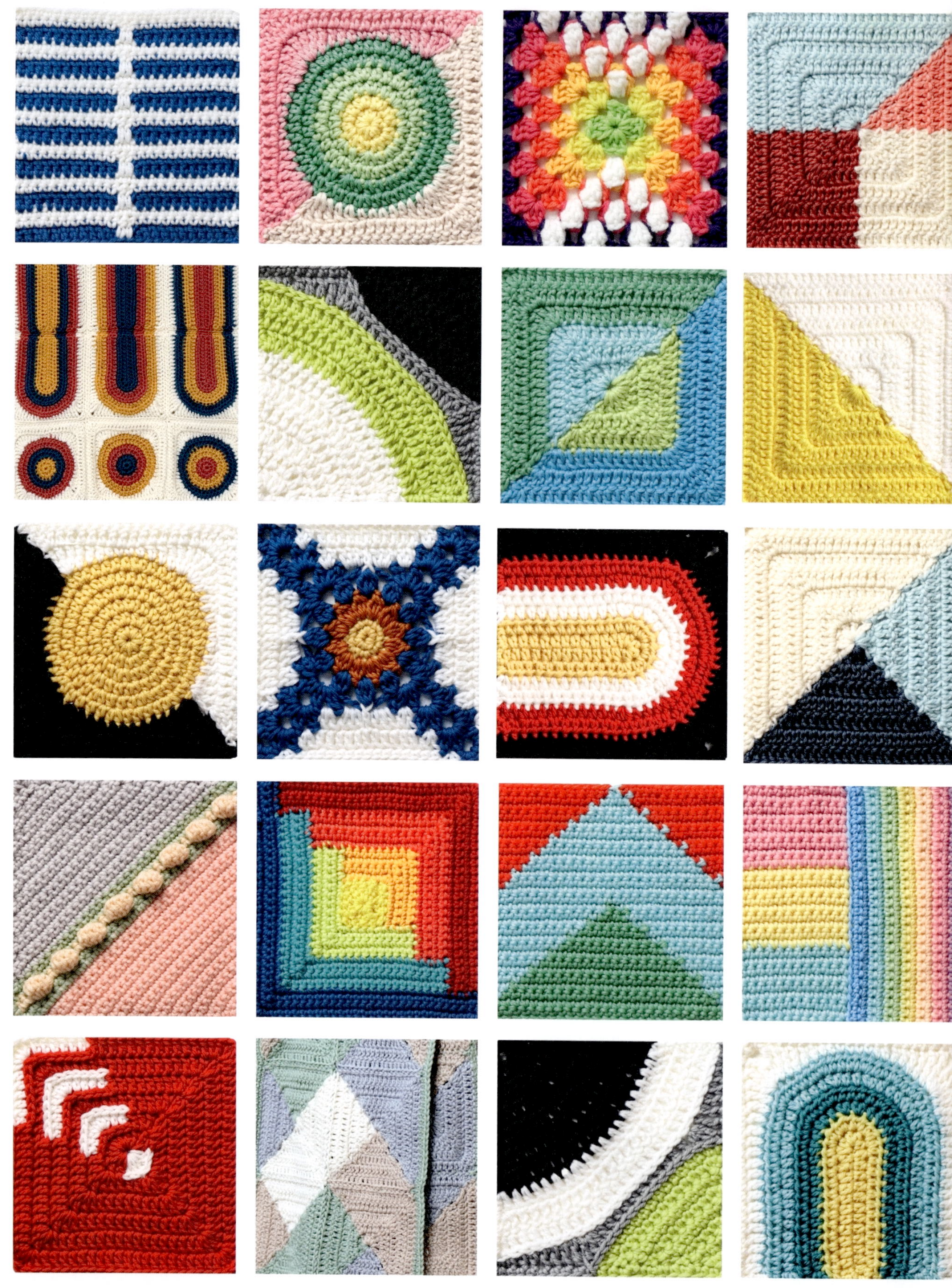

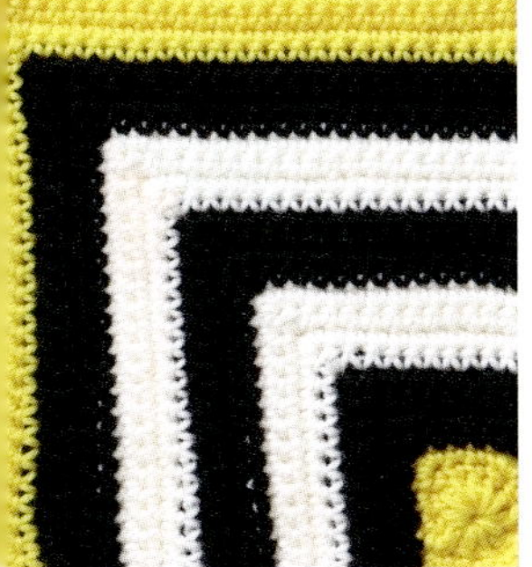
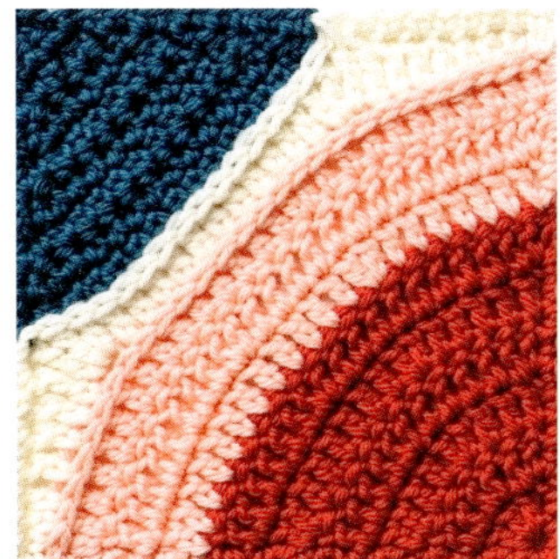
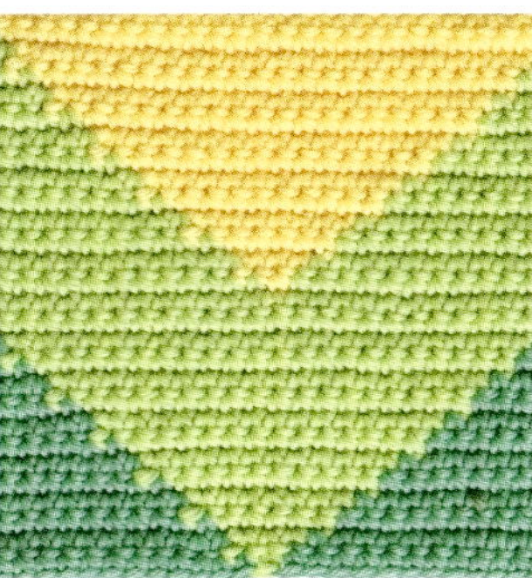
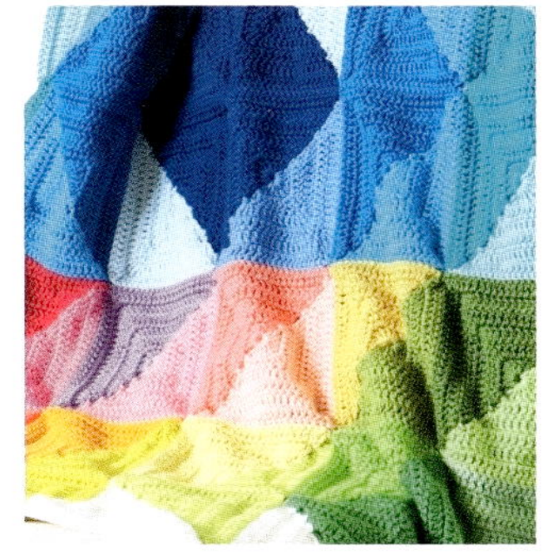
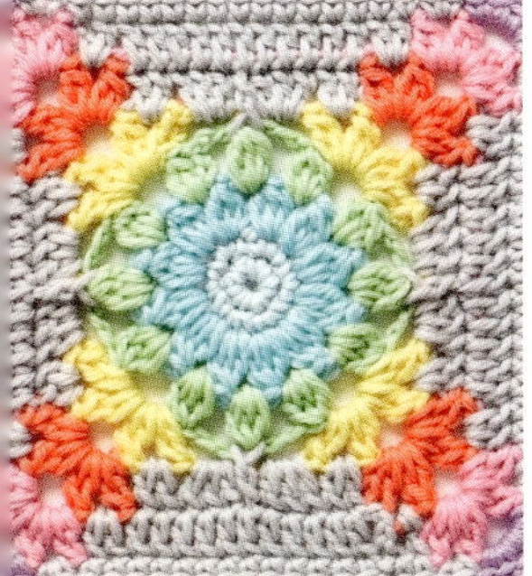
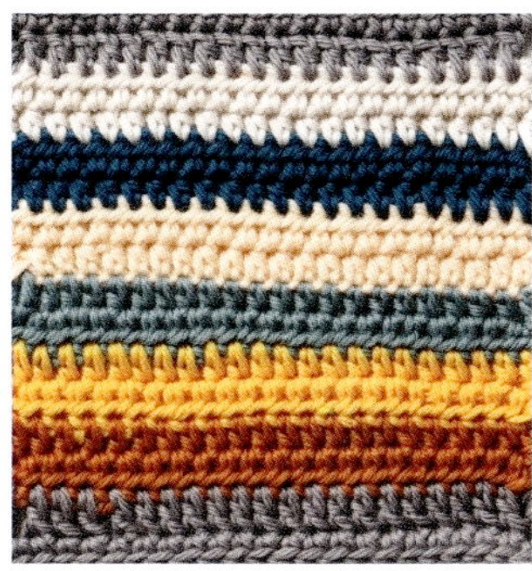

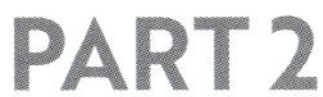

PART 2

Blocks and Projects

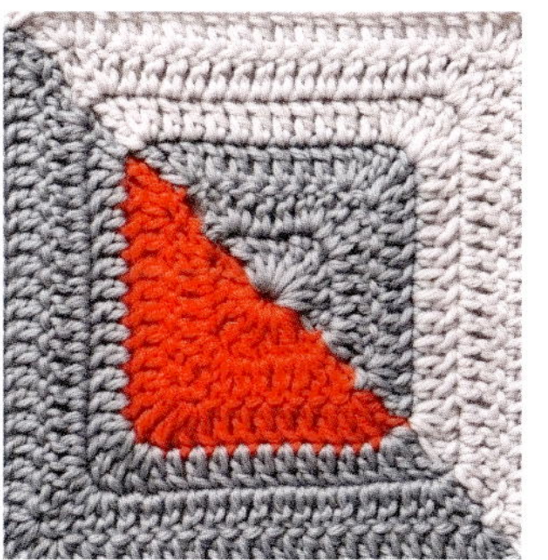
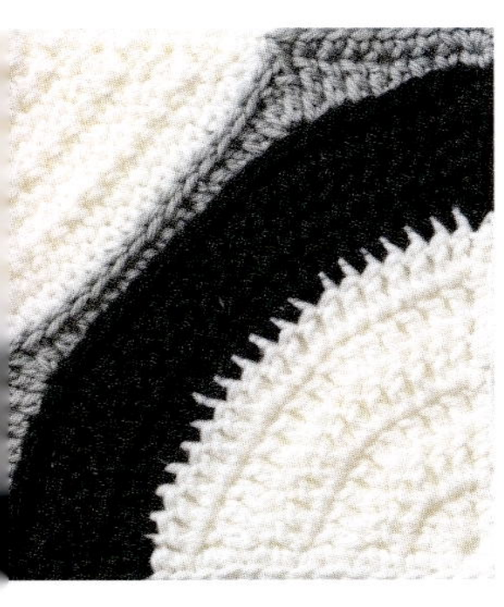
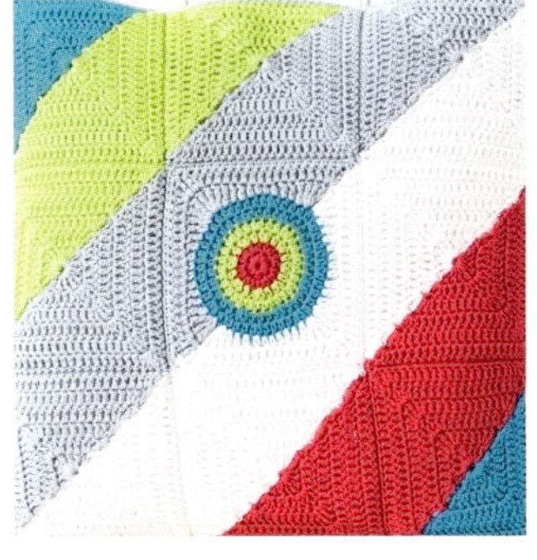
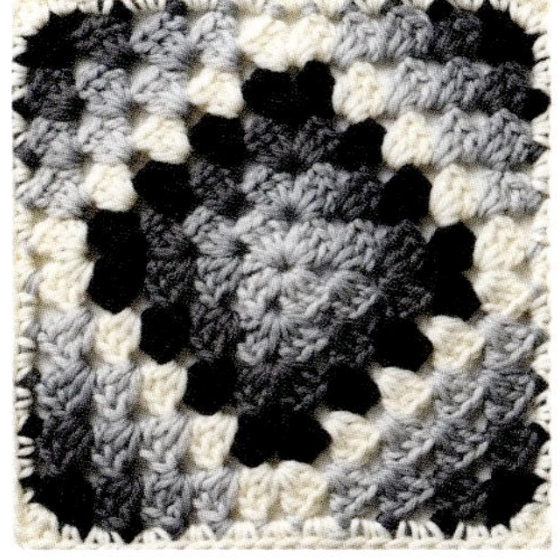
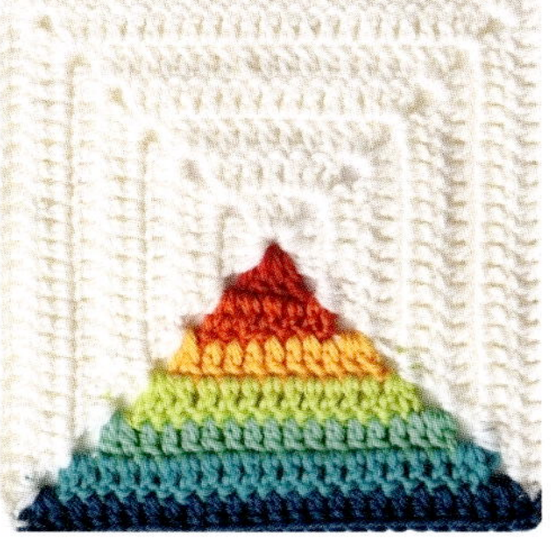
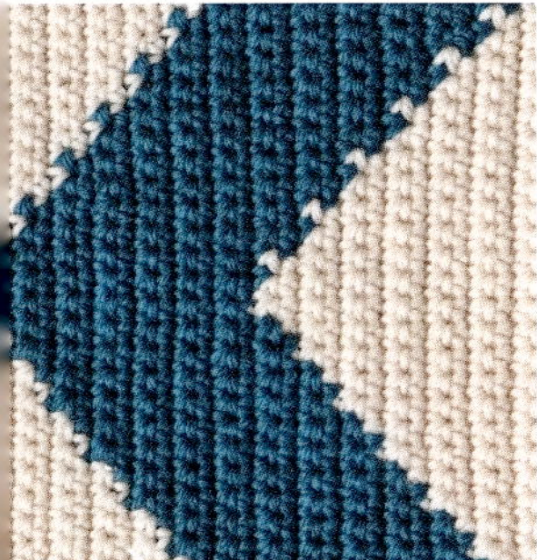
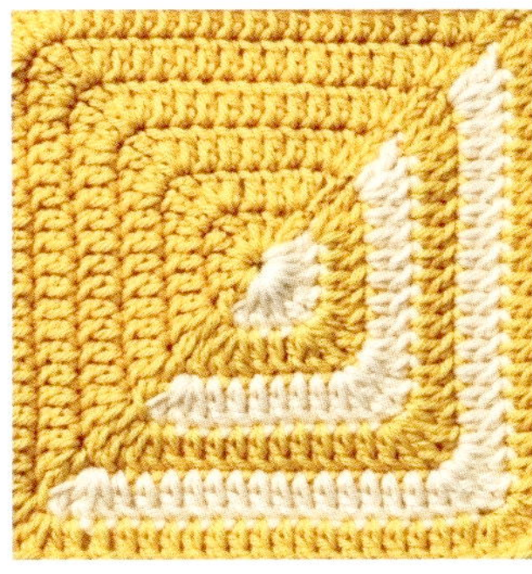
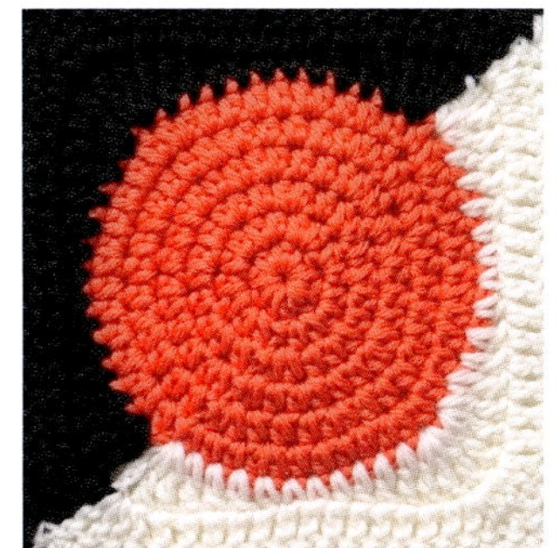
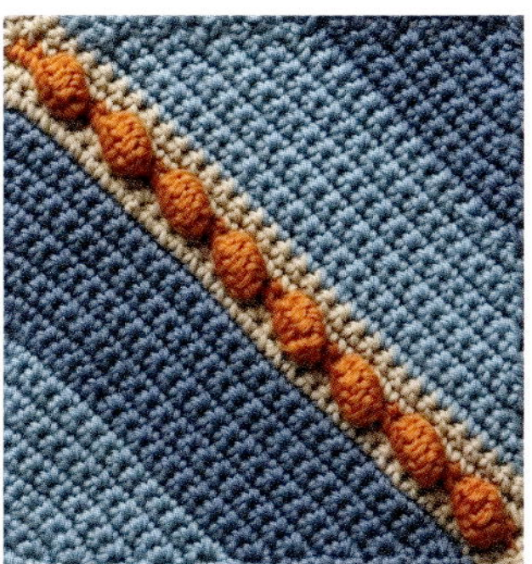

DIAGONAL DOUBLE SPLIT

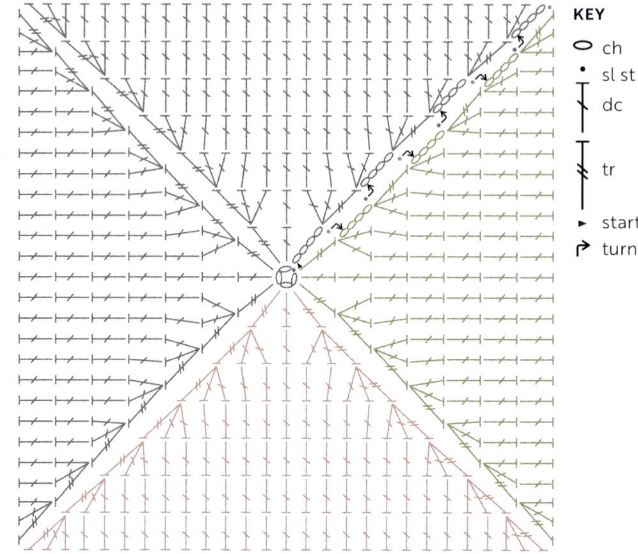

I've used three colors to make these blocks. For a patchwork look, make a selection of blocks where the larger halves are worked in the same color and the two smaller sections are worked in many different colors: perfect for using up scraps of yarn from your stash. The Scarf project on page 123 uses this block.

SKILL LEVEL: Easy

BLOCK SIZE: 6" x 6" (15 x 15 cm)

HOOK SIZE: G/6 (4 mm)

YARN WEIGHT: DK

YARN: Cascade 220 Superwash®

Main Block

Yarn Requirements

Color A: 24 yd (22 m)

Color B: 12 yd (11 m)

Color C: 12 yd (11 m)

A: 338 (Harbor Mist)

B: 365 (Silver Pink)

C: 250 (Laurel Green)

Variations

Yarn Requirements

Color A: 24 yd (22 m)

Color B: 12 yd (11 m)

Color C: 12 yd (11 m)

Colorway 1

A: 355 (Stormy Weather)

B: 1942 (Mint)

C: 817 (Ecru)

Colorway 2

A: 1942 (Mint); **B:** 355 (Stormy Weather); **C:** 817 (Ecru)

Colorway 3

A: 817 (Ecru); **B:** 355 (Stormy Weather); **C:** 1942 (Mint)

Abbreviations and Stitches

ch	chain
sl st	slip stitch
dc	double crochet
tr	treble crochet
beg	beginning
st(s)	stitch(es)
yo	yarn over
( )	work instructions within brackets in place indicated

Notes

- Change yarn colors at the last yo of a designated stitch.
- Leave unused yarn color hanging on the wrong side of the work throughout and pick up from there when needed.

Crochet Pattern

Foundation Ring: Using A, ch 4, join with sl st to first ch made to form a ring.

Rnd 1 (RS): Ch 4 (counts as tr here and throughout), (dc, 2 tr, dc), tr changing to B, (tr, dc), tr changing to C, (tr, dc, tr) into ring, join with sl st in top of beg ch-4, turn—12 sts.

Rnd 2 (WS): Ch 4, 2 dc in same place, dc in 1 st, (2 dc, tr) in next st changing to B when working last st, (tr, 2 dc) in next st, dc in 1 st, (2 dc, tr) in next st changing to A when working last st, (tr, 2 dc) in next st, dc in 1 st, (2 dc, tr) in next st, (tr, 2 dc) in next st, dc in 1 st, (2 dc, tr) in next st, join with sl st in top of beg ch-4, turn—28 sts.

Rnd 3: Ch 4, 2 dc in same place, dc in 5 sts, (2 dc, tr) in next st, (tr, 2 dc) in next st, dc in 5 sts, (2 dc, tr) in next st changing to B when working last st, (tr, 2 dc) in next st, dc in 5 sts, (2 dc, tr) in next st changing to C when working last st, (tr, 2 dc) in next st, dc in 5 sts, (2 dc, tr) in next st, join with sl st in top of beg ch-4, turn—44 sts.

Rnd 4: Ch 4, 2 dc in same place, dc in 9 sts, (2 dc, tr) in next st changing to B when working last st, (tr, 2 dc) in next st, dc in 9 sts, (2 dc, tr) in next st changing to A when working last st, (tr, 2 dc) in next st, dc in 9 sts, (2 dc, tr) in next st, (tr, 2 dc) in next st, dc in 9 sts, (2 dc, tr) in next st, join with sl st in top of beg ch-4, turn—60 sts.

Rnd 5: Ch 4, 2 dc in same place, dc in 13 sts, (2 dc, tr) in next st, (tr, 2 dc) in next st, dc in 13 sts, (2 dc, tr) in next st changing to B when working last st, (tr, 2 dc) in next st, dc in 13 sts, (2 dc, tr) in next st changing to C when working last st, (tr, 2 dc) in next st, dc in 13 sts, (2 dc, tr) in next st, join with sl st in top of beg ch-4, turn—76 sts.

Rnd 6: Ch 4, 2 dc in same place, dc in 17 sts, (2 dc, tr) in next st changing to B when working last st, (tr, 2 dc) in next st, dc in 17 sts, (2 dc, tr) in next st changing to A when working last st, (tr, 2 dc) in next st, dc in 17 sts, (2 dc, tr) in next st, (tr, 2 dc) in next st, dc in 17 sts, (2 dc, tr) in next st, join with sl st in top of beg ch-4, turn—92 sts.

Rnd 7: Ch 4, 2 dc in same place, dc in 21 sts, (2 dc, tr) in next st, (tr, 2 dc) in next st, dc in 21 sts, (2 dc, tr) in next st changing to B when working last st, (tr, 2 dc) in next st, dc in 21 sts, (2 dc, tr) in next st changing to C when working last st, (tr, 2 dc) in next st, dc in 21 sts, (2 dc, tr) in next st, join with sl st in top of beg ch-4. Fasten off—108 sts.

Weave in all ends and block to measure 6" x 6" (15 x 15 cm).

Main Block

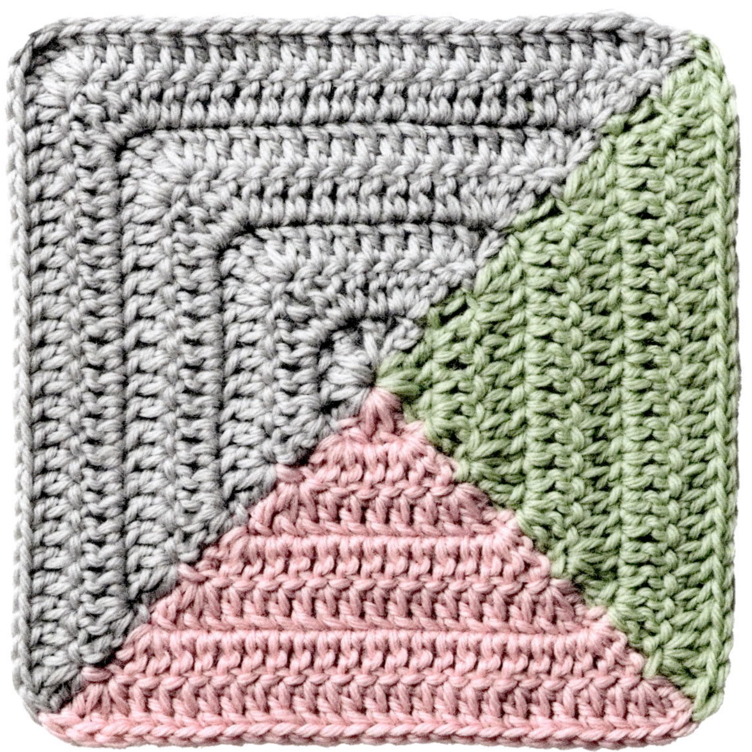

Variation Colorway 1

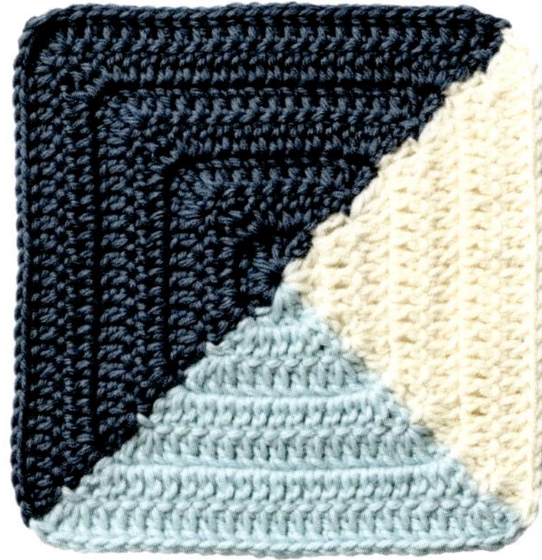

Here, I've used a neutral gray as the dominant color and two complementary colors in smaller quantities. This gives the piece a soft contrast overall.

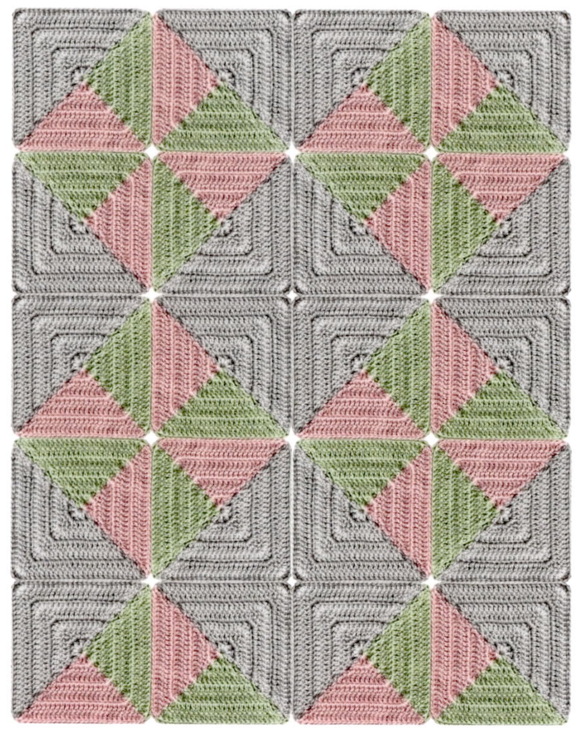

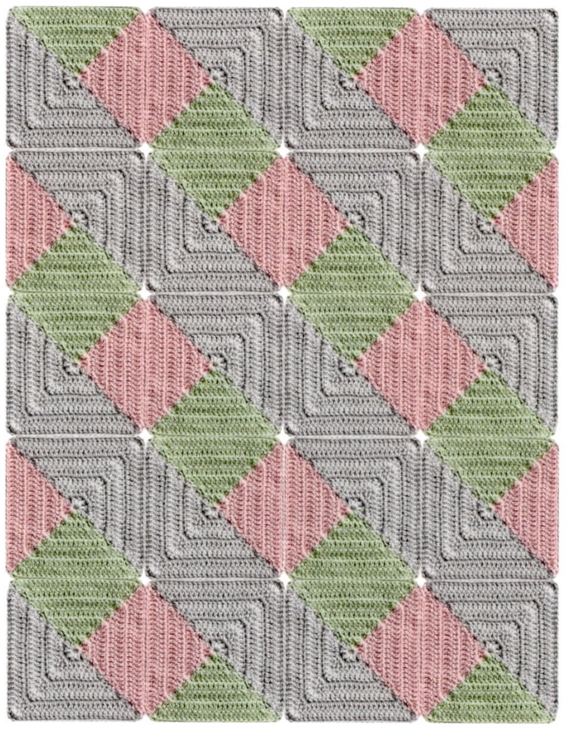

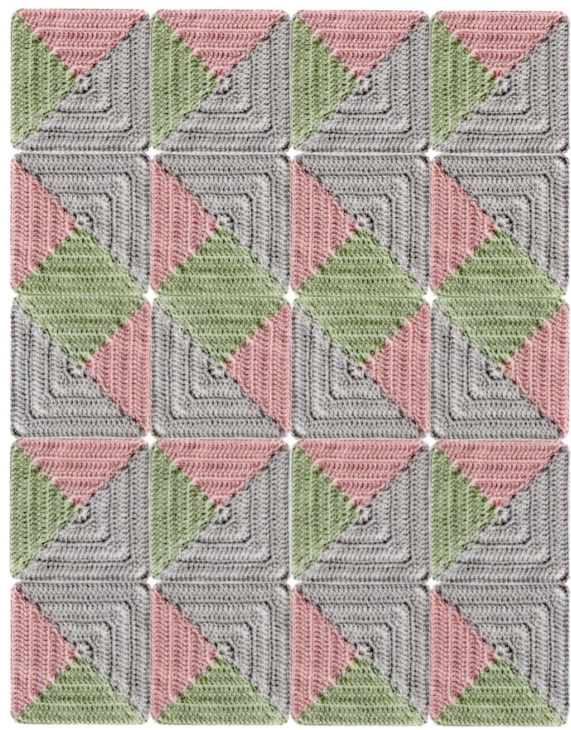

By using two tones of one color and pairing them with a neutral cream, you instantly achieve a more contrasting look. Creating three blocks, each with a different dominant color, allows for lots more opportunities for playing with the colors.

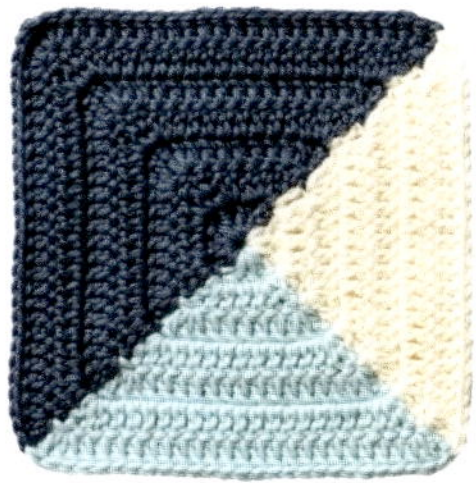

Variation Colorway 1

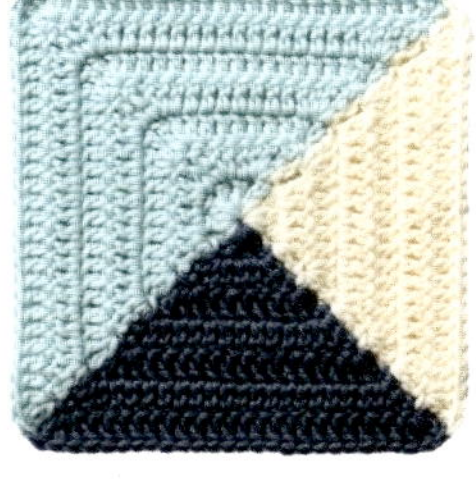

Variation Colorway 2

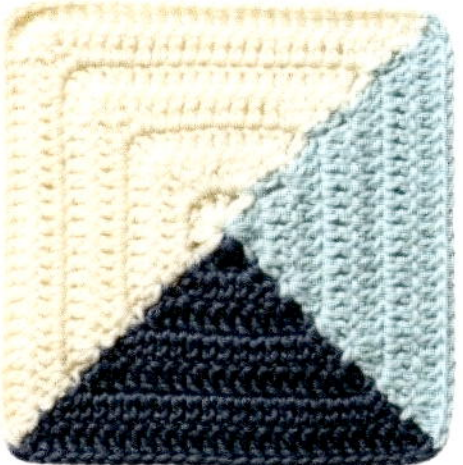

Variation Colorway 3

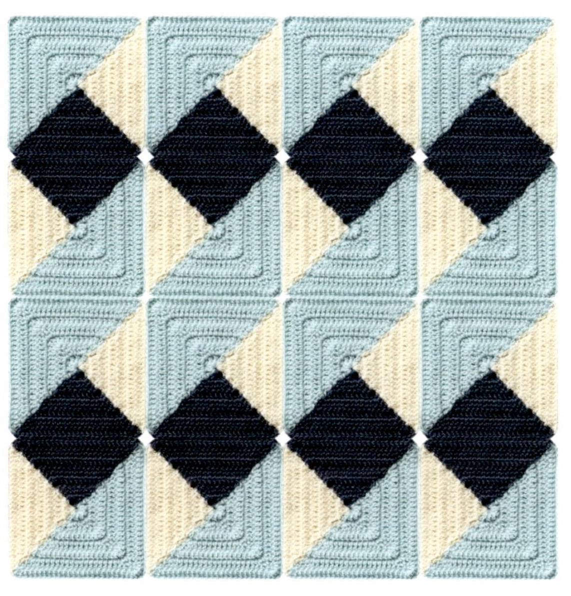

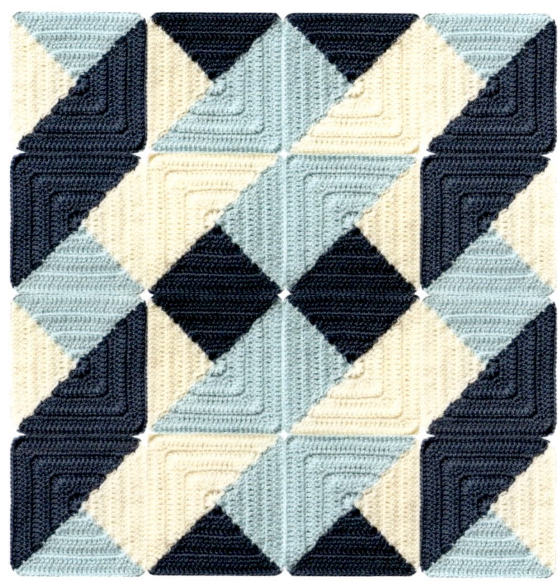

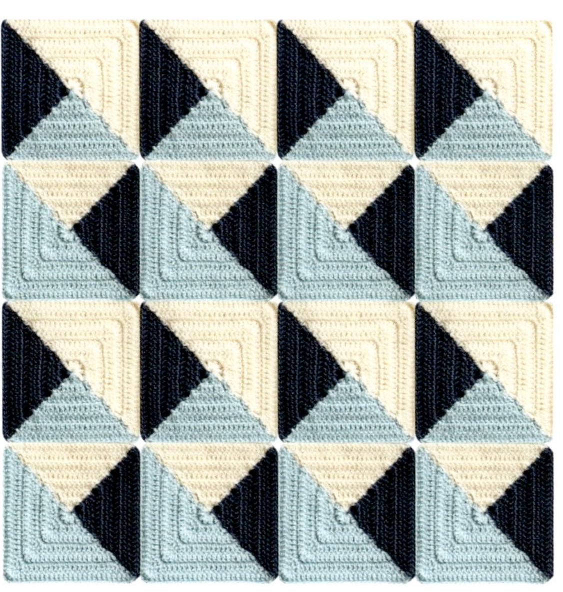

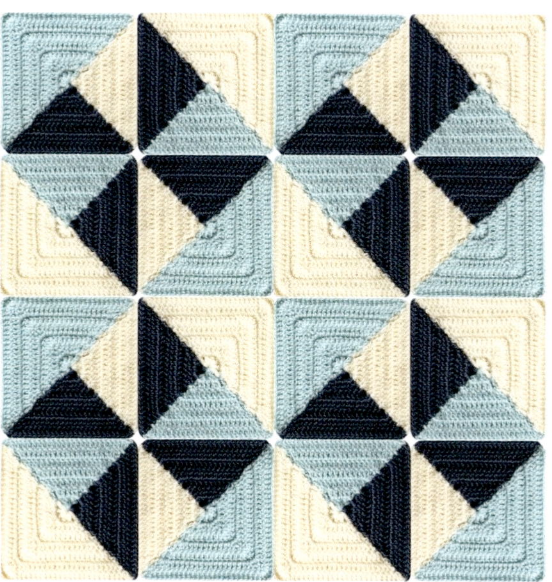

BEE CORNER

Whether vibrant and zingy with a cartoonish feel, or worked in a softer blend of analogous colors, this block has lots of potential for creating zigzags or squares.

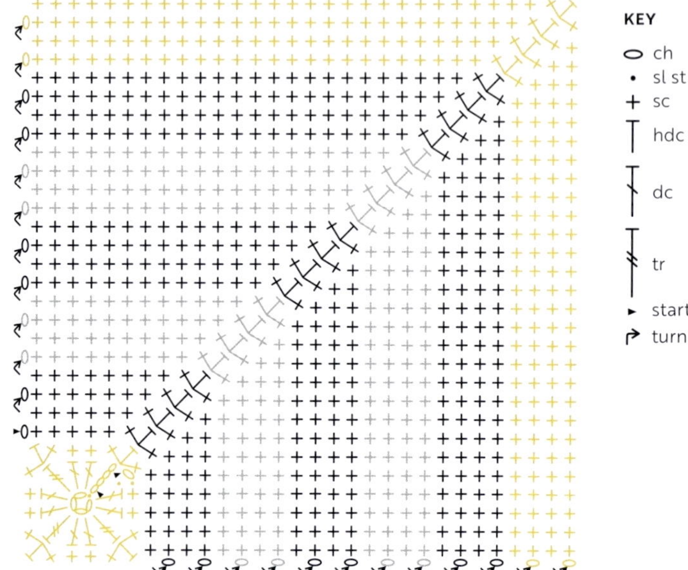

SKILL LEVEL: Easy

BLOCK SIZE: 6" x 6" (15 x 15 cm)

HOOK SIZE: E/4 (3.5 mm)

YARN WEIGHT: DK

YARN: Cascade 220 Superwash®

Main Block

Yarn Requirements

Color A: 15½ yd (14 m)
Color B: 23 yd (21 m)
Color C: 15½ yd (14 m)

Colorway 1

A: 346 (Daisy Yellow)
B: 815 (Black)
C: 871 (White)

Colorway 2

A: 346 (Daisy Yellow); **B:** 871 (White); **C:** 815 (Black)

Variations

Work until Row 10, then continue following instructions using the yarn colors below:

Rows 11–14: D
Rows 15–18: E
Rows 19–22: F
Rows 23–26: A

Yarn Requirements

Color A: 15½ yd (14 m)
Color B: 4½ yd (4 m)
Color C: 5½ yd (5 m)
Color D: 7¾ yd (7 m)
Color E: 10 yd (9 m)
Color F: 11 yd (10 m)

Colorway 1

A: 850 (Lime Sherbet)
B: 820 (Lemon)
C: 821 (Daffodil)
D: 835 (Pink Rose)
E: 282 (Mauve Mist)
F: 842 (Light Iris)

Colorway 2

A: 850 (Lime Sherbet); **B:** 842 (Light Iris); **C:** 282 (Mauve Mist); **D:** 835 (Pink Rose); **E:** 821 (Daffodil); **F:** 820 (Lemon)

Abbreviations and Stitches

ch	chain
sl st	slip stitch
sc	single crochet
hdc	half-double crochet
dc	double crochet
tr	treble crochet
beg	beginning
st(s)	stitch(es)
[ ]	repeat instructions within brackets the stated number of times
( )	work instructions within brackets in place indicated

Crochet Pattern

Foundation Ring: Using A, ch 4, join with sl st to first ch made to form a ring.

Rnd 1 (RS): Ch 4 (counts as tr), [2dc, tr] three times, 2 dc into ring, join with sl st in top of beg ch-4—12 sts.

Rnd 2 (RS): Ch 1 (does not count as a st here and throughout), (sc, hdc, sc) in same place, sc in next 2 sts, [(sc, hdc, sc), sc in next 2 sts] three times, join with sl st to first st made, fasten off A, turn—20 sts.

Row 3 (WS): Join in B in any corner hdc, ch 1, sc in next 5 sts, (sc, hdc, sc) in next st, sc in next 5 sts, turn—13 sts.

Rows 4–6: Ch 1, sc in each st to corner hdc, (sc, hdc, sc) in corner hdc, sc in each st to end, turn. Fasten off B at end of Row 6—19 sts.

Rows 7–10: Join in C, ch 1, sc in each st to corner hdc, (sc, hdc, sc) in corner hdc, sc in each st to end, turn. Fasten off C at end of Row 10—27 sts.

Rows 11–14: Repeat Rows 7–10 using B—35 sts.

Rows 15–18: Repeat Rows 7–10 using C—43 sts.

Rows 19–22: Repeat Rows 7–10 using B—51 sts.

Rows 23–26: Repeat Rows 7–10 using A. Fasten off—59 sts.

Weave in all ends and block to measure 6" x 6" (15 x 15 cm).

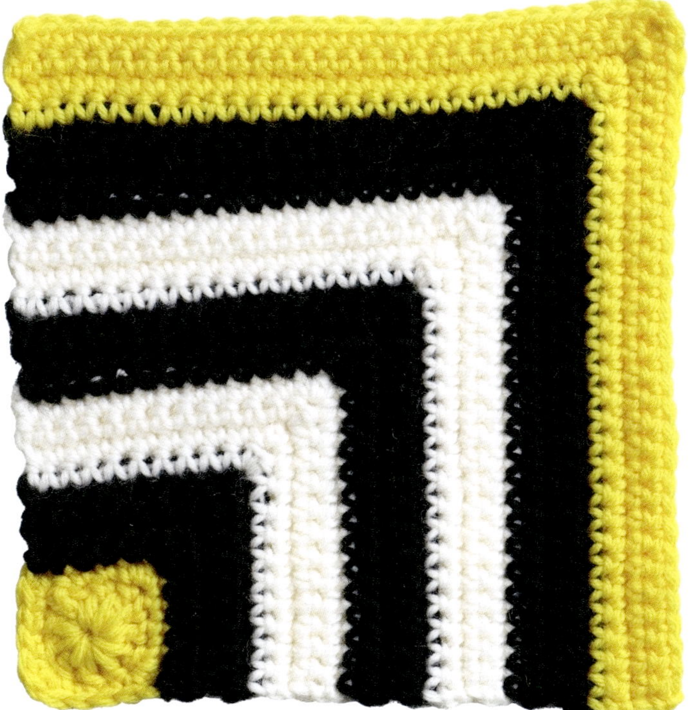

Main Block Colorway 1

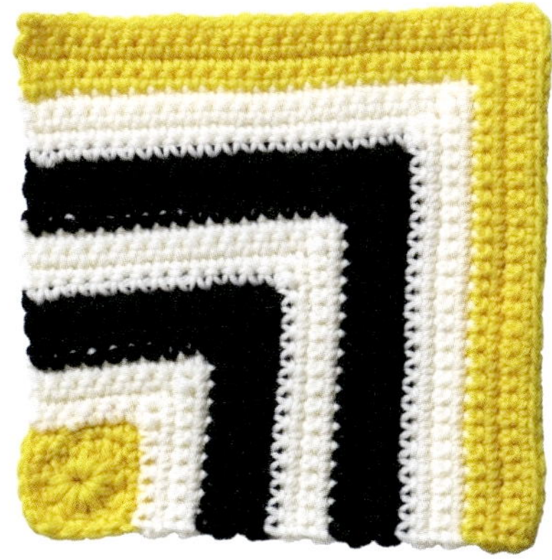

Main Block Colorway 2

In this fun, high contrast colorway you can create zigzags, blocks, or mitred squares in rows. You can join the blocks in some very eye-twizzling combos if you use both colorway options!

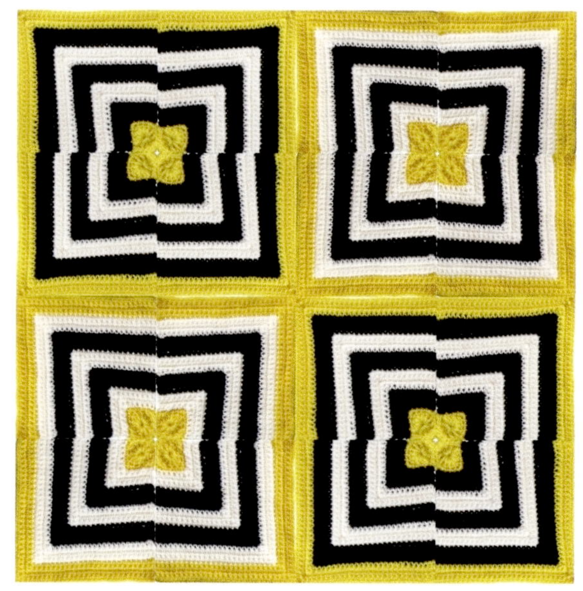

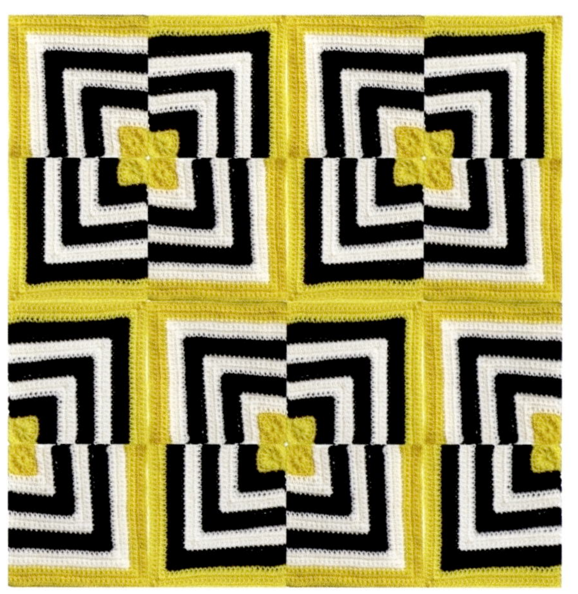

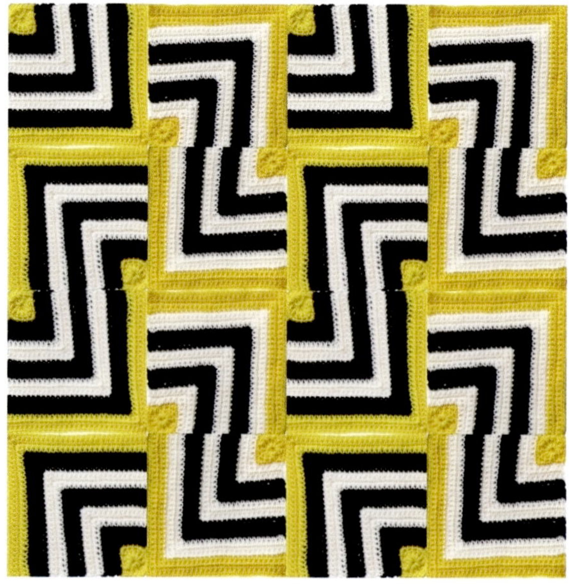

This lower contrast colorway is much softer on the eye when joined. By ensuring both the first few rounds and the last two rows are worked in the same color you can create lots of color patterns.

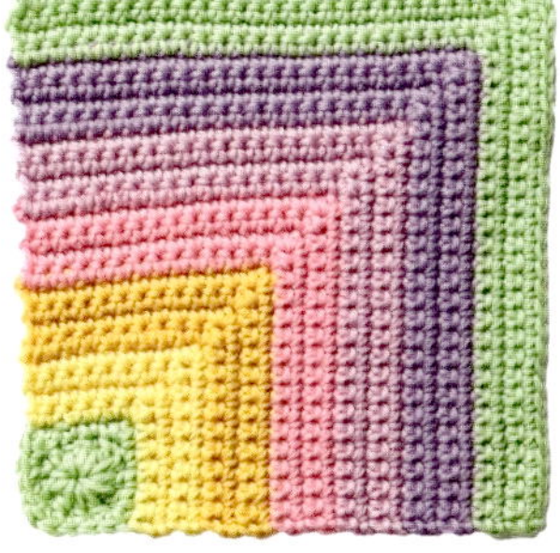

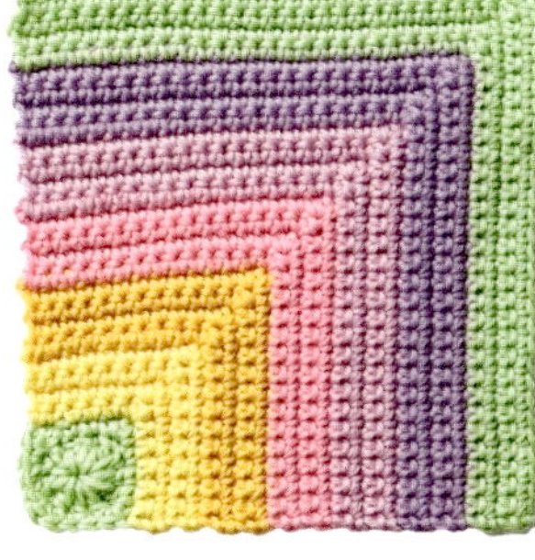

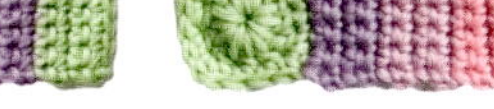

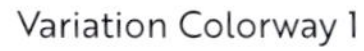

Variation Colorway 1

Variation Colorway 2

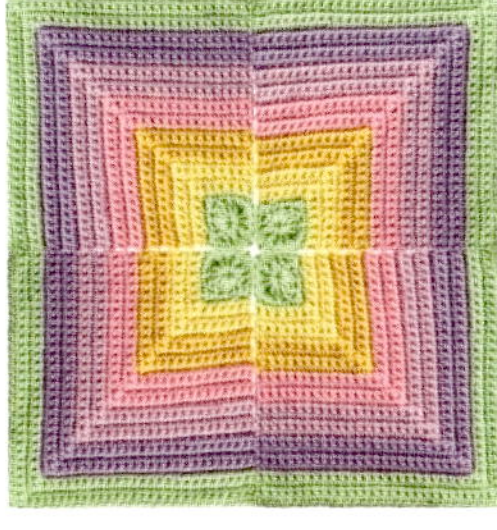

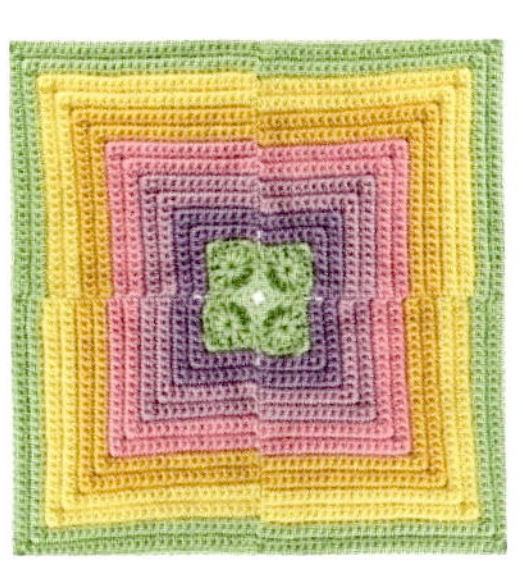

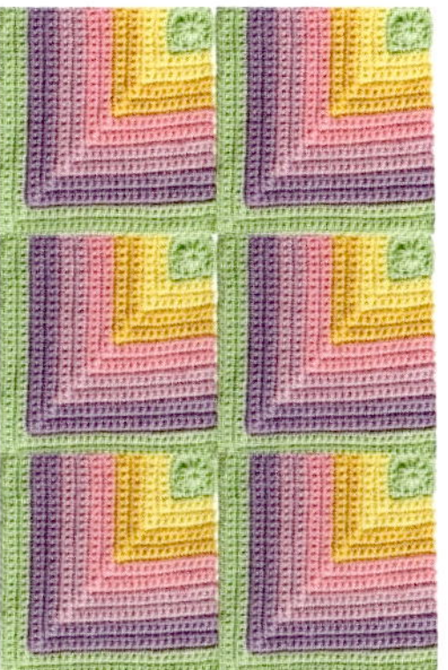

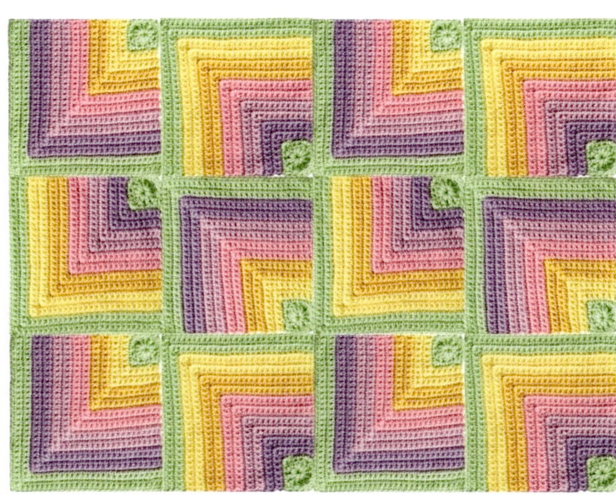

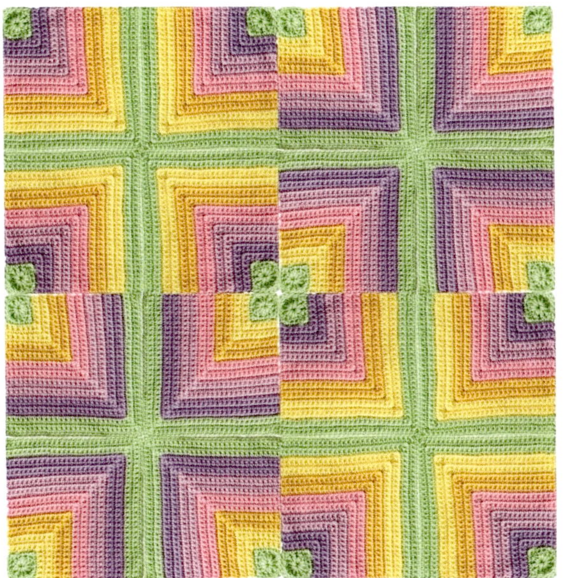

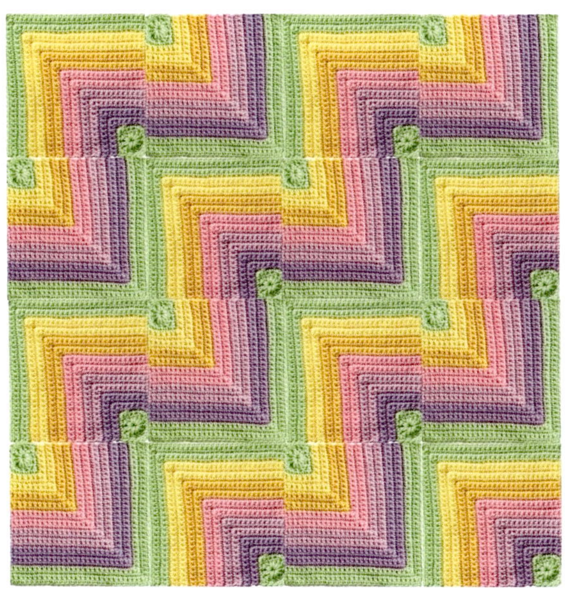

CENTRAL STRIPE

Begin this block in the center and work outward on one edge at a time. This block was designed to complement Arch (see page 56) and is used in the Wall Hanging project on page 118.

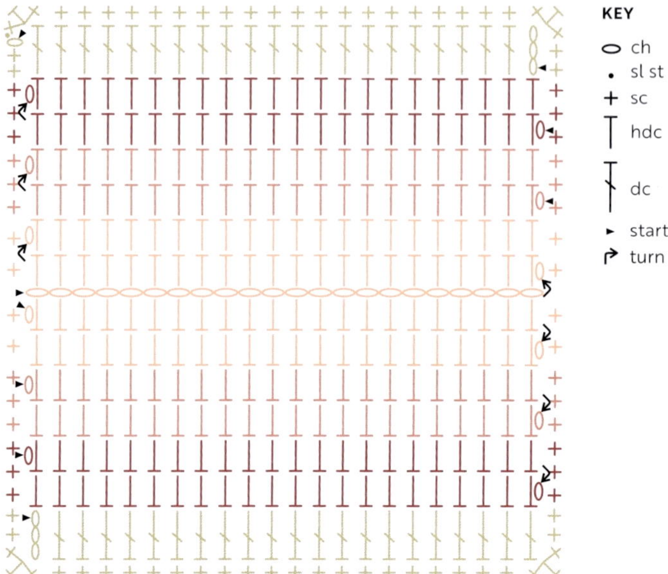

SKILL LEVEL: Easy

BLOCK SIZE: 6" x 6" (15 x 15 cm)

HOOK SIZE: G/6 (4 mm)

YARN WEIGHT: DK

YARN: Cascade 220 Superwash®

Main Block

Yarn Requirements

Each color: 13¼ yd (12 m)

Colorway 1

- **A:** 1941 (Salmon)
- **B:** 364 (Faded Rose)
- **C:** 314 (Garnet)
- **D:** 871 (White)

Colorway 2

A: 871 (White); **B:** 1941 (Salmon); **C:** 364 (Faded Rose); **D:** 314 (Garnet)

Variation

Work until Row 7, then continue following instructions using the yarn colors below:

Rows 8 and 9: E
Rows 10 and 11: F
Rows 12 and 13: G
Row 14: D

Yarn Requirements

Each color: 6½ yd (6m)

- **A:** 289 (Creampuff)
- **B:** 811 (Como Blue)
- **C:** 228 (Frosted Almond)
- **D:** 281 (Frost Grey)
- **E:** 371 (Chinois Green)
- **F:** 877 (Golden)
- **G:** 876 (Sandalwood)

Abbreviations and Stitches

ch	chain
sl st	slip stitch
sc	single crochet
hdc	half-double crochet
dc	double crochet
st(s)	stitch(es)
[ ]	repeat instructions within brackets the stated number of times
( )	work instructions within brackets in place indicated

Notes

- When working the edging, make sure to change to the color of the row end you'll be working into next.
- You can carry unused yarns by holding them toward the back of the work and crocheting over them. This will add a bit of bulk to the edging. Alternatively, you can use separate strands of each color.

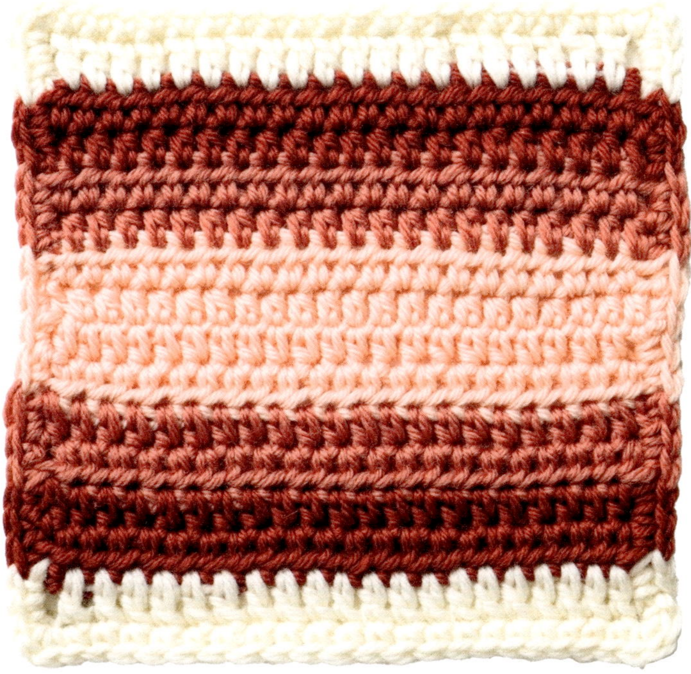

Main Block Colorway 1

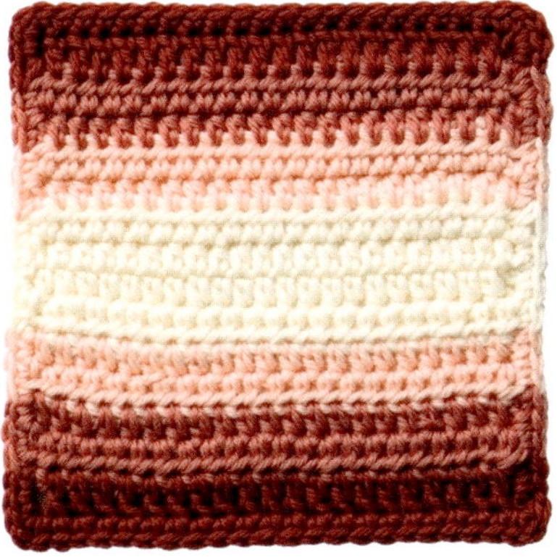

Main Block Colorway 2

Crochet Pattern

Foundation Row: Using A, ch 23.
Row 1 (RS): hdc in second ch from hook and in next 21 ch, turn—22 sts.
Row 2 (WS): Ch 1 (does not count as a st here and throughout), hdc in next 22 sts, fasten off A, turn.
Row 3: Join in B, ch 1, hdc in next 22 sts, turn.
Row 4: Repeat Row 2, fasten off B.
Row 5: Join in C, ch 1, hdc in next 22 sts, turn.
Row 6: Repeat Row 2, fasten off C.
Row 7: Join in D, ch 3 (counts as 1 dc), dc in next 21 sts, fasten off D.
Rotate piece to work along the other side of the foundation chain.
Row 8 (RS): Join in A in first foundation chain, ch 1, hdc in next 22 foundation ch, turn.
Row 9 (WS): Ch 1, hdc in next 22 sts, turn.
Rows 10–14: Repeat Rows 3–7.

Edging (RS): Join in D around post of last st on Row 7, ch 1, [2 sc around post of dc changing to C when working last st, 3 sc across next 2 row ends changing to B when working last st, 3 sc across next 2 row ends changing to A when working last st, 4 sc across next 4 row ends changing to B when working last st, 3 sc across next 2 row ends changing to C when working last st, 3 sc across next 2 row ends changing to D when working last st, 2 sc in next row end, (sc, hdc, sc) in top of next st] twice, join with sl st to first st made. Fasten off all yarns.

Weave in all ends and block to measure 6" x 6" (15 x 15 cm).

You can use this block in just one colorway for some nice layouts, but when you work the block in two colorways you'll have a few more options.

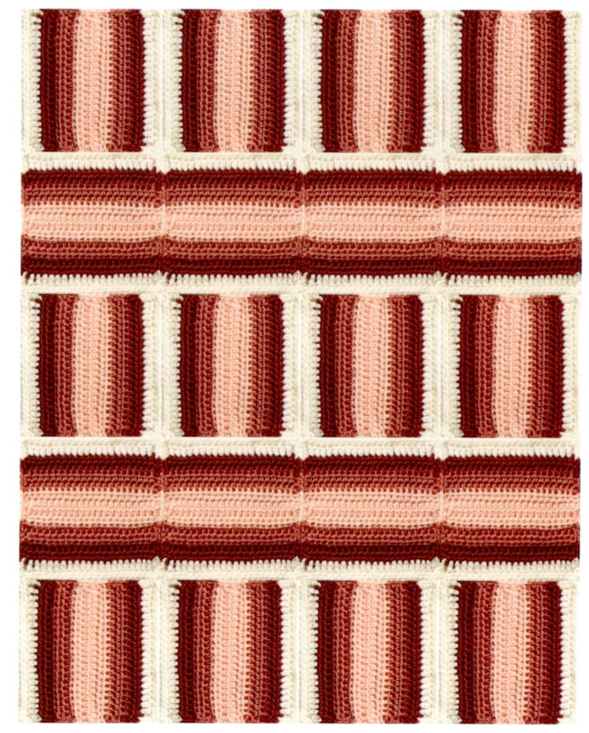

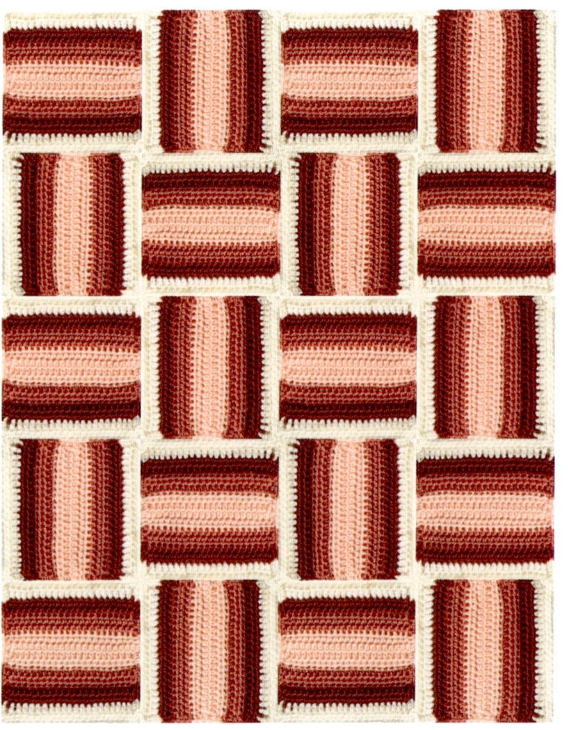

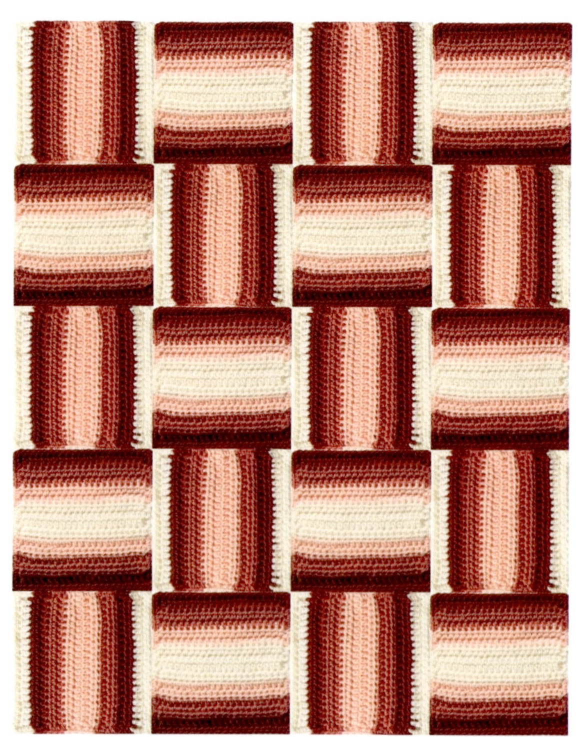

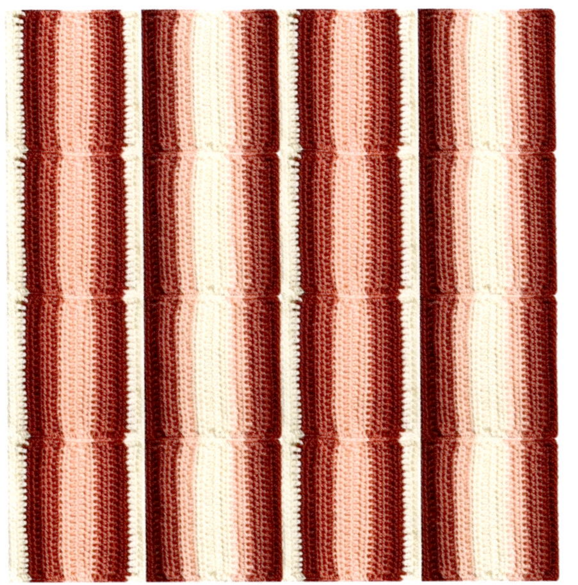

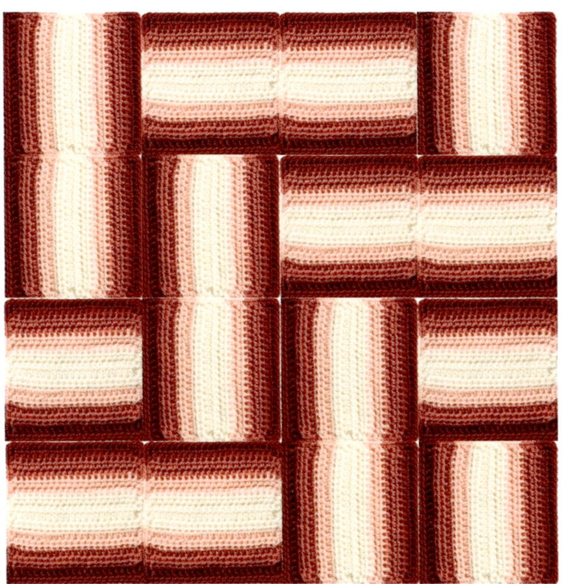

When worked in a range of colors the blocks take on a very different look. For a patchwork look you could work each stripe in leftover yarns from your yarn stash.

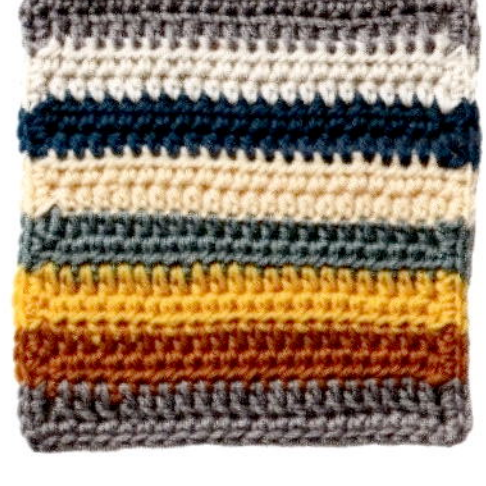

Variation

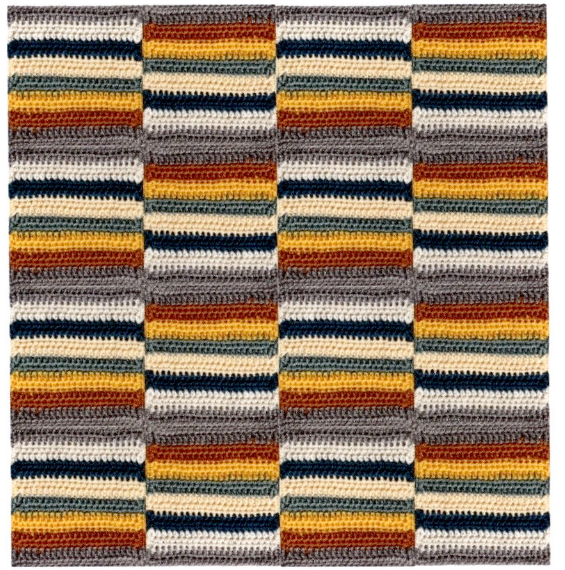

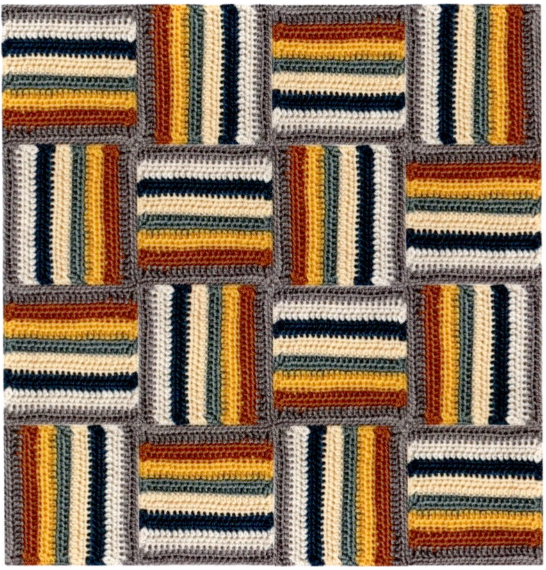

DIAMOND GRANNY

This block is a different take on the traditional granny square. Working the corners in one block of color allows for some interesting color layouts. You could pair this block with a traditional granny square for an alternative granny afghan.

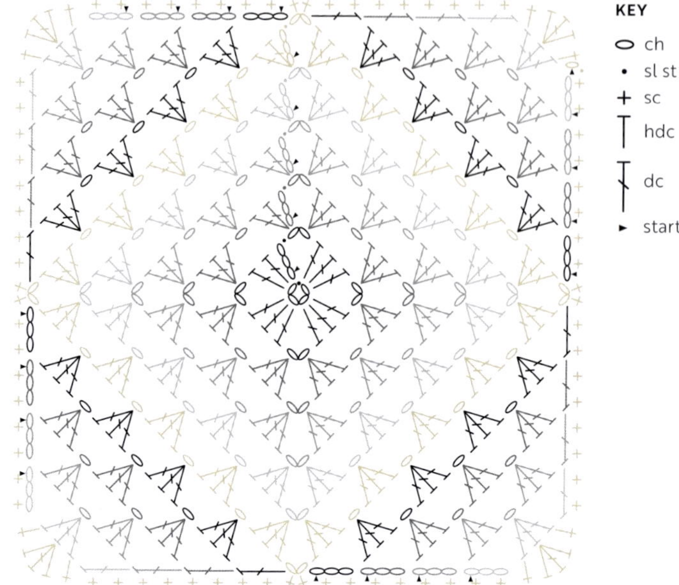

SKILL LEVEL: Easy

BLOCK SIZE: 6" x 6" (15 x 15 cm)

HOOK SIZE: E/4 (3.5 mm)

YARN WEIGHT: DK

YARN: Cascade 220 Superwash®

Main Block

Yarn Requirements

Color A: 10 yd (9 m)

Color B: 10 yd (9 m)

Color C: 10 yd (9 m)

Color D: 10 yd (9 m)

Color E: 14 yd (13 m)

Colorway 1

A: 815 (Black)

B: 816 (Grey)

C: 339 (Sleet)

D: 338 (Harbor Mist)

E: 817 (Ecru)

Colorway 2

A: 338 (Harbor Mist); **B:** 339 (Sleet); **C:** 816 (Grey); **A:** 815 (Black); **E:** 817 (Ecru)

Variation

Work corners in one color only.

Yarn Requirements

Color A: 10 yd (9 m)

Color B: 10 yd (9 m)

Color C: 10 yd (9 m)

Color D: 10 yd (9 m)

Color E: 14 yd (13 m)

A: 310 (Dark Violet)

B: 259 (Blue Turquoise)

C: 837 (Berry Pink)

D: 370 (Sulfur)

E: 809 (Really Red)

Abbreviations and Stitches

ch	chain
sp	space
sl st	slip stitch
sc	single crochet
hdc	half-double crochet
dc	double crochet
beg	beginning
st(s)	stitch(es)
[ ]	repeat instructions within brackets the stated number of times
( )	work instructions within brackets in place indicated

Note

- All rows and rounds are worked with RS facing.

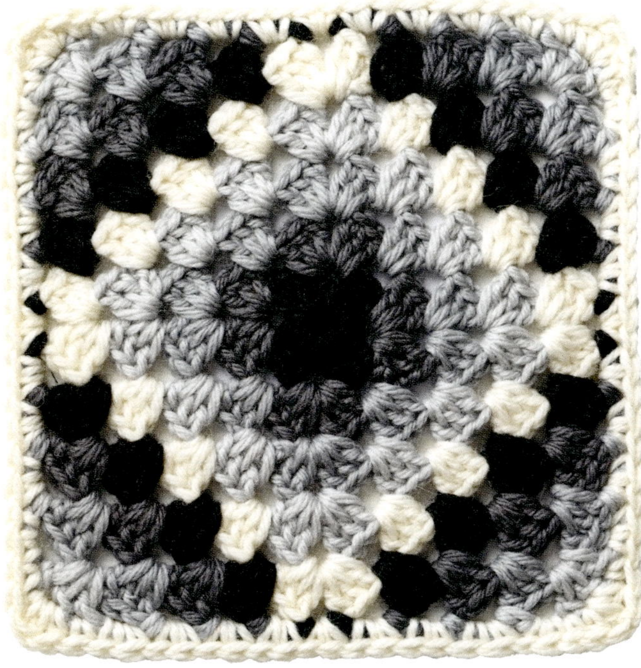

Main Block Colorway 1

Crochet Pattern

Foundation Ring: Using A, ch 4, join with sl st to first ch made to form a ring.
Rnd 1: Ch 3 (counts as dc here and throughout), 2 dc, [ch 2, 3 dc] three times, ch 2, join with sl st to top of beg ch-3, fasten off A—12 sts.
Rnd 2: Join in B in ch-2 sp, ch 3, 2 dc in same place, [ch 1, (3 dc, ch 2, 3 dc) in next ch-2 sp] three times, ch 1, 3 dc in next ch-2 sp, ch 2, join with sl st to top of beg ch-3, fasten off B—24 sts.
Rnd 3: Join in C in ch-2 sp, ch 3, 2 dc in same place, [ch 1, 3 dc in next ch sp, ch 1, (3 dc, ch 2, 3 dc) in next ch-2 sp] three times, ch 1, 3 dc in next ch sp, ch 1, 3 dc in next ch-2 sp, ch 2, join with sl st to top of beg ch-3, fasten off C—36 sts.
Rnd 4: Join in D in ch-2 sp, ch 3, 2 dc in same place, [[ch 1, 3 dc in next ch sp] twice, ch 1, (3 dc, ch 2, 3 dc) in next ch-2 sp] three times, [ch 1, 3 dc in next ch sp] three times, ch 2, join with sl st to top of beg ch-3, fasten off D—48 sts.
Rnd 5: Join in E in ch-2 sp, ch 3, 2 dc in same place, [[ch 1, 3 dc in next ch sp] three times, ch 1, (3 dc, ch 2, 3 dc) in ch-2 sp] three times, [ch 1, 3 dc in next ch sp] three times, ch 1, 3 dc in ch-2 sp, ch 2, join with sl st to top of beg ch-3, fasten off E—60 sts.
Work Rows 6–9 across each edge until all four corners are complete.
Row 6: Join in A in corner ch-2 sp, ch 3, [3 dc in next ch sp, ch 1] three times, 3 dc in next ch sp, dc in next ch-2 sp, fasten off A—14 sts.
Row 7: Join in B in gap between ch 3 and 3-dc group on previous row, ch 3, [3 dc in ch sp, ch 1] twice, 3 dc in next ch sp, dc in gap between last 3-dc group and last dc on previous row, fasten off B—11 sts.
Row 8: Join in C in gap between ch 3 and 3-dc group on previous row, ch 3, 3 dc in ch sp, ch 1, 3 dc in ch sp, dc in gap between last 3-dc group and last dc on previous row, fasten off B—8 sts.
Row 9: Join in D in gap between ch 3 and 3-dc group on previous row, ch 3, 3 dc in ch sp, dc in gap between last 3-dc group and last dc on previous row, fasten off D—5 sts.
Now work around the whole block.
Edging: Join in E in first of 3-dc group in any corner, ch 1 (does not count as a st), sc in same place, [(hdc, dc, hdc) in next st, sc in next st, 2 sc around post of next 4 sts, 2 sc into next ch-2 sp, 2 sc around post of next 4 sts, sc in next st] four times, join with sl st to first st made. Fasten off—96 sts.

Weave in all ends and block to measure 6" x 6" (15 x 15 cm).

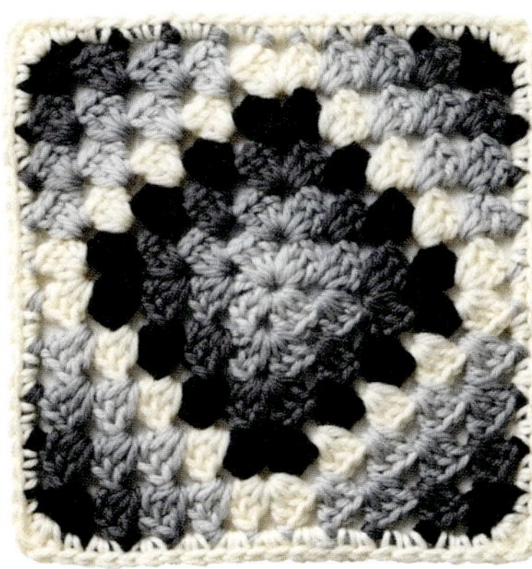

Main Block Colorway 2

This block worked in one colorway looks great when joined. By reversing the colors, you can a create a subtly different color layout.

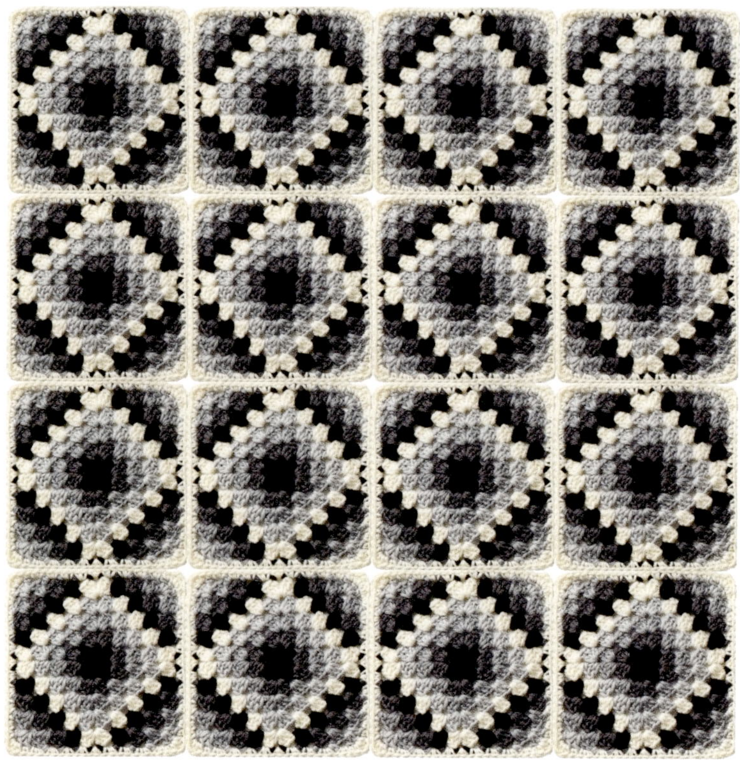

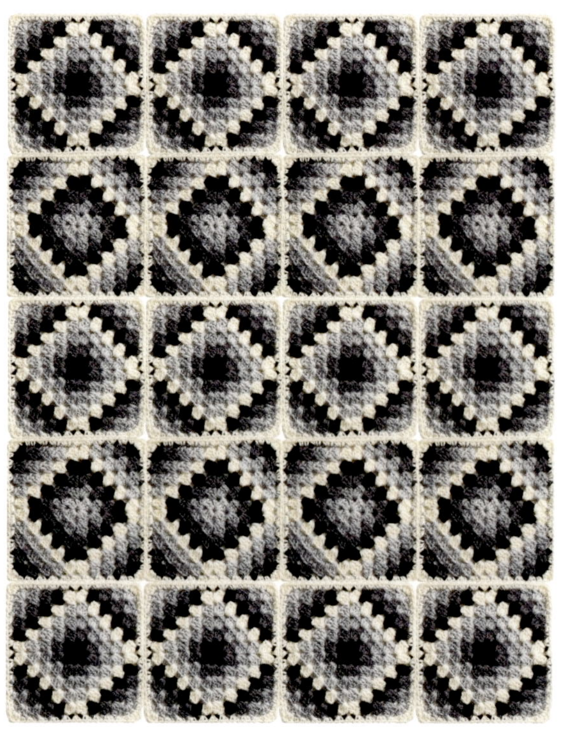

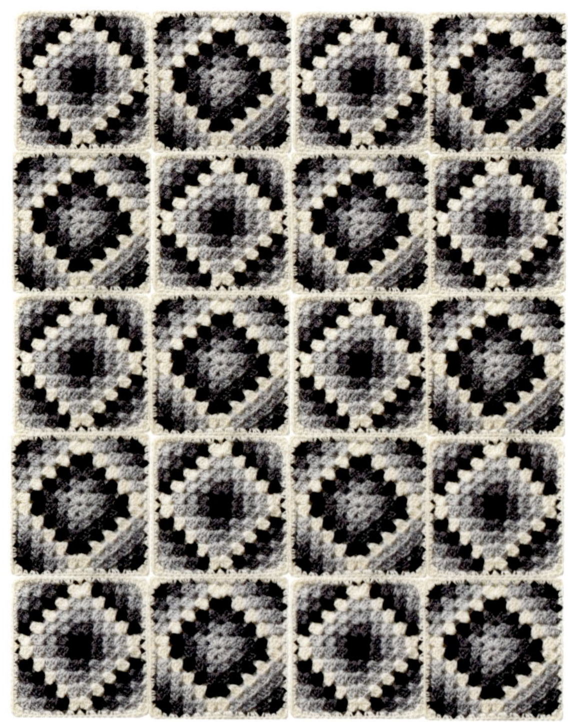

You can create more color shapes in this design by working the corners all in one color rather than stripes.

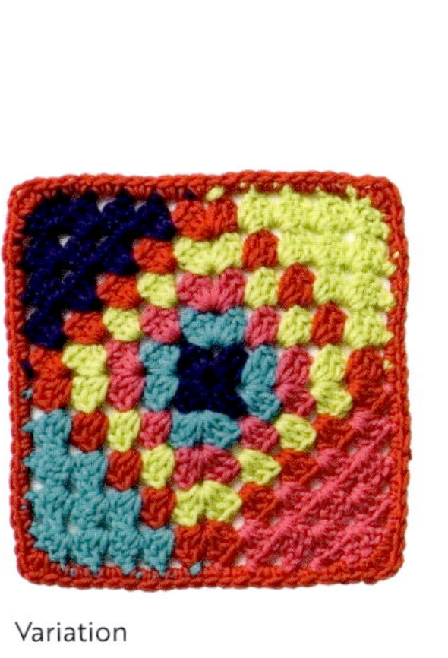

Variation

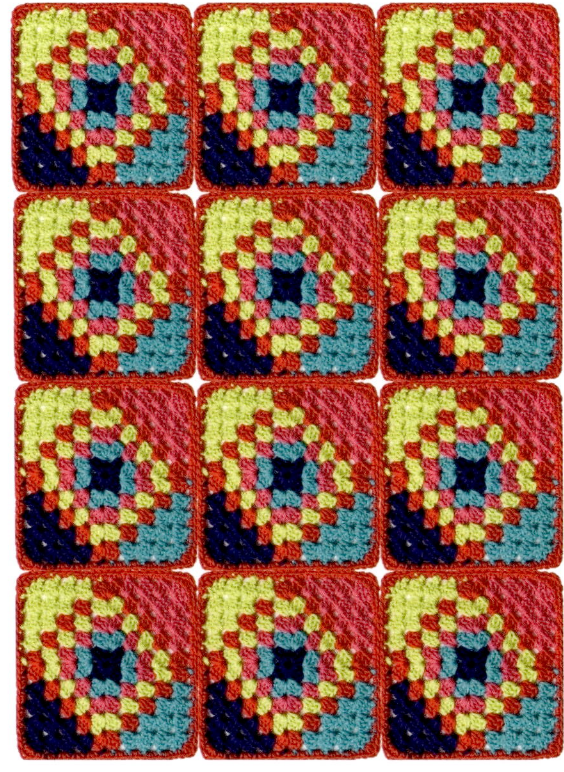

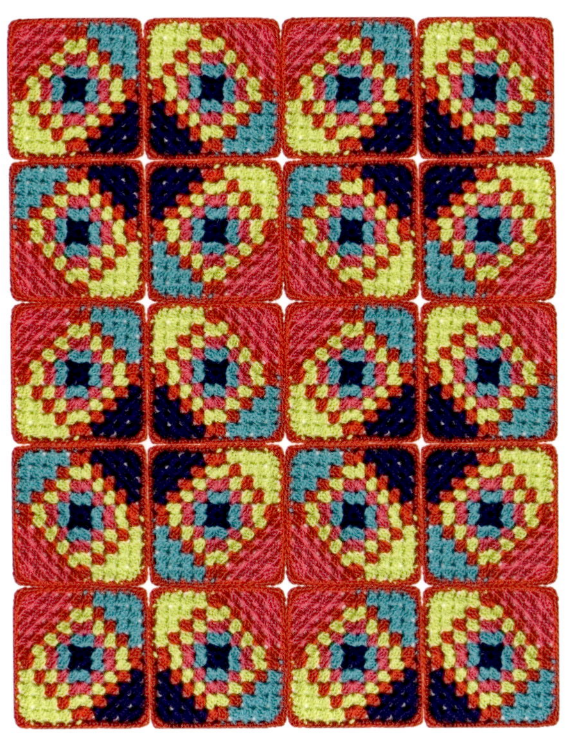

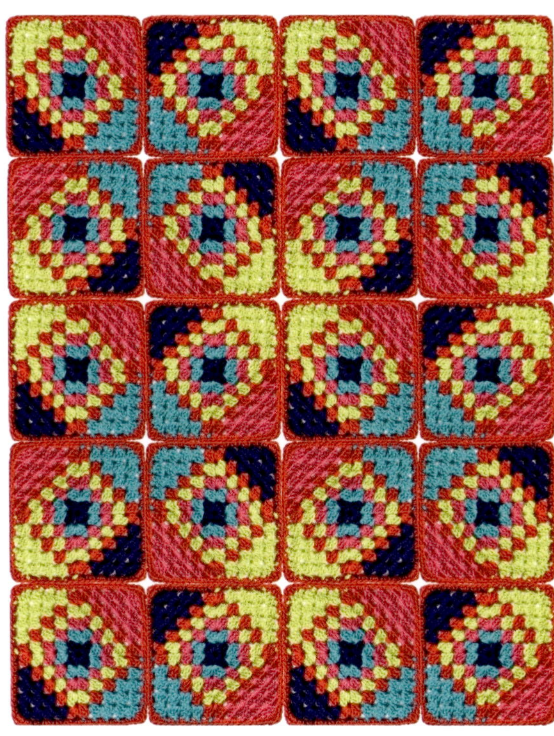

LOG CABIN

You can work this design in all sorts of colorways and lay the squares out in different ways to create a huge variety of designs. Log cabin is a well-known pattern in the quilting world, where you will find lots of inspiration for different color options and layouts.

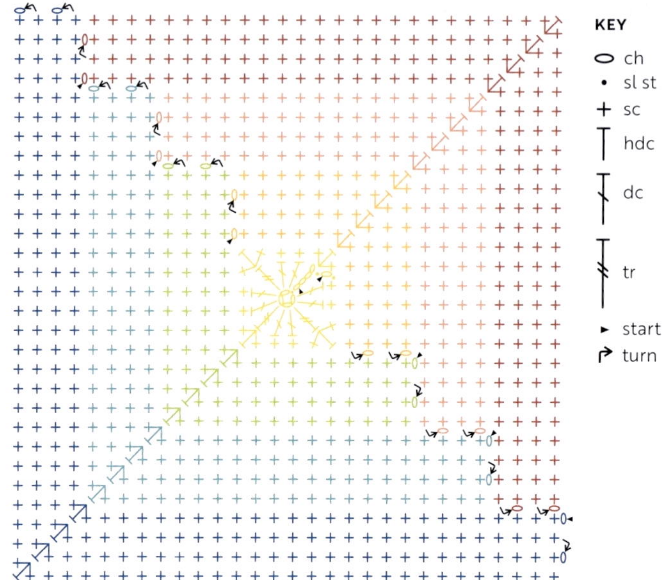

SKILL LEVEL: Easy

BLOCK SIZE: 6" x 6" (15 x 15 cm)

HOOK SIZE: E/4 (3.5 mm)

YARN WEIGHT: DK

YARN: Cascade 220 Superwash®

Main Block

Yarn Requirements

Color A: 3¼ yd (3 m)
Color B: 4½ yd (4 m)
Color C: 5½ yd (5 m)
Color D: 7¾ yd (7 m)
Color E: 10 yd (9 m)
Color F: 11 yd (10 m)
Color G: 12 yd (11 m)

A: 346 (Daisy Yellow)
B: 263 (Gold Fusion)
C: 370 (Sulfur)
D: 290 (Chrysanthemum)
E: 259 (Blue Turquoise)
F: 809 (Really Red)
G: 311 (Blue Sapphire)

Variation

Yarn Requirements

Color A: 4 yd (3 m)
Color B: 4½ yd (4 m)
Color C: 5½ yd (5 m)
Color D: 7¾ yd (7 m)
Color E: 10 yd (9 m)
Color F: 11 yd (10 m)
Color G: 12 yd (11 m)

A: 821 (Daffodil)
B: 1941 (Salmon)
C: 1942 (Mint)
D: 1940 (Peach)
E: 371 (Chinois Green)
F: 364 (Faded Rose)
G: 354 (Mallard Blue)

Abbreviations and Stitches

ch	chain
sl st	slip stitch
sc	single crochet
hdc	half-double crochet
dc	double crochet
tr	treble crochet
beg	beginning
st(s)	stitch(es)
[ ]	repeat instructions within brackets the stated number of times
( )	work instructions within brackets in place indicated

Crochet Pattern

Foundation Ring: Using A, ch 4 and join with sl st in first ch made to form a ring.

Rnd 1 (RS): Ch 4 (counts as tr), [2 dc, tr] three times, 2 dc, join with sl st to top of beg ch-4—12 sts.

Rnd 2: Ch 1 (does not count as a st here and throughout), [(sc, hdc, sc) in corner tr, sc in next 2 sts] four times, join with sl st to first st made, fasten off A—20 sts.

Row 3 (WS): Join in B in corner hdc, ch 1, sc in 5 sts, (sc, hdc, sc) in hdc, sc in 5 sts, turn.

Rows 4–6: Ch 1, sc in each st to corner hdc, (sc, hdc, sc) in corner hdc, sc in each st to end of row, turn. Fasten off B at end of Row 6.

Row 7 (WS): Join in C in row end at beg of Row 6, ch 1, sc in next 4 row ends, sc in next 5 sts, (sc, hdc, sc) in corner hdc, sc in next 5 sts, sc in next 4 row ends, turn.

Rows 8–10: Ch 1, sc in each st to corner hdc, (sc, hdc, sc) in corner hdc, sc in each st to end, turn. Fasten off C at end of Row 10.

Row 11 (WS): Join in D in row end at beg of Row 10, ch 1, sc in next 4 row ends, sc in next 9 sts, (sc, hdc, sc) in corner hdc, sc in next 9 sts, sc in next 4 row ends, turn.

Rows 12–14: Ch 1, sc in each st to corner hdc, (sc, hdc, sc) in corner hdc, sc in each st to end, turn. Fasten off D at end of Row 14.

Row 15 (WS): Join in E in row end at beg of Row 14, ch 1, sc in next 4 row ends, sc in next 13 sts, (sc, hdc, sc) in corner hdc, sc in next 13 sts, sc in next 4 row ends, turn.

Rows 16–18: Ch 1, sc in each st to corner hdc, (sc, hdc, sc) in corner hdc, sc in each st to end, turn. Fasten off E at end of Row 18.

Row 19 (WS): Join in F in row end at beg of Row 18, ch 1, sc in next 4 row ends, sc in next 17 sts, (sc, hdc, sc) in corner hdc, sc in next 17 sts, sc in next 4 row ends, turn.

Rows 20–22: Ch 1, sc in each st to corner hdc, (sc, hdc, sc) in corner hdc, sc in each st to end, turn. Fasten off F at end of Row 22.

Row 23 (WS): Join in G in row end at beg of Row 22, ch 1, sc in next 4 row ends, sc in 21 sts, (sc, hdc, sc) in corner hdc, sc in next 21 sts, sc in next 4 row ends, turn.

Rows 24–26: Ch 1, sc in each st to corner hdc, (sc, hdc, sc) in corner hdc, sc in each st to end, turn. Fasten off G at end of Row 26.

Weave in all ends and block to measure 6" x 6" (15 x 15 cm).

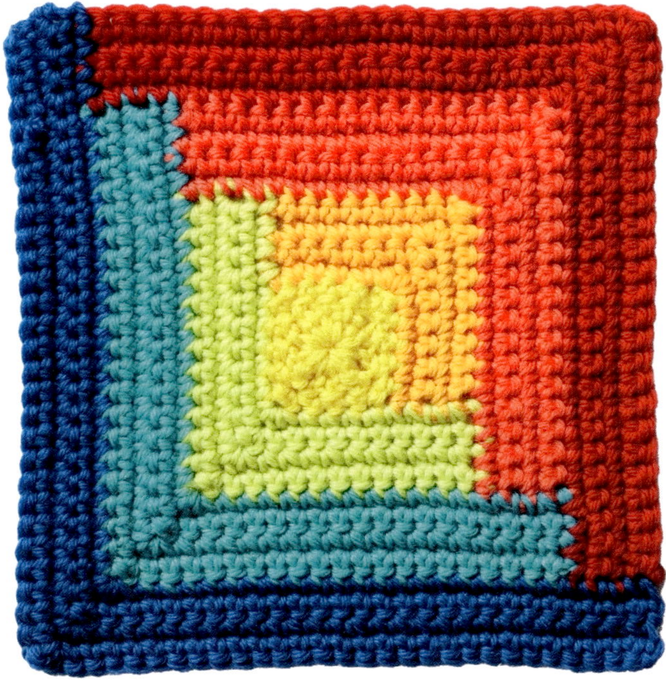

Main Block

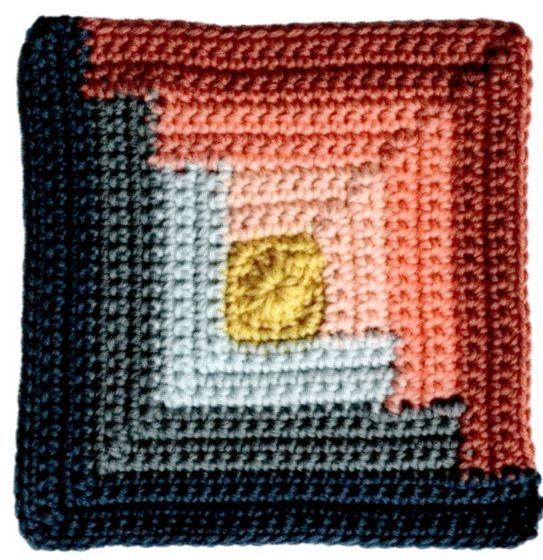

Variation

This block, worked in warm and cool colors with strong saturation, creates a striking color layout. There are oodles of colorplay options for the log cabin in the world of quilting, which I recommend you browse online—there just isn't enough space to showcase them all here!

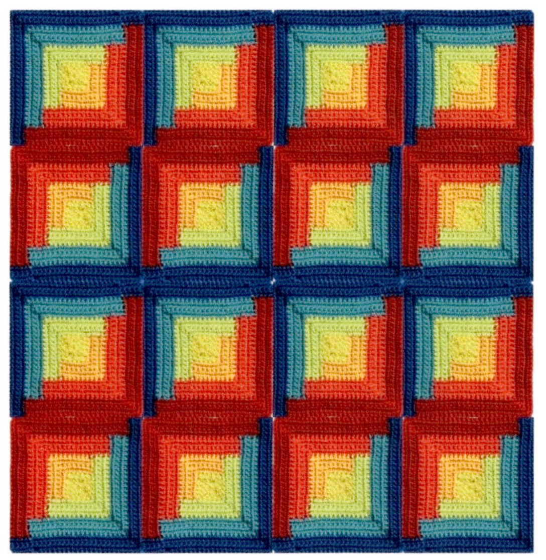

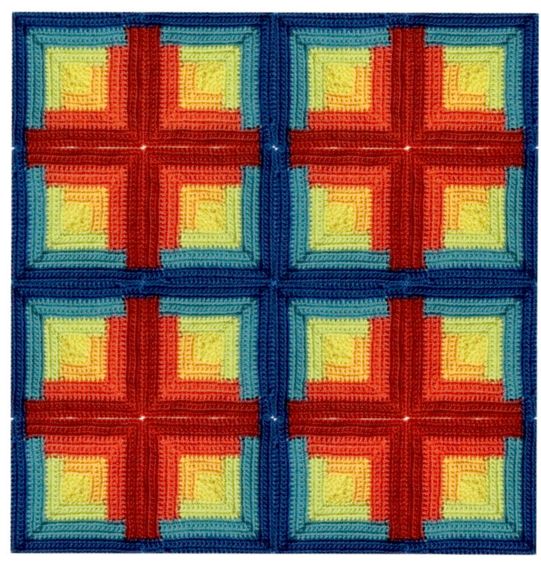

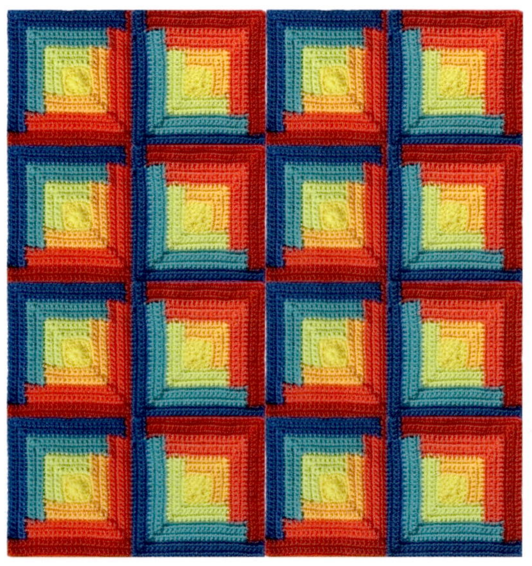

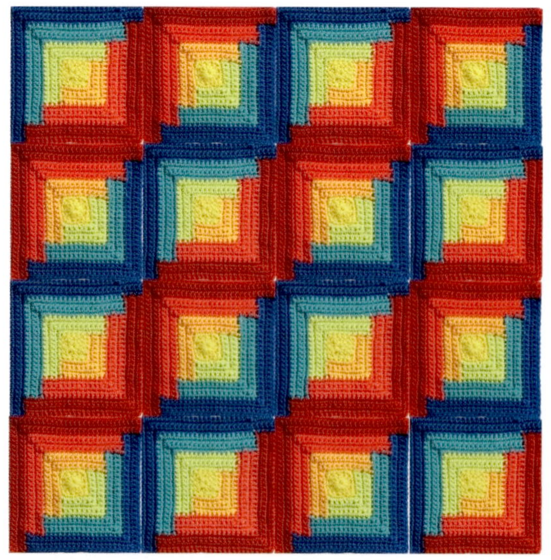

Using less saturated colors gives a calmer feel to the finished piece. If teals and corals aren't your favorite you can pick your own palette by choosing split-complementary colors in a range of saturation levels.

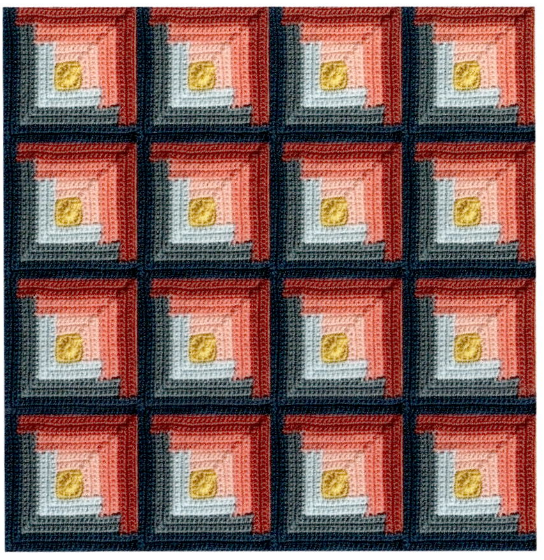

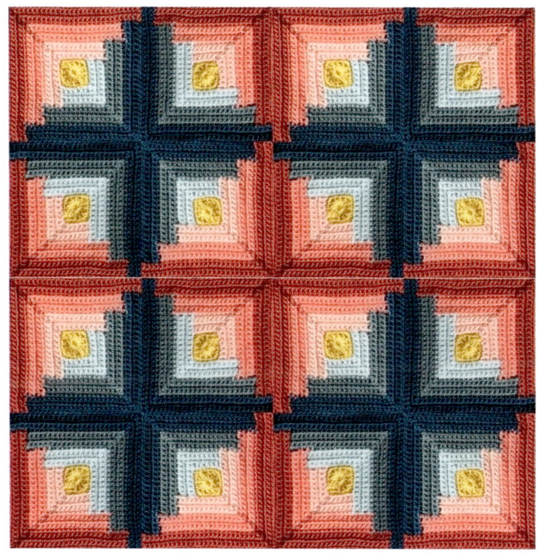

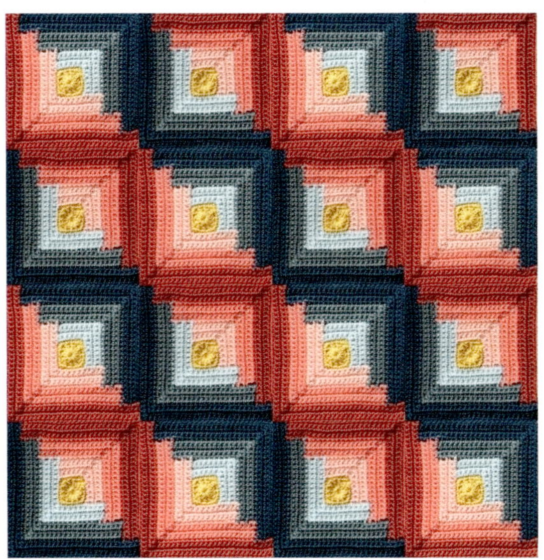

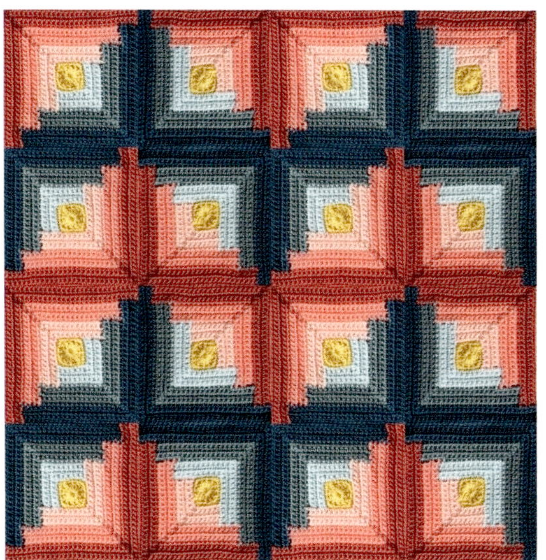

PLEACH

Inspired by the gardening technique of pleaching, in which tree branches are trained horizontally on a frame, this is an easy striped block. When worked in two colors, it creates a broken line pattern. Use a variety of colors for more of a rainbow effect.

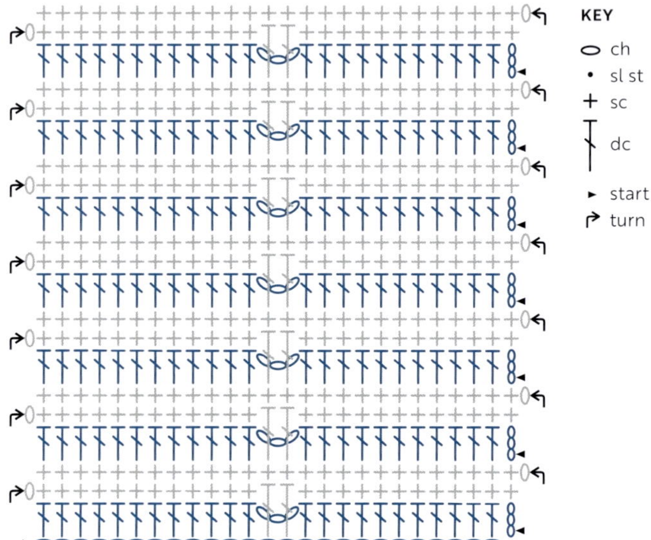

SKILL LEVEL: Easy

BLOCK SIZE: 6" x 6" (15 x 15 cm)

HOOK SIZE: G/6 (4 mm)

YARN WEIGHT: DK

YARN: Cascade 220 Superwash®

Main Block

Yarn Requirements

Color A: 15¼ yd (14 m)
Color B: 23 yd (21 m)

Colorway 1

A: 311 (Blue Sapphire)
B: 871 (White)

Colorway 2

A: 871 (White); **B:** 311 (Blue Sapphire)

Variations

Yarn Requirements

Color A: 2¼ yd (2 m)
Color B: 23 yd (21 m)
Color C: 2¼ yd (2 m)
Color D: 2¼ yd (2 m)
Color E: 2¼ yd (2 m)
Color F: 2¼ yd (2 m)
Color G: 2¼ yd (2 m)
Color H: 2¼ yd (2 m)

Colorway 1

A: 311 (Blue Sapphire)
B: 871 (White)
C: 259 (Blue Turquoise)
D: 370 (Sulfur)
E: 346 (Daisy Yellow)
F: 287 (Deep Sea Coral)
G: 809 (Really Red)
H: 815 (Black)

Colorway 2

Work as for main block, changing color for each repeat of Row 4.

Abbreviations and Stitches

ch	chain
sp	space
sl st	slip stitch
sc	single crochet
dc	double crochet
st(s)	stitch(es)

Crochet Pattern

Foundation Row: Using A, ch 28.
Row 1 (RS): Work dc in fourth ch from hook (first ch-3 counts as dc) and in each of next 10 ch, ch 3, skip 2 ch, dc in next 12 ch, fasten off A, turn—24 sts.
Row 2 (WS): Join in B, ch 1 (does not count as a st here and throughout), sc in 12 sts, dc into each of skipped 2 ch on previous row and working over the ch-3 sp, sc in 12 sts, turn—26 sts.
Row 3: Ch 1, sc in 26 sts, fasten off B—26 sts.
Row 4 (RS): Join in A, ch 3 (counts as dc), dc in 11 sts, ch 3, skip 2 sts, dc in 12 sts, fasten off A, turn—24 sts.
Rows 5–21: Repeat Rows 2–4 five times then repeat Rows 2 and 3 once. Fasten off.

Weave in all ends and block to measure 6" x 6" (15 x 15 cm).

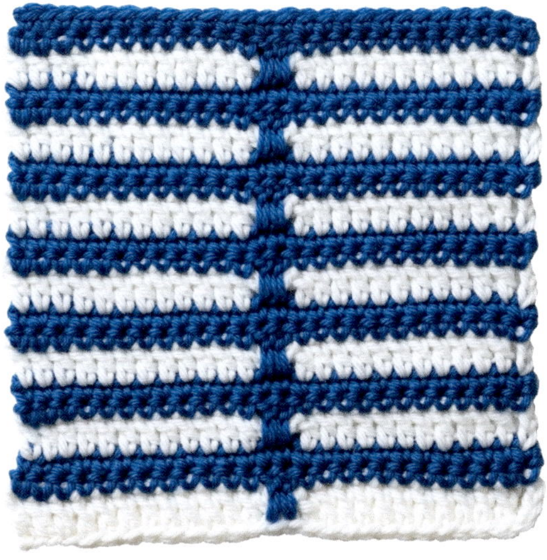

Main Block Colorway 2

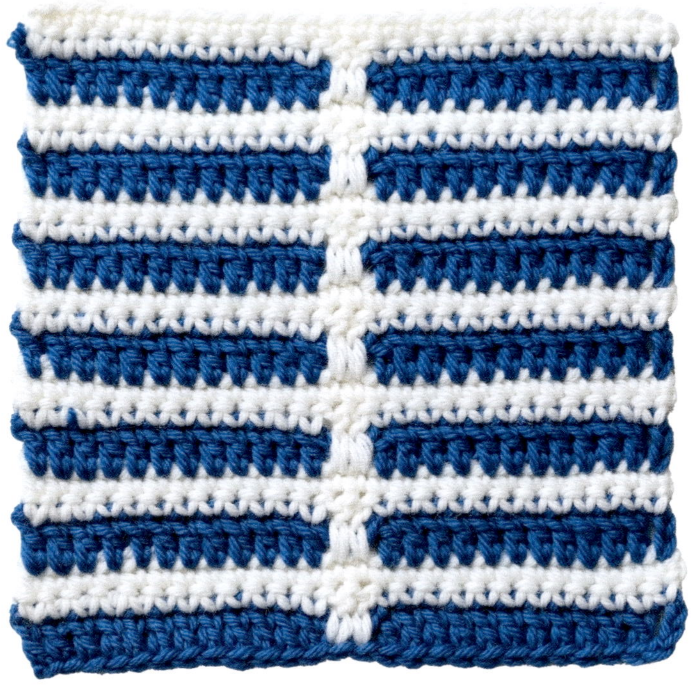

Main Block Colorway 1

This block looks great when worked in just one colorway. When you use both colorways you can create a staggered stripy pattern or a lovely basketweave design.

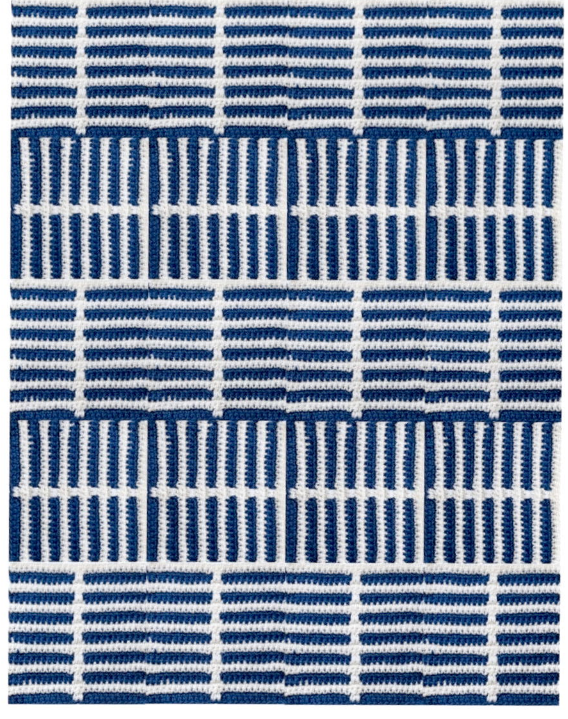

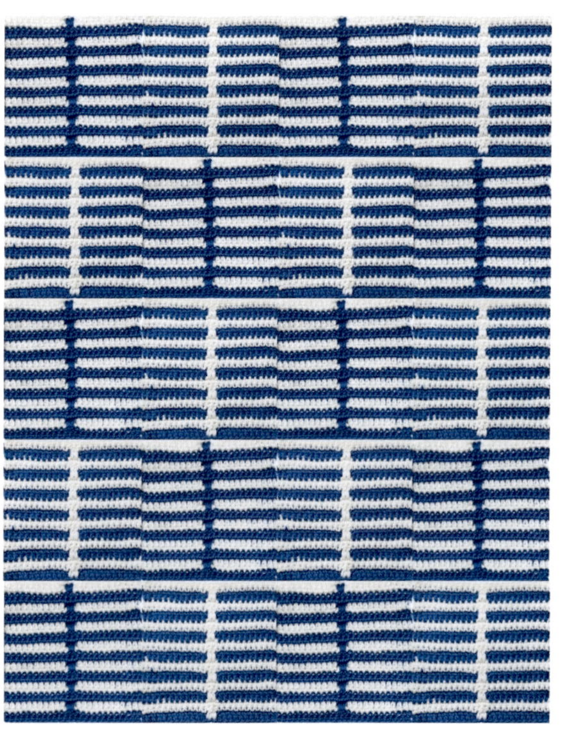

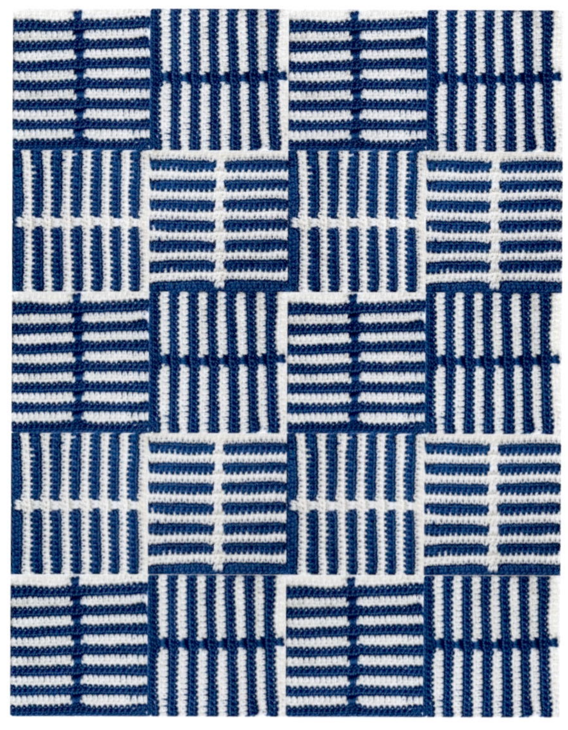

When worked in rainbow colors the finished layout is vibrant. This block would also work well in a monochromatic color palette in a range of tones.

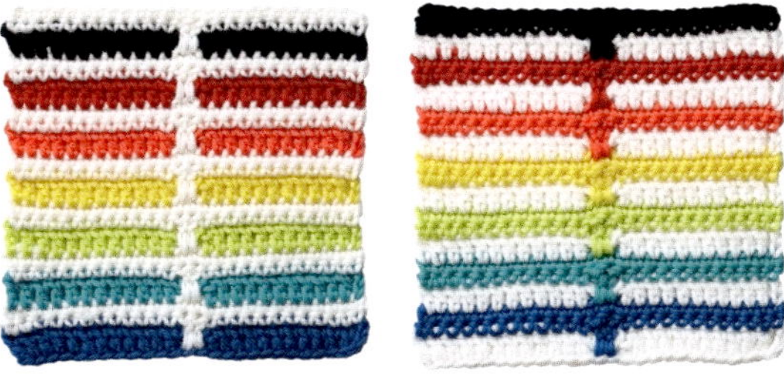

Variation Colorway 1

Variation Colorway 2

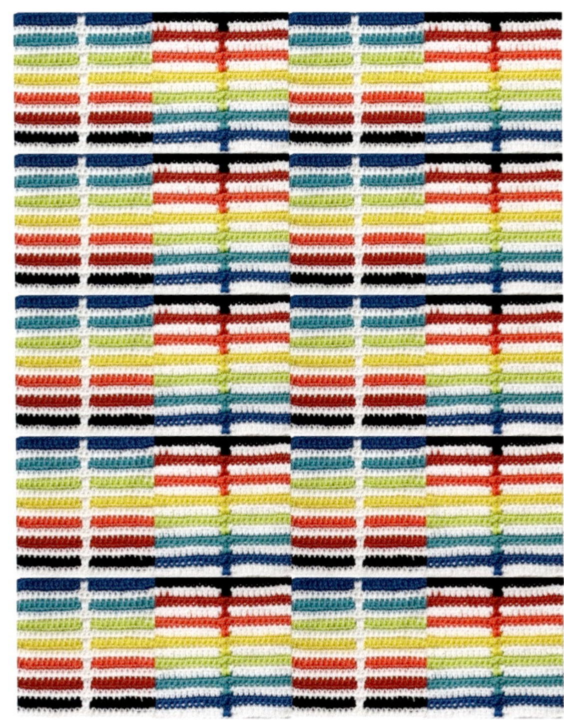

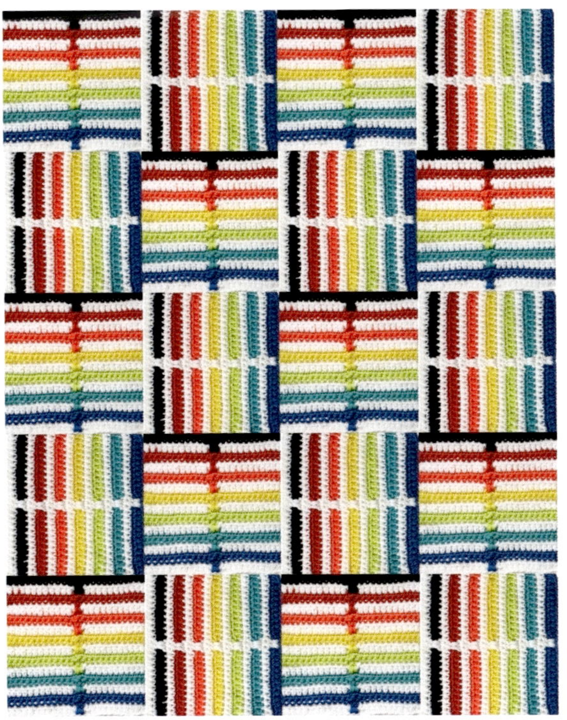

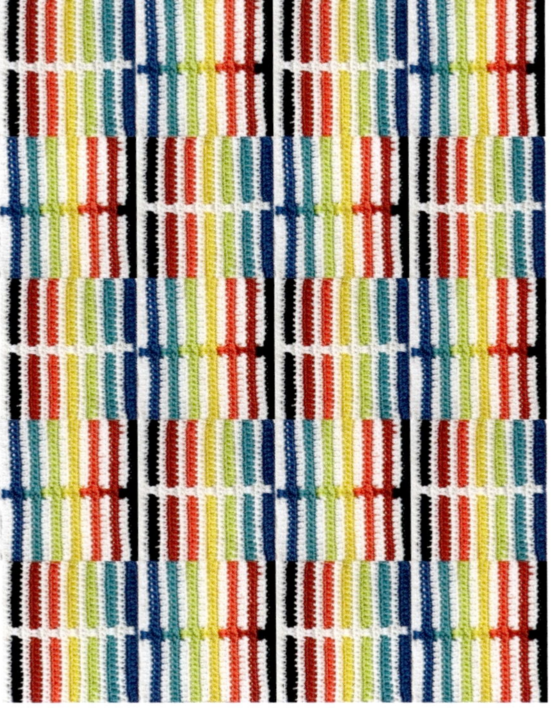

ARCH

I've used three colors for the arch on this block, but you could work each row of the arch in a different color to create a rainbow. See the Wall Hanging project on page 118, which uses this block.

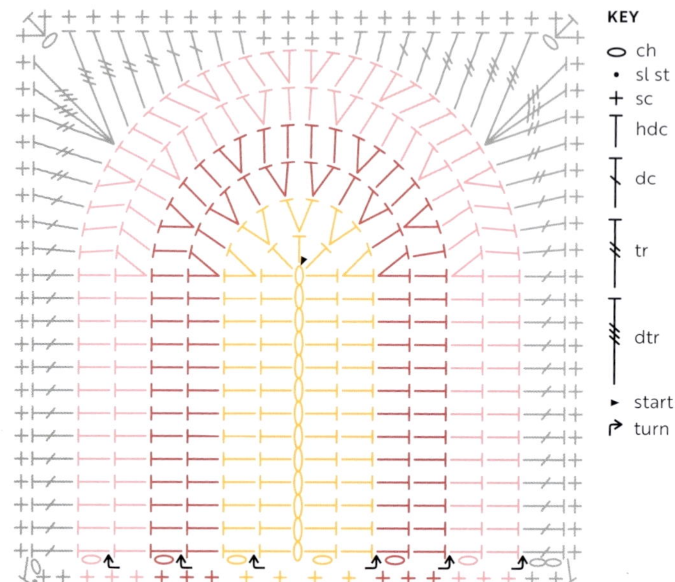

SKILL LEVEL: Intermediate

BLOCK SIZE: 6" x 6" (15 x 15 cm)

HOOK SIZE: G/6 (4 mm)

YARN WEIGHT: DK

YARN: Cascade 220 Superwash®

Main Block

Yarn Requirements

Color A: 5½ yd (5 m)

Color B: 7¼ yd (6.5 m)

Color C: 8¾ yd (8 m)

Color D: 14 yd (13 m)

Colorway 1

A: 820 (Lemon)

B: 837 (Berry Pink)

C: 835 (Pink Rose)

D: 871 (White)

For colorways 2, 3, and 4, use the following combinations for yarns B and C:

Colorway 2

B: 887 (Wasabi)

C: 370 (Sulfur)

Colorway 3

B: 259 (Blue Turquoise)

C: 1973 (Seafoam Heather)

Colorway 4

B: 842 (Light Iris)

C: 282 (Mauve Mist)

Variations

Yarn Requirements

Color A: 5½ yd (5 m)

Color B: 7¼ yd (6.5 m)

Color C: 8¾ yd (8 m)

Color D: 14 yd (13 m)

Colorway 1

A: 281 (Frost Grey)

B: 817 (Ecru)

C: 876 (Sandalwood)

D: 349 (Irish Cream)

Colorway 2

A: 876 (Sandalwood); **B:** 817 (Ecru); **C:** 281 (Frost Grey); **D:** 349 (Irish Cream)

Colorway 3

A: 821 (Daffodil)

B: 871 (White)

C: 809 (Really Red)

D: 815 (Black)

Abbreviations and Stitches

ch	chain
sp	space
sl st	slip stitch
sc	single crochet
hdc	half-double crochet
dc	double crochet
tr	treble crochet
dtr	double treble crochet
beg	beginning
st(s)	stitch(es)
[ ]	repeat instructions within brackets the stated number of times
( )	work instructions within brackets in place indicated

Main Block Colorway 1

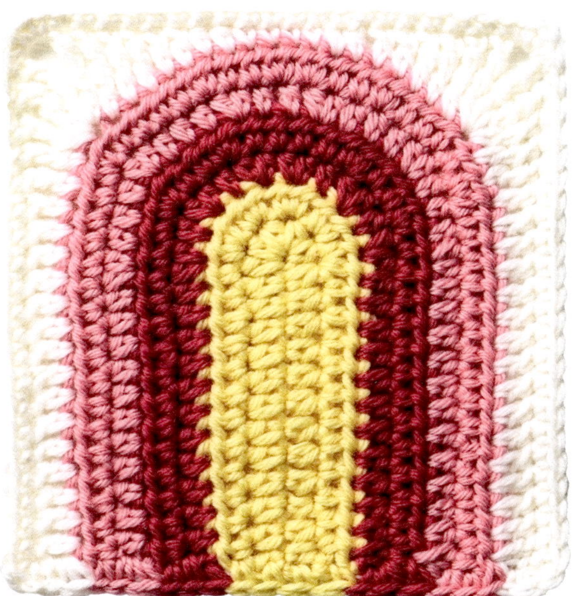

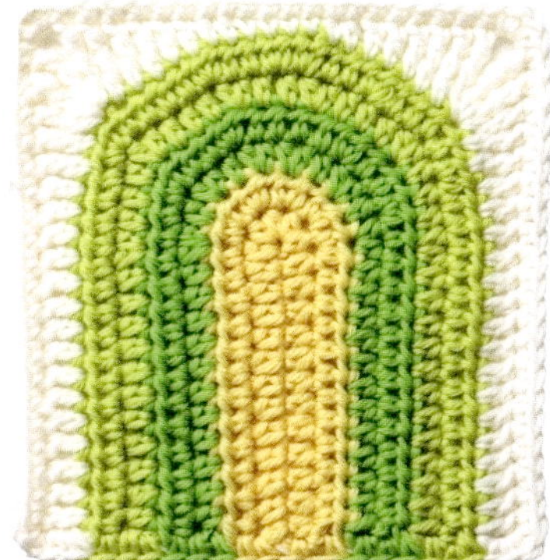

Main Block Colorway 2

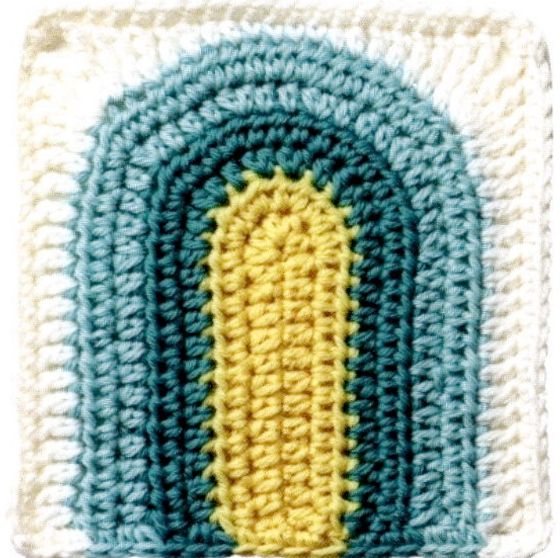

Main Block Colorway 3

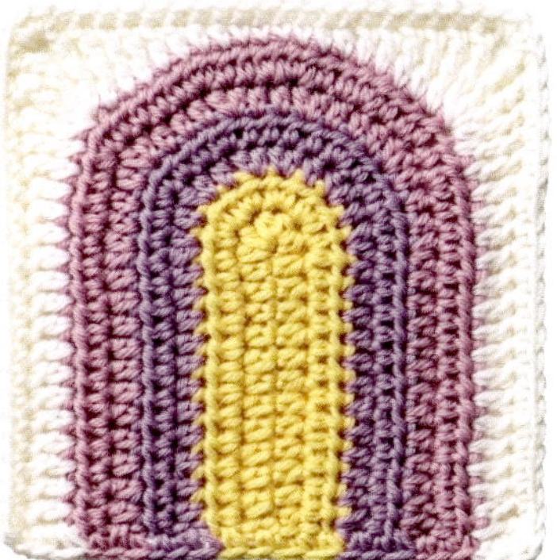

Main Block Colorway 4

Crochet Pattern

Foundation Row: Using A, ch 14.

Row 1 (RS): hdc in second ch from hook, hdc in next 11 ch, 5 hdc in next ch, turn to work back along the opposite side of the foundation chain, hdc in each of next 12 ch, turn—29 sts.

Row 2 (WS): Ch 1 (does not count as a st here and throughout), hdc in 12 sts, 2 hdc in next 5 sts, hdc in 12 sts, changing to B when working last st, fasten off A, turn—34 sts.

Row 3: Ch 1, hdc in 12 sts, [2 hdc in 1 st, hdc in 1 st] twice, 2 hdc in next 2 sts, [hdc in 1 st, 2 hdc in 1 st] twice, hdc in 12 sts, turn—40 sts.

Row 4: Ch 1, hdc in 14 sts, [2 hdc in 1 st, hdc in 2 sts] twice, [hdc in 2 sts, 2 hdc in 1 st] twice, hdc in 14 sts, changing to C when working last st, fasten off B, turn—44 sts.

Row 5: Ch 1, hdc in 12 sts, [2 hdc in 1 st, hdc in 3 sts] twice, 2 hdc in 1 st, hdc in 2 sts, 2 hdc in 1 st, [hdc in 3 sts, 2 hdc in 1 st] twice, hdc in 12 sts, turn—50 sts.

Row 6: Ch 1, hdc in 16 sts, 2 hdc in 1 st, hdc in 4 sts, 2 hdc in 1 st, hdc in 2 sts, 2 hdc in 2 sts, hdc in 2 sts, 2 hdc in 1 st, hdc in 4 sts, 2 hdc in 1 st, hdc in 16 sts, changing to D when working last st, fasten off C, turn—56 sts.

Row 7: Ch 2 (does not count as a st), dc in 16 sts, tr in 2 sts, (tr, 2 dtr, ch 1, dtr) in next st, dtr in 1 st, tr in 2 sts, dc in 2 sts, hdc in 2 sts, sc in 4 sts, hdc in 2 sts, dc in 2 sts, tr in 2 sts, dtr in 1 st, (dtr, ch 1, 2 dtr, tr) in next st, tr in 2 sts, dc in 16 sts, do not turn—62 sts 2 ch-1 sp.

Edging (RS): Rotate to work along the bottom edge of the block, ch 1, 2 sc in row end changing to C when working last st, 3 sc across next 2 row ends changing to B when working last st, 3 sc across next 2 row ends changing to A when working last st, 4 sc across next 4 row ends changing to B when working last st, 3 sc across next 2 row ends changing to C when working last st, 3 sc across next 2 row ends changing to D when working last st, 2 sc in last row end. Rotate to work across next edge, (hdc, sc) in top of next st, [sc in 20 sts, (sc, hdc, sc) in ch sp] twice, sc in 20 sts, (sc, hdc) in last st, join by working sl st into sc at beg of round, fasten off D—90 sts.

Weave in all ends and block to measure 6" x 6" (15 x 15 cm).

You can use the block worked in one colorway or in four colorways. Layouts include arches or lozenges, and you can play with color in the way you lay out the blocks.

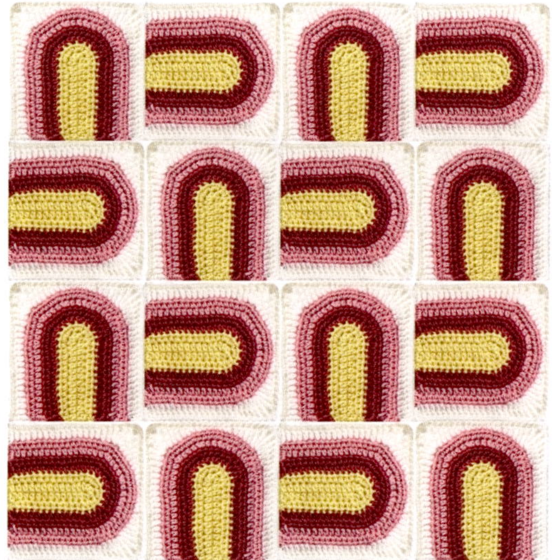

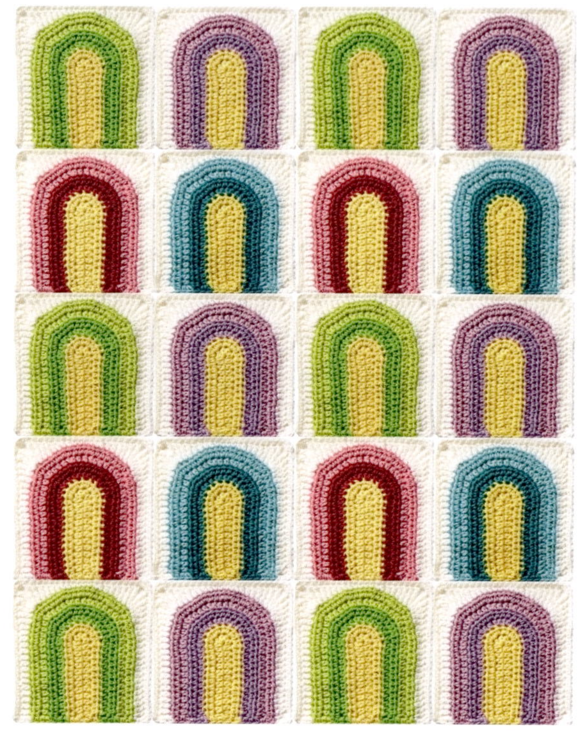

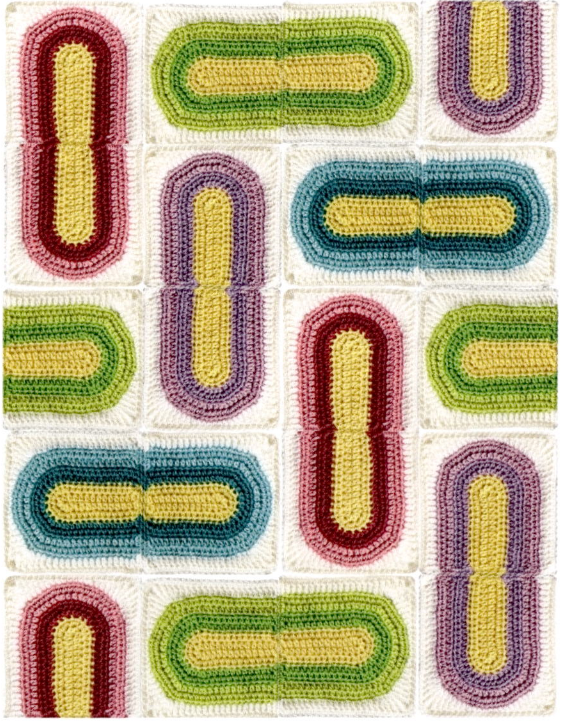

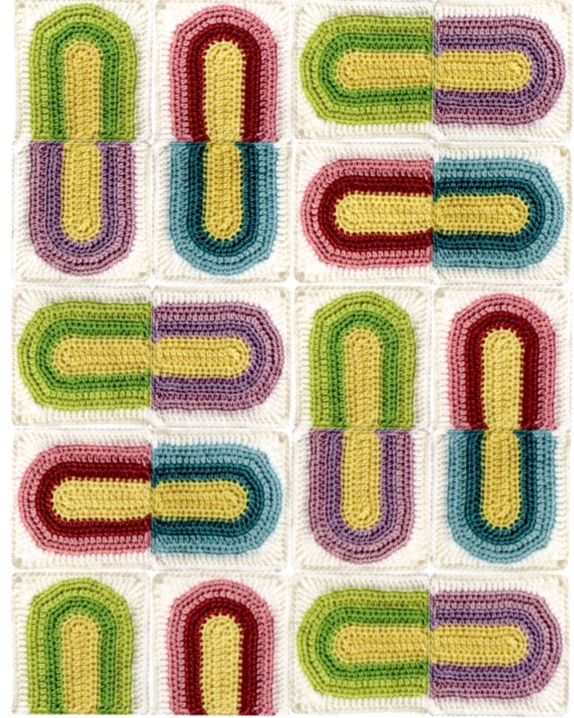

The earthy colors used for these two colorways give the finished piece a calm vibe. Perfect for draping over the sofa.

Variation Colorways 1 and 2

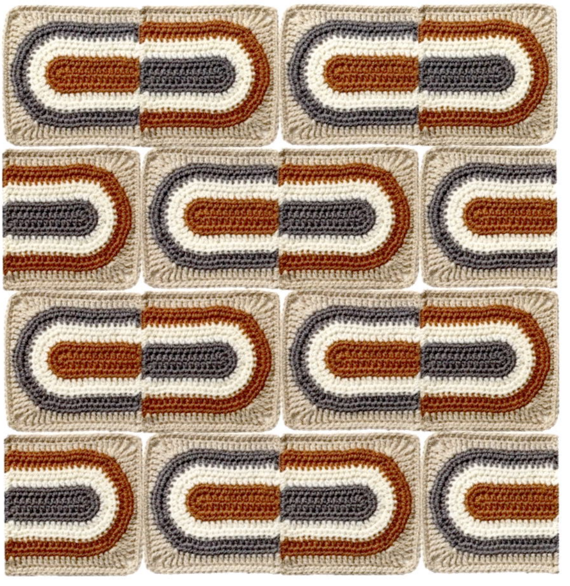

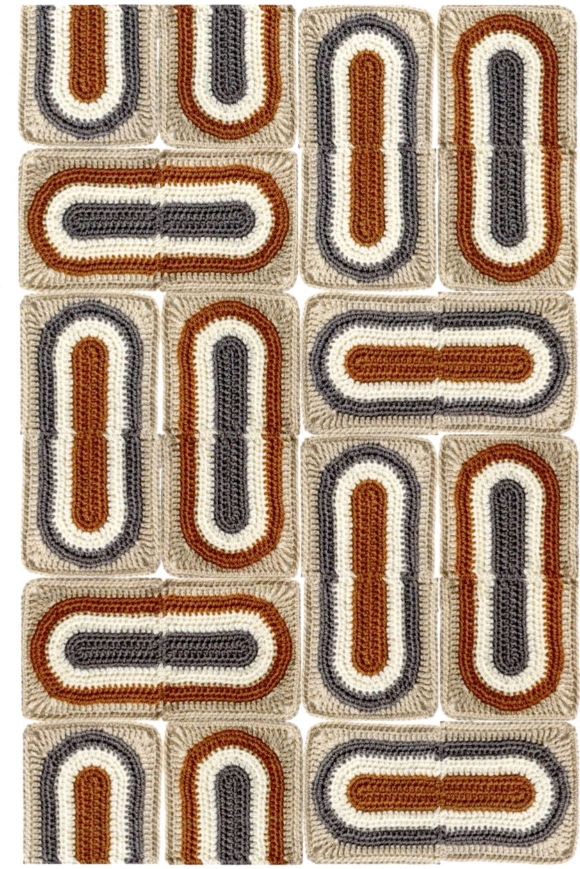

Here the blocks are all worked in one colorway but using black as the background color gives the finished piece a more dramatic look.

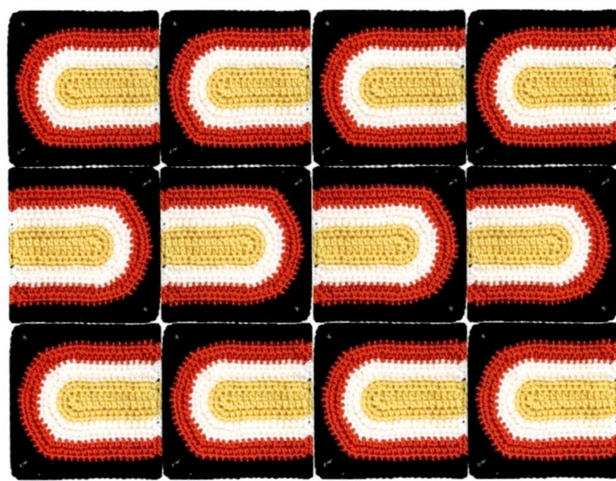

Variation Colorway 3

DIAGONAL SPLIT

This pattern is worked in the round using two colors and is an easy square to make. Hook up a load of these in a riot of colors and you will be well on your way to a stunning project. See the Afghan on page 112 and the Pillow on page 115 for projects that use this block.

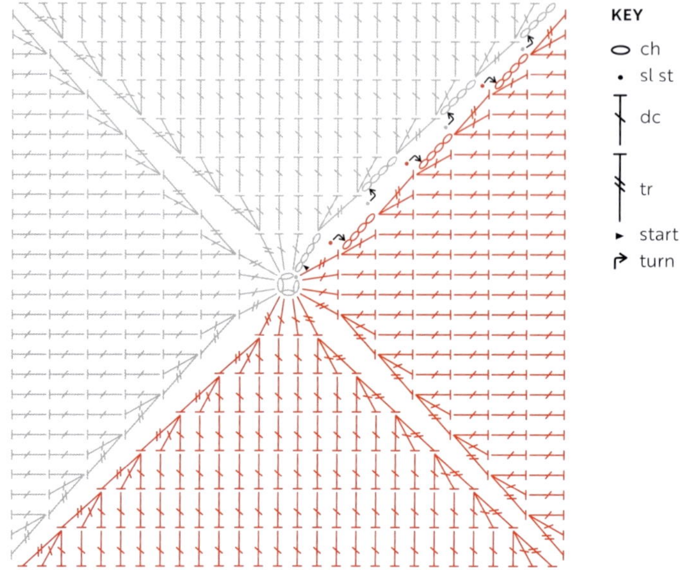

SKILL LEVEL: Intermediate

BLOCK SIZE: 6" x 6" (15 x 15 cm)

HOOK SIZE: E/4 (3.5 mm)

YARN WEIGHT: DK

YARN: Cascade 220 Superwash®

Main Block

Yarn Requirements

Each color: 24 yd (22 m)

Colorway 1

A: 871 (White)

B: 344 (Cherry Tomato)

Colorway 2

For yarn B use either:

815 (Black)

252 (Celestial)

346 (Daisy Yellow)

Variations

Make one block using yarn B and yarn C.

Make one block using yarn A and yarn C.

Make one block using yarn A and yarn B.

Yarn Requirements

Each color: 24 yd (22 m)

A: 287 (Deep Sea Coral)

B: 1940 (Peach)

C: 827 (Coral)

Abbreviations and Stitches

ch	chain
sl st	slip stitch
dc	double crochet
tr	treble crochet
beg	beginning
st(s)	stitch(es)
( )	work instructions within brackets in place indicated

Note

- Leave unused yarn color hanging on the wrong side of the work throughout and pick up from there when needed.

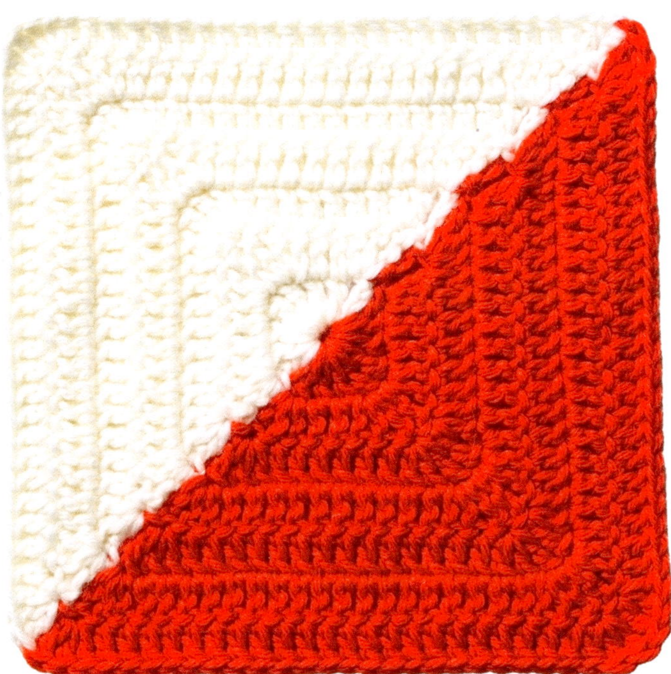

Main Block Colorway 1

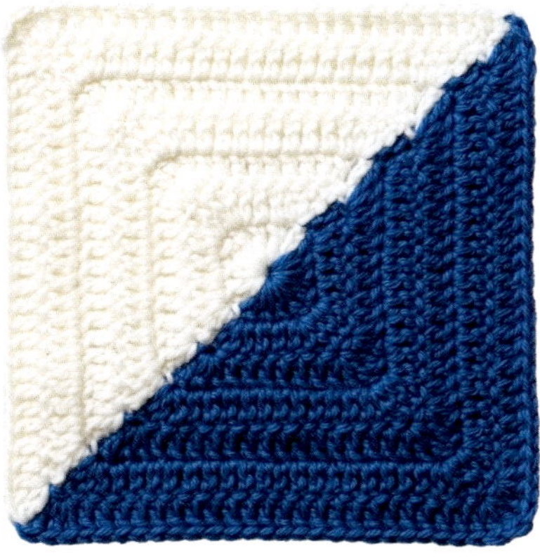

Main Block Colorway 2

Crochet Pattern

Foundation Ring: Using A, ch 4, join with sl st to first ch made to form a ring.

Rnd 1 (RS): Ch 4 (counts as tr here and throughout), (2 dc, 2 tr, 2 dc), tr changing to B, (tr, 2 dc, 2 tr, 2dc tr) into ring, join with sl st to top of beg ch-4, turn—16 sts.

Rnd 2 (WS): Ch 4, 2 dc in same place, dc in 2 sts, (2 dc, tr) in next st, (tr, 2 dc) in next st, dc in 2 sts, (2 dc, tr) in next st changing to A when working tr, (tr, 2 dc) in next st, dc in 2 sts, (2 dc, tr) in next st, (tr, 2 dc) in next st, dc in 2 sts, (2 dc, tr) in next st, join with sl st to top of beg ch-4, turn—32 sts.

Rnd 3: Ch 4, 2 dc in same place, dc in 6 sts, (2 dc, tr) in next st, (tr, 2 dc) in next st, dc in 6 sts, (2 dc, tr) in next st changing to B when working tr, (tr, 2 dc) in next st, dc in 6 sts, (2 dc, tr) in next st, (tr, 2 dc) in next st, dc in 6 sts, (2 dc, tr) in next st, join with sl st to top of beg ch-4, turn—48 sts.

Rnd 4: Ch 4, 2 dc in same place, dc in 10 sts, (2 dc, tr) in next st, (tr, 2 dc) in next st, dc in 10 sts, (2 dc, tr) in next st changing to A when working tr, (tr, 2 dc) in next st, dc in 10 sts, (2 dc, tr) in next st, (tr, 2 dc) in next st, dc in 10 sts, (2 dc, tr) in next st, join with sl st to top of beg ch-4, turn—64 sts.

Rnd 5: Ch 4, 2 dc in same place, dc in 14 sts, (2 dc, tr) in next st, (tr, 2 dc) in next st, dc in 14 sts, (2 dc, tr) in next st changing to B when working tr, (tr, 2 dc) in next st, dc in 14 sts, (2 dc, tr) in next st, (tr, 2 dc) in next st, dc in 14 sts, (2 dc, tr) in next st, join with sl st to top of beg ch-4, turn—80 sts.

Rnd 6: Ch 4, 2 dc in same place, dc in 18 sts, (2 dc, tr) in next st, (tr, 2 dc) in next st, dc in 18 sts, (2 dc, tr) in next st changing to A when working tr, (tr, 2 dc) in next st, dc in 18 sts, (2 dc, tr) in next st, (tr, 2 dc) in next st, dc in 18 sts, (2 dc, tr) in next st, join with sl st to top of beg ch-4, turn—96 sts.

Rnd 7: Ch 4, 2 dc in same place, dc in 22 sts, (2 dc, tr) in next st, (tr, 2 dc) in next st, dc in 22 sts, (2 dc, tr) in next st changing to B when working tr, (tr, 2 dc) in next st, dc in 22 sts, (2 dc, tr) in next st, (tr, 2 dc) in next st, dc in 22 sts, (2 dc, tr) in next st, join with sl st to top of beg ch-4. Fasten off—112 sts.

Weave in all ends, and block to measure 6" x 6" (15 x 15 cm).

Working with one colorway means you'll have lots of layout options with this block. When you combine four colorways you can experiment with even more shapes and combinations.

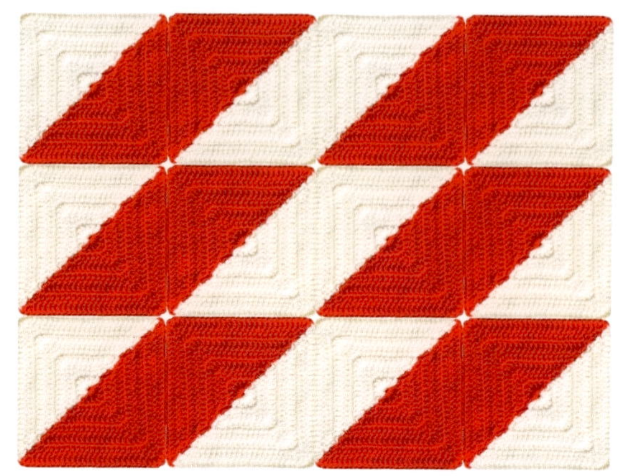

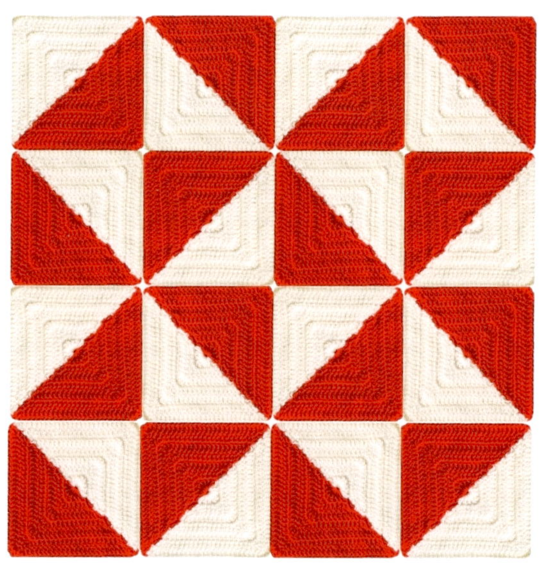

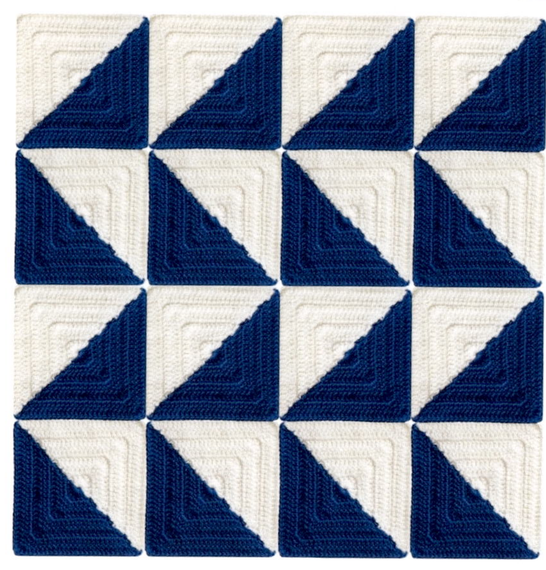

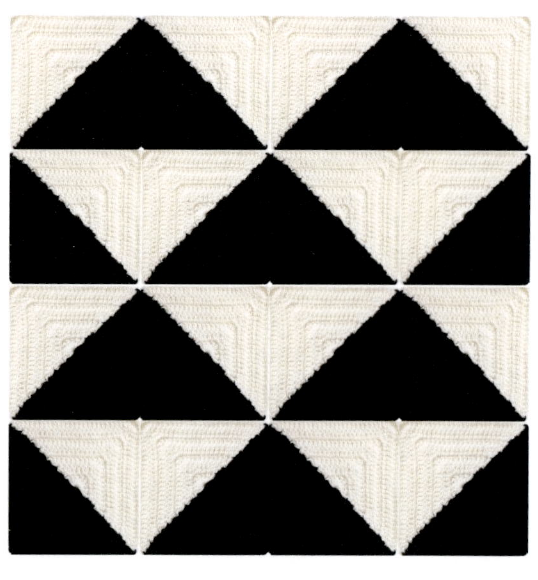

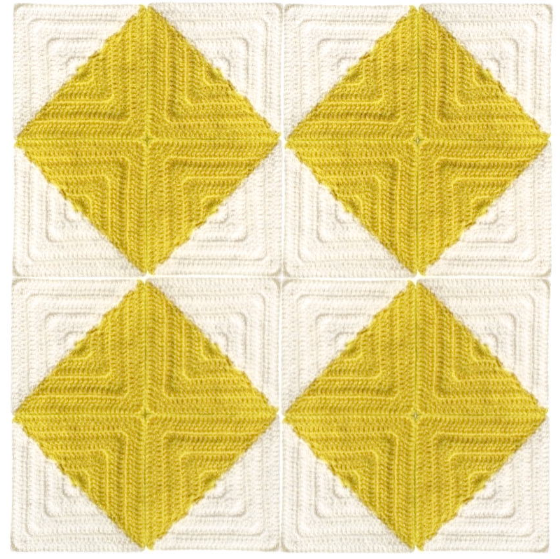

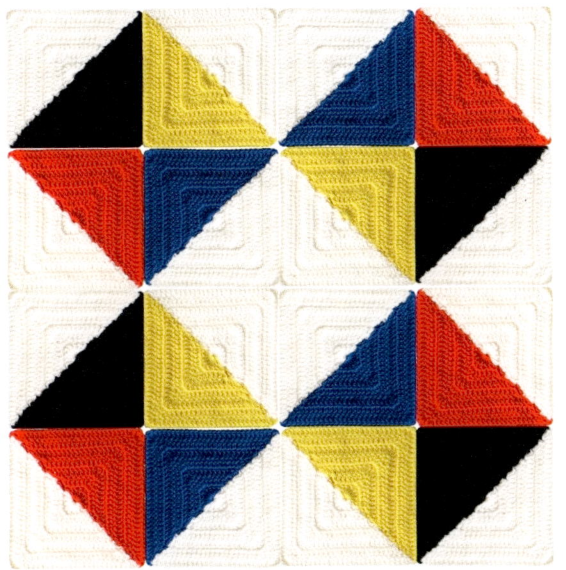
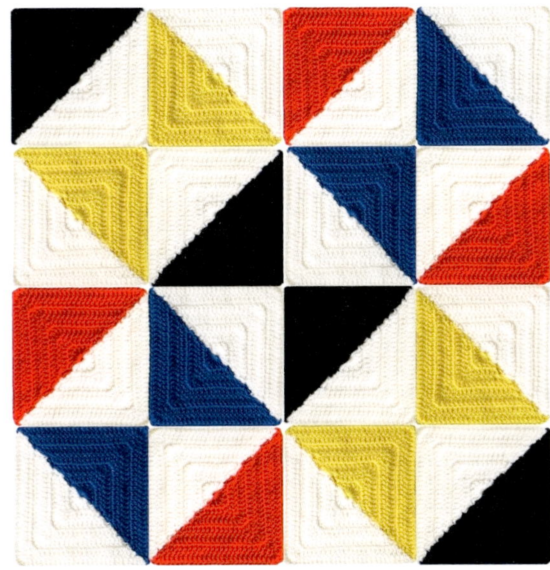

Worked in a monochromatic scheme, these blocks have a lower contrast when joined, giving a softer overall look.

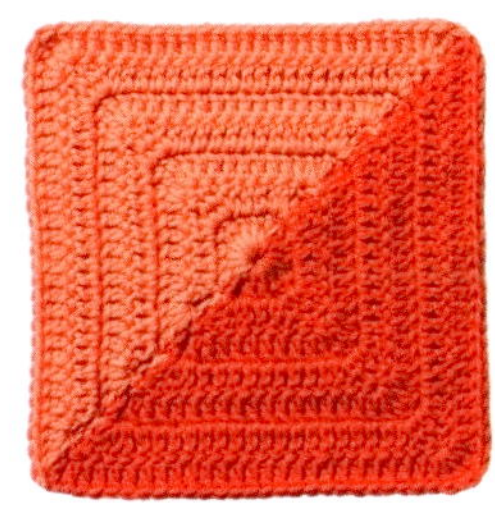
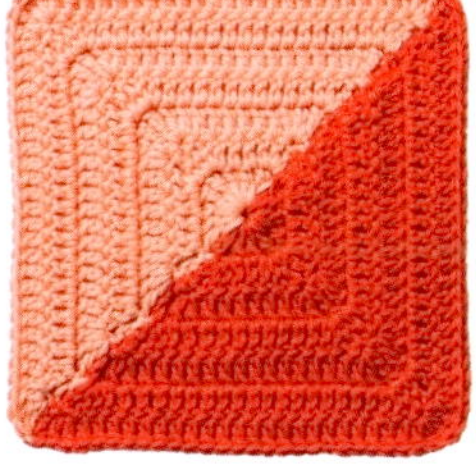
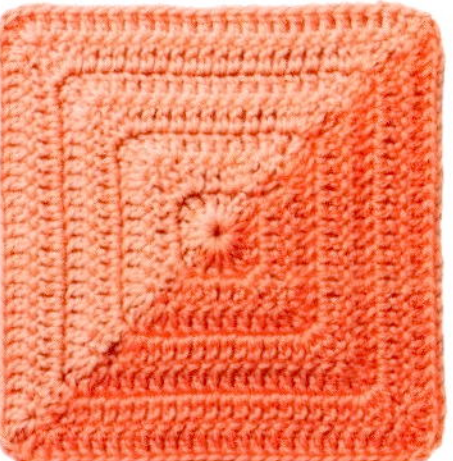

Variation Colorways

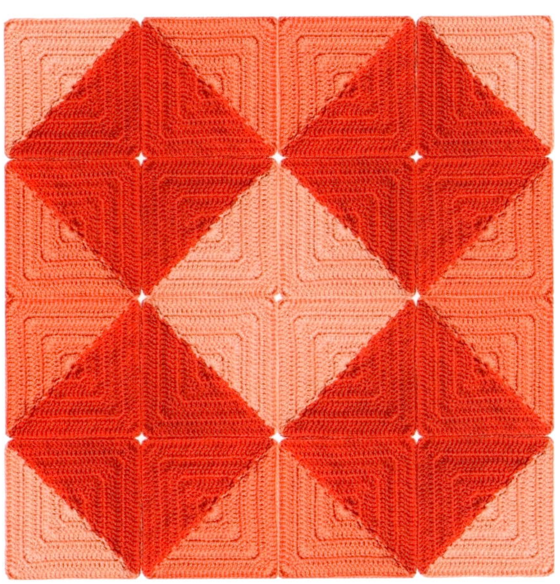
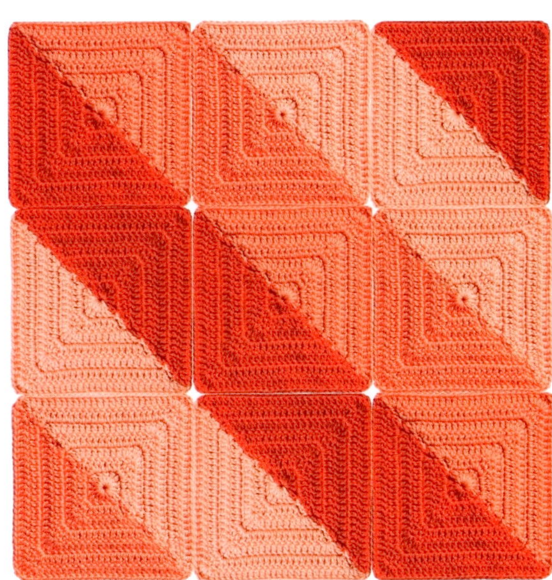

SQUARE AND TRIANGLE

This block allows for some interesting geometric layouts. I've used three and four colors for the samples shown here, but you could also try working the block in just two colors for a bolder option.

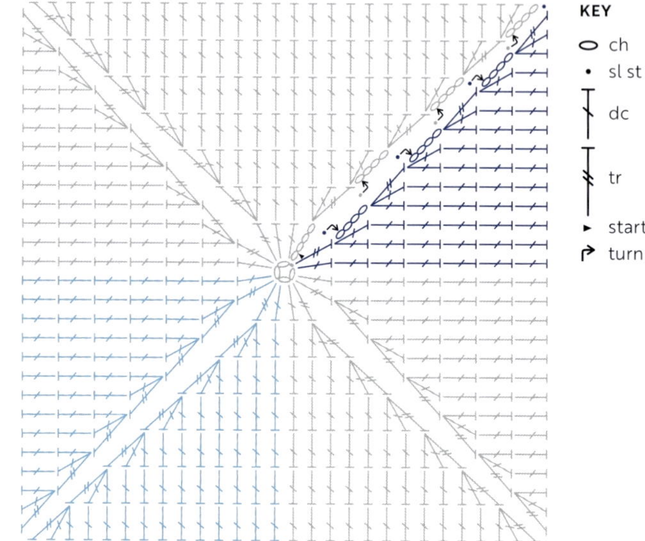

SKILL LEVEL: Intermediate

BLOCK SIZE: 6" x 6" (15 x 15 cm)

HOOK SIZE: E/4 (3.5 mm)

YARN WEIGHT: DK

YARN: Cascade 220 Superwash®

Main Block

Yarn Requirements

Color A: 27 yd (25 m)

Color B: 12 yd (11 m)

Color C: 6 yd (5.5 m)

Colorway 1

A: 871 (White)

B: 847 (Caribbean)

C: 311 (Blue Sapphire)

Colorway 2

A: 871 (White); **B:** 311 (Blue Sapphire); **C:** 847 (Caribbean)

Variations

Yarn Requirements

Color A: 15¼ yd (14 m)

Color B: 12 yd (11 m)

Color C: 12 yd (11 m)

Color D: 6 yd (5.5 m)

Colorway 1

A: 1942 (Mint)

B: 364 (Faded Rose)

C: 817 (Ecru)

D: 1940 (Peach)

Colorway 2

A: 817 (Ecru); **B:** 1940 (Peach)
C: 1942 (Mint); **D:** 364 (Faded Rose)

Abbreviations and Stitches

ch	chain
sl st	slip stitch
dc	double crochet
tr	treble crochet
beg	beginning
st(s)	stitch(es)
( )	work instructions within brackets in place indicated

Notes

- You will be changing yarn colors mid-round from Rnd 1 onward.
- Leave unused yarn color hanging on the wrong side of the work throughout and pick up from there when needed.

Crochet Pattern

Foundation Ring: Using A, ch 4, join with sl st to first ch made to form a ring.

Rnd 1 (RS): Ch 4 (counts as tr here and throughout), 2 dc, 2 tr, dc, changing to B when working last st, dc, 2 tr, dc, changing to a new strand of A, dc, 2 tr, dc, changing to C, dc, tr, join with sl st to top of beg ch-4, turn—16 sts.

Rnd 2 (WS): Ch 4, 2 dc in same place, dc in next st changing to A, dc in next st, (2 dc, tr) in next st, (tr, 2 dc) in next st, dc in next st changing to B, dc in 1 st, (2 dc, tr) in next st, (tr, 2 dc) in next st, dc in next st changing to A, dc in next st, (2 dc, tr) in next st, (tr, 2 dc) in next st, dc in 2 sts, (2 dc, tr) in next st, join with sl st to top of beg ch-4, turn—32 sts.

Rnd 3: Ch 4, 2 dc in same place, dc in 6 sts, (2 dc, tr) in next st, (tr, 2 dc) in next st, dc in 3 sts changing to B when working last st, dc in 3 sts, (2 dc, tr) in next st, (tr, 2 dc) in next st, dc in 3 sts changing to A when working last st, dc in 3 sts, (2 dc, tr) in next st, (tr, 2 dc) in next st, dc in 3 sts changing to C when working last st, dc in 3 sts, (2 dc, tr) in next st, join with sl st to top of beg ch-4, turn—48 sts.

Rnd 4: Ch 4, 2 dc in same place, dc in 5 sts changing to A when working last st, dc in 5 sts, (2 dc, tr) in next st, (tr, 2 dc) in next st, dc in 5 sts changing to B when working last st, dc in 5 sts, (2 dc, tr) in next st, (tr, 2 dc) in next st, dc in 5 sts changing to A when working last st, dc in 5 sts, (2 dc, tr) in next st, (tr, 2 dc) in next st, dc in 10 sts, (2 dc, tr) in next st, join with sl st to top of beg ch-4, turn—64 sts.

Rnd 5: Ch 4, 2 dc in same place, dc in 14 sts, (2 dc, tr) in next st, (tr, 2 dc) in next st, dc in 7 sts changing to B when working last st, dc in 7 sts, (2 dc, tr) in next st, (tr, 2 dc) in next st, dc in 7 sts changing to A when working last st, dc in 7 sts, (2 dc, tr) in next st, (tr, 2 dc) in next st, dc in 7 sts changing to C when working last st, dc in 7 sts, (2 dc, tr) in next st, join with sl st to top of beg ch-4, turn—80 sts.

Rnd 6: Ch 4, 2 dc in same place, dc in 9 sts changing to A when working last st, dc in 9 sts, (2 dc, tr) in next st, (tr, 2 dc) in next st, dc in 9 sts changing to B when working last st, dc in 9 sts, (2 dc, tr) in next st, (tr, 2 dc) in next st, dc in 9 sts changing to A when working last st, dc in 9 sts, (2 dc, tr) in next st, (tr, 2 dc) in next st, dc in 18 sts, (2 dc, tr) in next st, join with sl st to top of beg ch-4, turn—96 sts.

Rnd 7: Ch 4, 2 dc in same place, dc in 22 sts, (2 dc, tr) in next st, (tr, 2 dc) in next st, dc in 11 sts changing to B when working last st, dc in 11 sts, (2 dc, tr) in next st, (tr, 2 dc) in next st, dc in 11 sts changing to A when working last st, dc in 11 sts, (2 dc, tr) in next st, (tr, 2 dc) in next st, dc in 11 sts changing to C when working last st, dc in 11 sts, (2 dc, tr) in next st, join with sl st to top of beg ch-4. Fasten off—112 sts.

Weave in all ends, and block to measure 6" x 6" (15 x 15 cm).

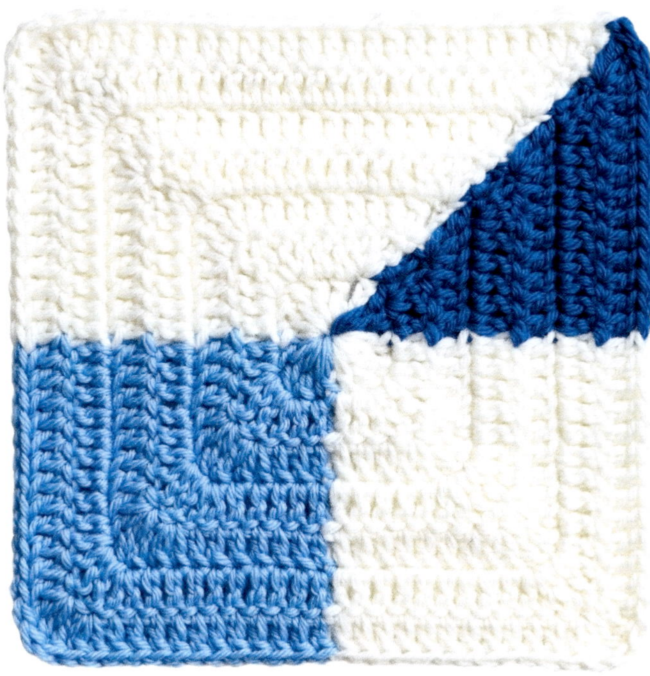

Main Block Colorway 1

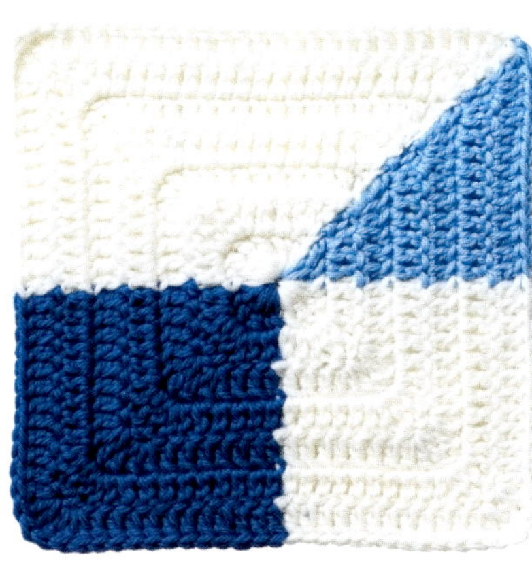

Main Block Colorway 2

Whether you use just one colorway or two, this block has plenty of geometric layouts. As you lay out the blocks you'll find new shapes appearing. Try working these blocks in just two colors for a whole different look.

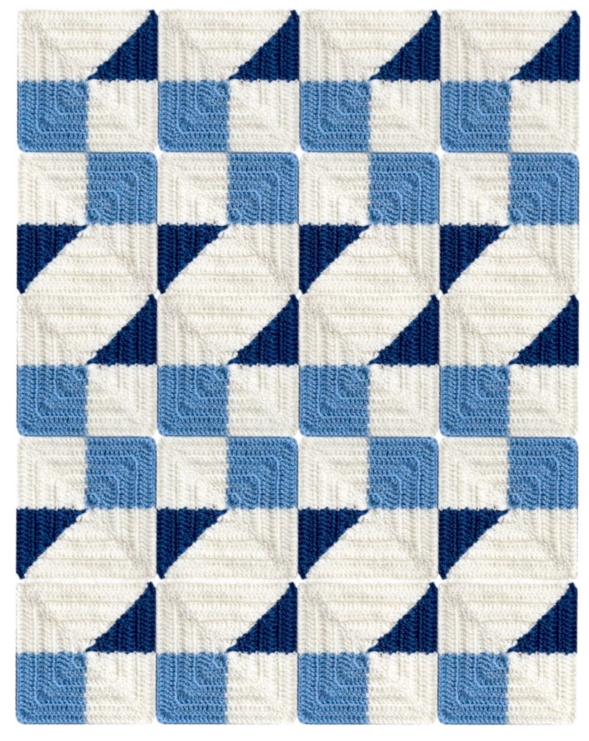

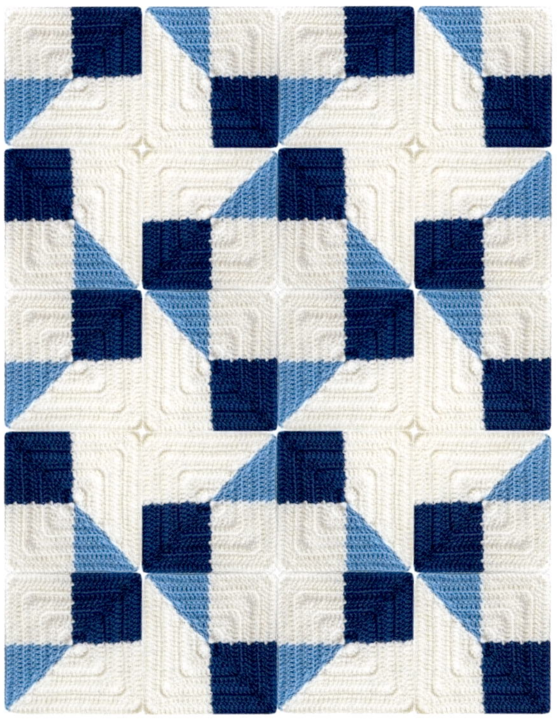

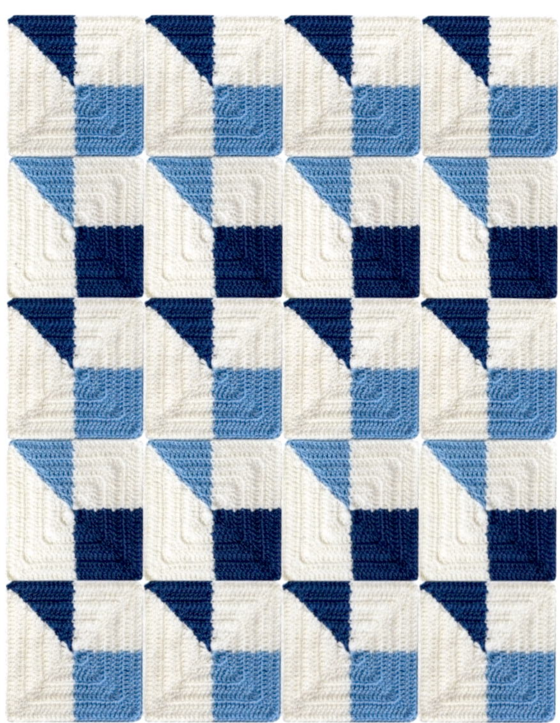

The first two layouts use just one of the variation colorways. The other two layouts use both colorways. Use a split-complementary color palette for a contrasting finish, or you could try a monochromatic color palette for a softer effect.

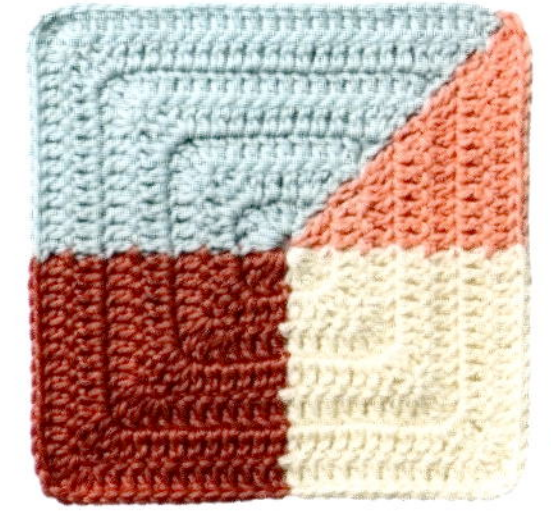

Variation Colorway 1

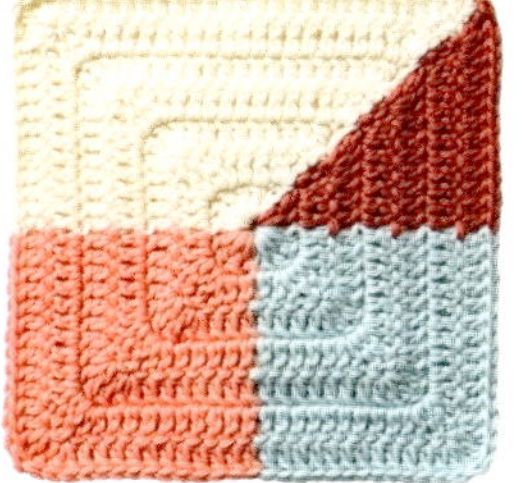

Variation Colorway 2

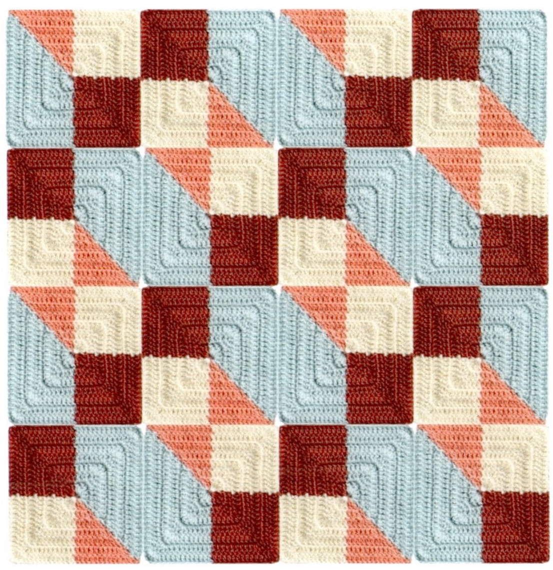

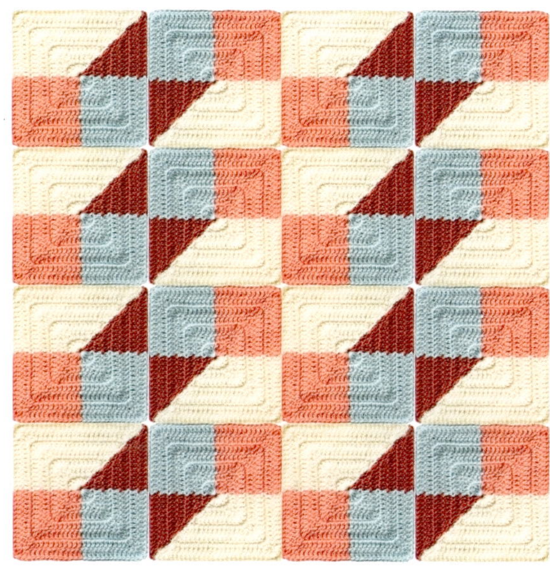

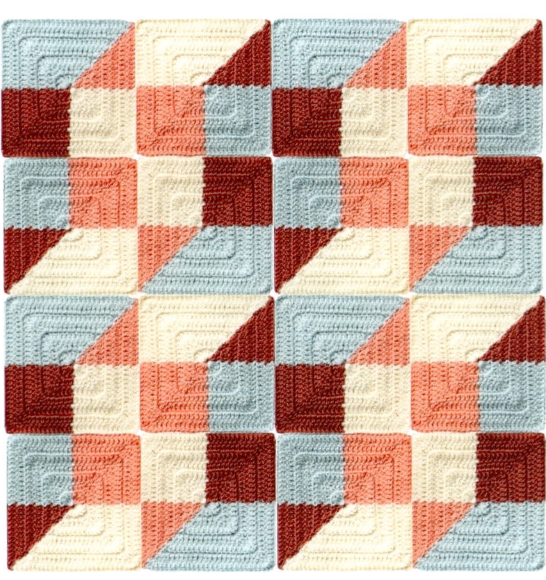

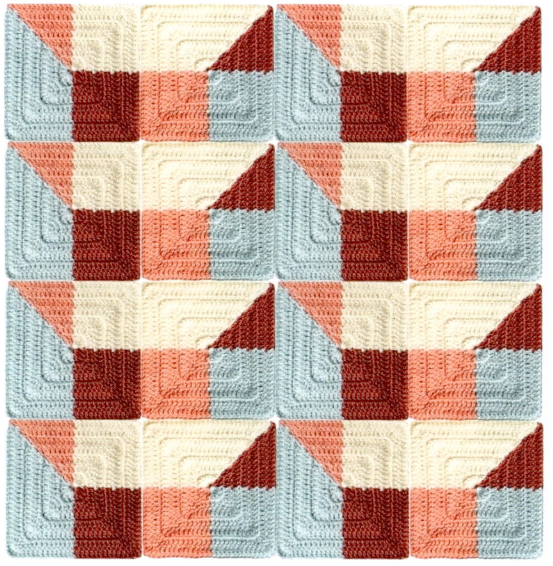

SPLIT STRIPES

This block is created by working in rows, then turning the piece 90 degrees and working rows of single crochet in the other direction. There are lots of opportunities for playing with color with this block. Join with mattress stitch for a hidden join or use a crochet join in the dominant color.

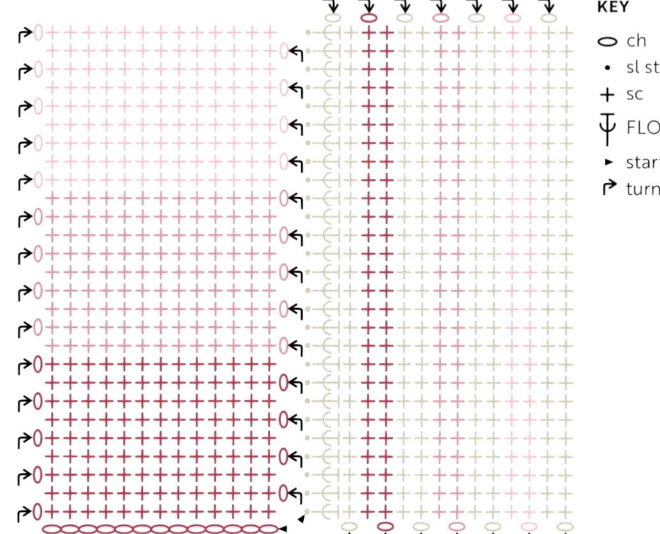

SKILL LEVEL: Intermediate

BLOCK SIZE: 6" x 6" (15 x 15 cm)

HOOK SIZE: G/6 (4mm)

YARN WEIGHT: DK

YARN: Cascade 220 Superwash®

Main Block

Yarn Requirements

Color A: 10 yd (9 m)
Color B: 10 yd (9 m)
Color C: 10 yd (9 m)
Color D: 13¼ yd (12 m)

Colorway 1

A: 837 (Berry Pink)
B: 901 (Cotton Candy)
C: 835 (Pink Rose)
D: 817 (Ecru)

Colorway 2

A: 835 (Pink Rose); **B:** 901 (Cotton Candy); **C:** 837 (Berry Pink); **D:** 817 (Ecru)

Variations

Yarn Requirements

Color A: 10 yd (9 m)
Color B: 10 yd (9 m)
Color C: 10 yd (9 m)
Color D: 3¼ yd (3 m)
Color E: 3¼ yd (3 m)
Color F: 3¼ yd (3 m)
Color G: 3¼ yd (3 m)

Colorway 1

Start Row 28 in yarn D and change to the next yarn listed when repeating Rows 31 and 32.

A: 1973 (Seafoam Heather)
B: 820 (Lemon)
C: 835 (Pink Rose)
D: 842 (Light Iris)
E: 289 (Creampuff)
F: 850 (Lime Sherbet)
G: 847 (Caribbean)

Colorway 2

A: 1973 (Seafoam Heather); **B:** 820 (Lemon); **C:** 835 (Pink Rose); **D:** 847 (Caribbean); **E:** 850 (Lime Sherbet); **F:** 289 (Creampuff); **G:** 842 (Light Iris)

Abbreviations and Stitches

ch	chain
sl st	slip stitch
sc	single crochet
st(s)	stitch(es)
FLO	front loop only

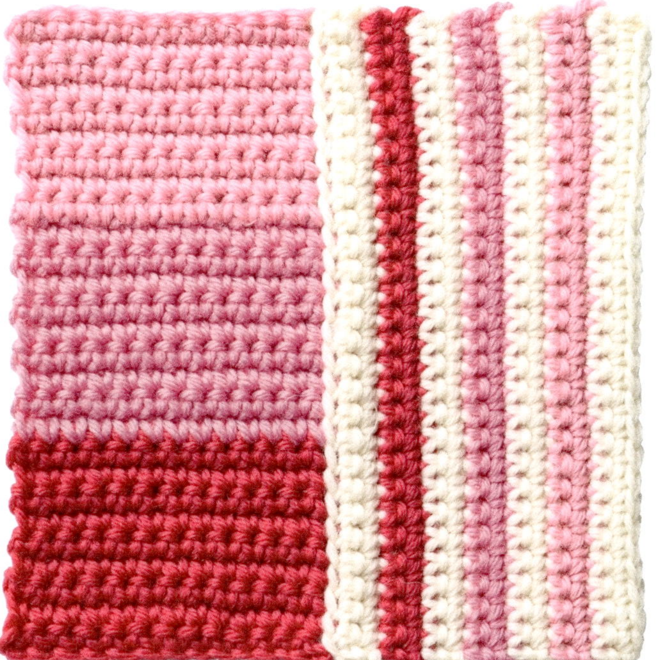

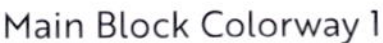

Main Block Colorway 1

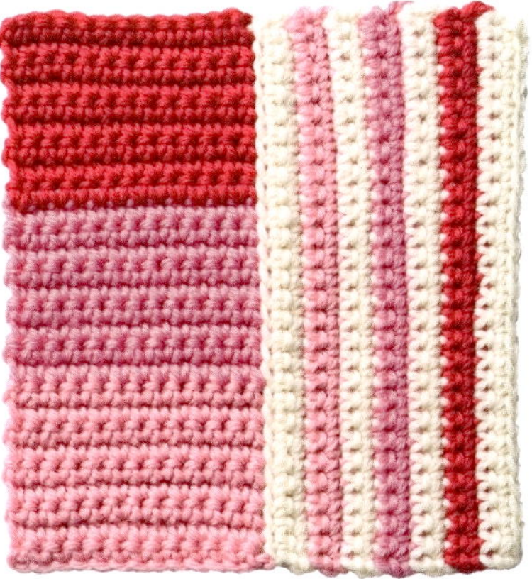

Main Block Colorway 2

Crochet Pattern

Foundation Row: Using A, ch 14.

Row 1 (WS): sc in second ch from hook and in next 12 ch, turn—13 sts.

Rows 2–9: Ch 1 (does not count as a st here and throughout), sc in next 13 sts, fasten off A, turn.

Row 10 (RS): Join in B, ch 1, sc in next 13 sts, turn.

Rows 11–18: Repeat Rows 2–9, fasten off B.

Row 19 (WS): Join in C and repeat Row 10.

Rows 20–27: Repeat Rows 2–9, fasten off C.

With RS facing, turn piece to work along right-hand edge.

Row 28 (RS): Using D, work sl st into the side of each row, turn—27 sts.

Row 29 (WS): Ch 1, sc FLO in 27 sts, turn.

Row 30: Ch 1, sc in each st to end, fasten off D, turn.

Row 31: Join in A, ch 1, sc in each st to end, turn.

Row 32: Ch 1, sc in each st to end, fasten off A.

Rows 33–34: Repeat Rows 31 and 32 using D.

Rows 35–36: Repeat Rows 31 and 32 using B.

Rows 37–38: Repeat Rows 31 and 32 using D.

Rows 39–40: Repeat Rows 31 and 32 using C.

Rows 41–42: Repeat Rows 31 and 32 using D.

Weave in all ends and block to measure 6" x 6" (15 x 15 cm).

When worked in a monochromatic color palette, you can create some fun checkerboard and stripe layouts with this block.

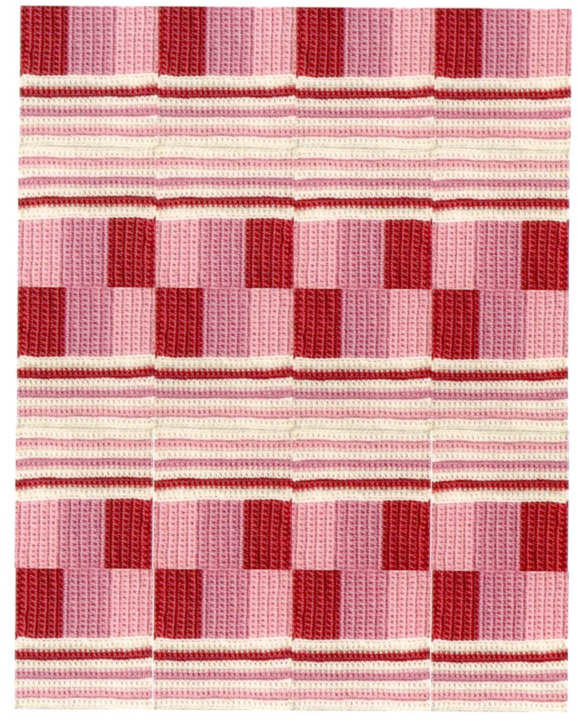

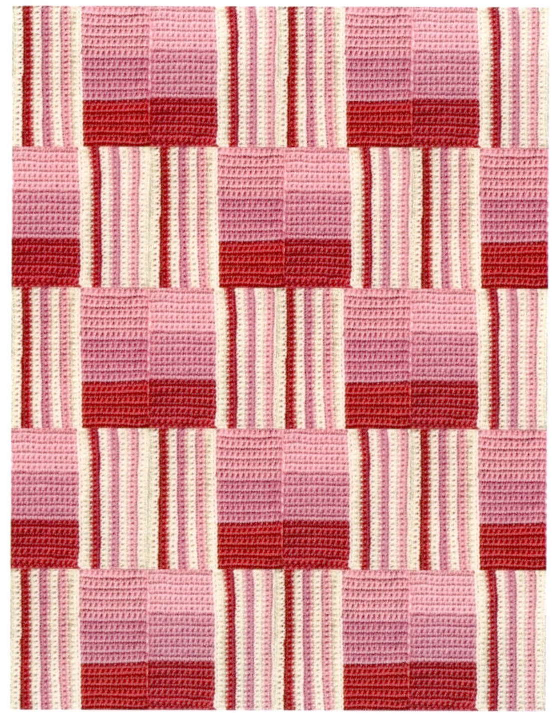

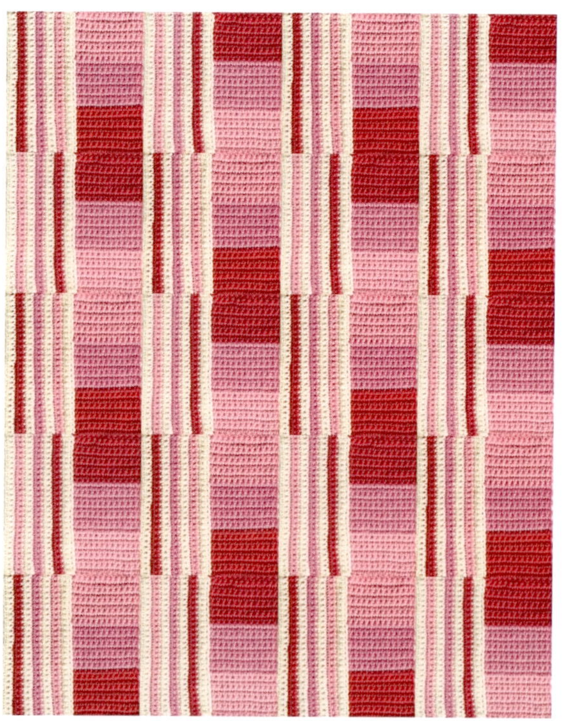

This block uses a split-complementary color palette with the addition of some extra colors in the stripes section. Try working this block in a triadic color palette for a bolder look.

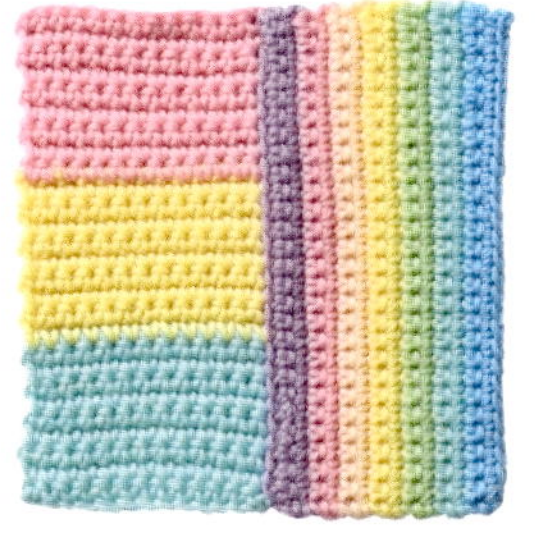

Variation Colorway 1

Variation Colorway 2

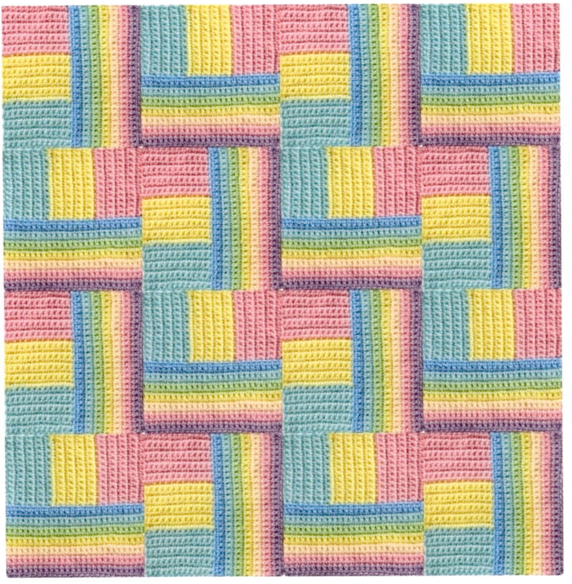

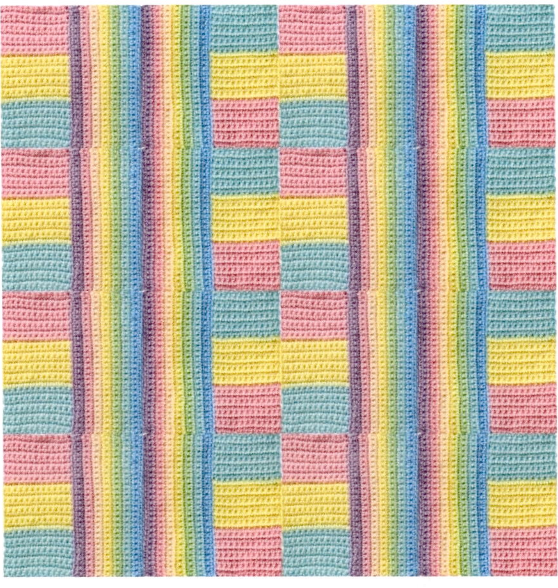

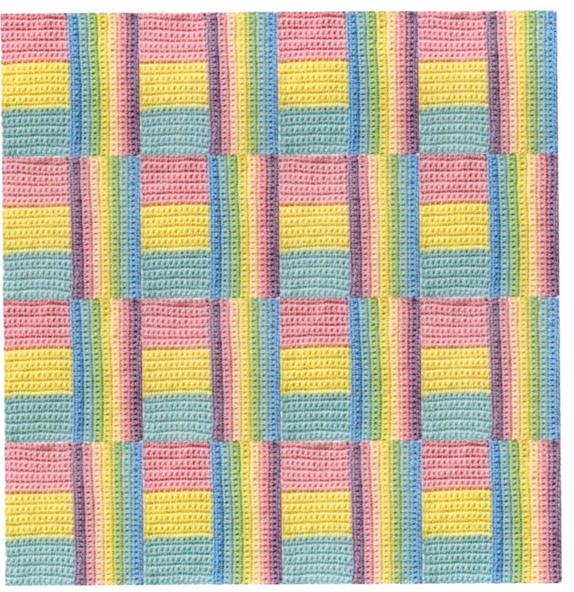

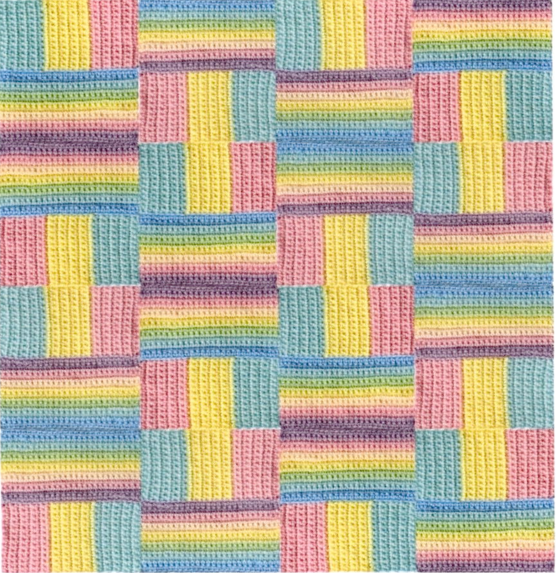

CORNER STRIPES

The colors in these blocks roughly form a square on the color wheel. Square color palettes are not used as often in color theory as some of the other methods, but you can create some fun and unexpected color combinations using this method.

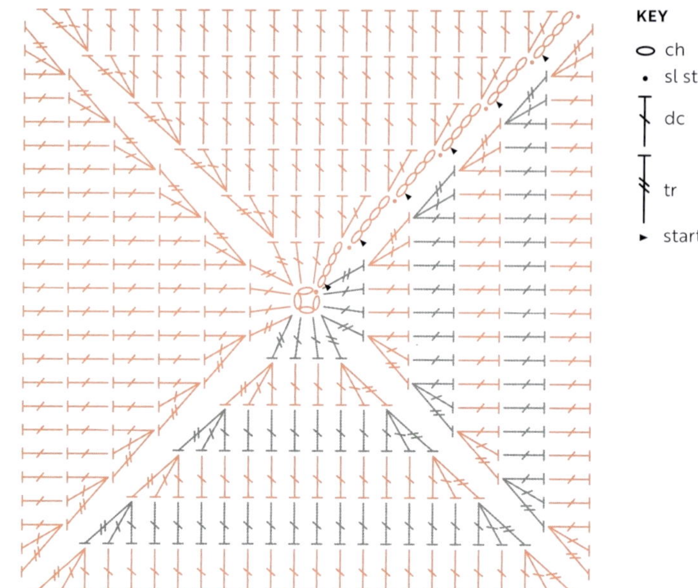

SKILL LEVEL: Intermediate

BLOCK SIZE: 6" x 6" (15 x 15 cm)

HOOK SIZE: G/6 (4mm)

YARN WEIGHT: DK

YARN: Cascade 220 Superwash®

Main Block

Yarn Requirements

Color A: 29½ yd (27 m)

Color B: 8¾ yd (8 m)

Colorway 1

A: 1940 (Peach)

B: 871 (White)

Colorway 2

A: 1973 (Seafoam Heather)

B: 871 (White)

Colorway 3

A: 842 (Light Iris)

B: 871 (White)

Colorway 4

A: 821 (Daffodil)

B: 871 (White)

Variations

Follow Variation Crochet Pattern (see page 73).

Yarn Requirements

Color A: 19¾ yd (18 m)

Color B: 8¾ yd (8 m)

Color C: 11 yd (10 m)

Colorway 1

A: 1922 (Christmas Red Heather)

B: 290 (Chrysanthemum)

C: 1940 (Peach)

Colorway 2

A: 1960 (Pacific)

B: 810 (Teal)

C: 1973 (Seafoam Heather)

Colorway 3

A: 803 (Royal Purple)

B: 1986 (Purple Hyacinth)

C: 842 (Light Iris)

Colorway 4

A: 876 (Sandalwood)

B: 263 (Gold Fusion)

C: 821 (Daffodil)

Abbreviations and Stitches

ch	chain
sl st	slip stitch
dc	double crochet
tr	treble crochet
beg	beginning
st(s)	stitch(es)
[ ]	repeat instructions within brackets the stated number of times
( )	work instructions within brackets in place indicated

Notes

- Carry unused yarn color unless otherwise stated.
- All rounds are worked with right side facing.

Main Block Crochet Pattern

Foundation Ring: Using A, ch 4, join with sl st to first ch made to form a ring.
Rnd 1: Ch 4 (counts as tr throughout), 2 dc, 2 tr, 2 dc, tr changing to B, tr, 2 dc, 2 tr, 2 dc, tr changing to A, join with sl st to top of beg ch-4, fasten off B—16 sts.
Rnd 2: Ch 4, 2 dc in same place, [dc in 2 sts, (2 dc, tr) in next st, (tr, 2 dc) in next st] three times, dc in next 2 sts, (2 dc, tr) in next st, join with sl st to top of beg ch-4—32 sts.
Rnd 3: Ch 4, 2 dc in same place, dc in next 6 sts, (2 dc, tr) in next st, (tr, 2 dc) in next st, dc in next 6 sts, (2 dc, tr) in next st changing to B, (tr, 2 dc) in next st, dc in next 6 sts, (2 dc, tr) in next st, (tr, 2 dc) in next st, dc in next 6 sts, (2 dc, tr) in next st changing to A, join with sl st to top of beg ch-4, fasten off B—48 sts.
Rnd 4: Ch 4, 2 dc in same place, [dc in next 10 sts, (2 dc, tr) in next st, (tr, 2 dc) in next st] three times, dc in next 10 sts, (2 dc, tr) in next st, join with sl st to top of beg ch-4—64 sts.
Rnd 5: Ch 4, 2 dc in same place, dc in next 14 sts, (2 dc, tr) in next st, (tr, 2 dc) in next st, dc in next 14 sts, (2 dc, tr) in next st changing to B, (tr, 2 dc) in next st, dc in next 14 sts, (2 dc, tr) in next st, (tr, 2 dc) in next st, dc in next 14 sts, (2 dc, tr) in next st changing to A, join with sl st to top of beg ch-4, fasten off B—80 sts.
Rnd 6: Ch 4, 2 dc in same place, [dc in next 18 sts, (2 dc, tr) in next st, (tr, 2 dc) in next st] three times, dc in next 18 sts, (2 dc, tr) in next st, join with sl st to top of beg ch-4, fasten off A—96 sts.

Weave in all ends and block to measure 6" x 6" (15 x 15 cm).

Variation Crochet Pattern

Work as for the main block making the following changes:
Rnd 2: Ch 4, 2 dc in same place, dc in next 2 sts, (2 dc, tr) in next st, (tr, 2 dc) in next st, dc in next 2 sts, (2 dc, tr) in next st changing to C, (tr, 2 dc) in next st, dc in next 2 sts, (2 dc, tr) in next st, (tr, 2 dc) in next st, dc in next 2 sts, (2 dc, tr) in next st changing to A, join with sl st to top of beg ch-4, fasten off C—32 sts.
Rnd 4: Ch 4, 2 dc in same place, dc in next 10 sts, (2 dc, tr) in next st, (tr, 2 dc) in next st, dc in next 10 sts, (2 dc, tr) in next st changing to C, (tr, 2 dc) in next st, dc in next 10 sts, (2 dc, tr) in next st, (tr, 2 dc) in next st, dc in next 10 sts, (2 dc, tr) in next st changing to A, join with sl st to top of beg ch-4, fasten off C—64 sts.
Rnd 6: Ch 4, 2 dc in same place, dc in next 18 sts, (2 dc, tr) in next st, (tr, 2 dc) in next st, dc in next 18 sts, (2 dc, tr) in next st changing to C, (tr, 2 dc) in next st, dc in next 18 sts, (2 dc, tr) in next st, (tr, 2 dc) in next st, dc in next 18 sts, (2 dc, tr) in next st changing to A, join with sl st to top of beg ch-4, fasten off C—96 sts.
Fasten off A.

Weave in all ends and block to measure 6" x 6" (15 x 15 cm).

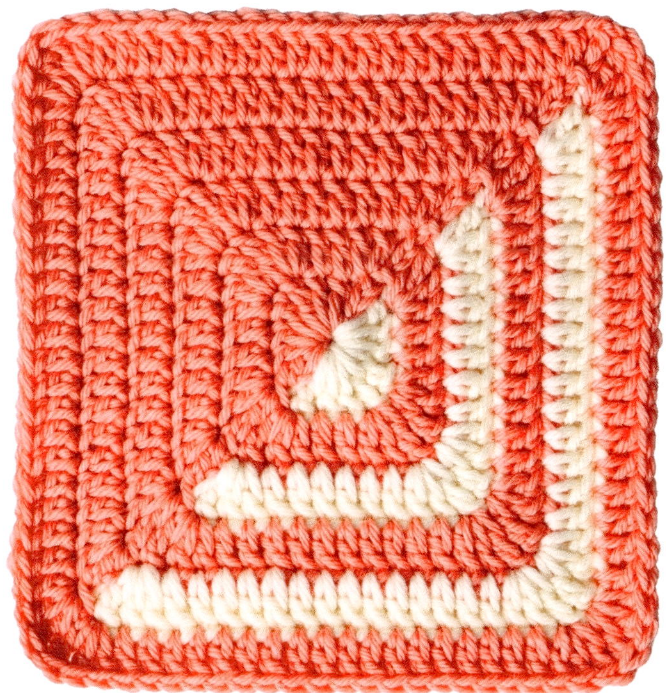

Main Block Colorway 1

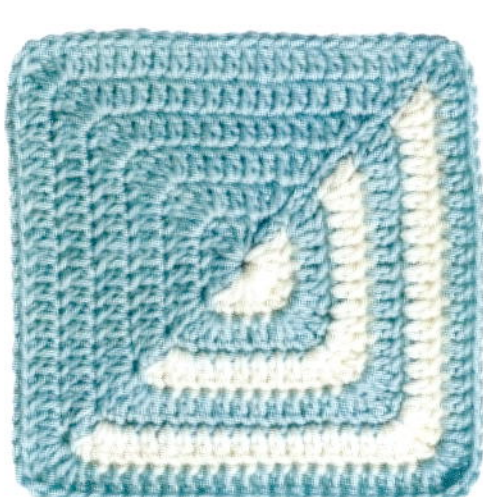

Main Block Colorway 2

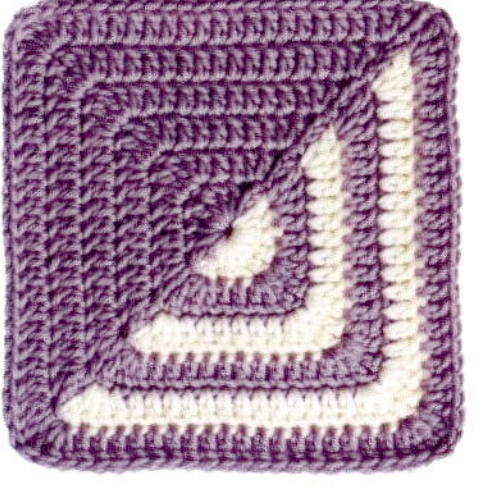

Main Block Colorway 3

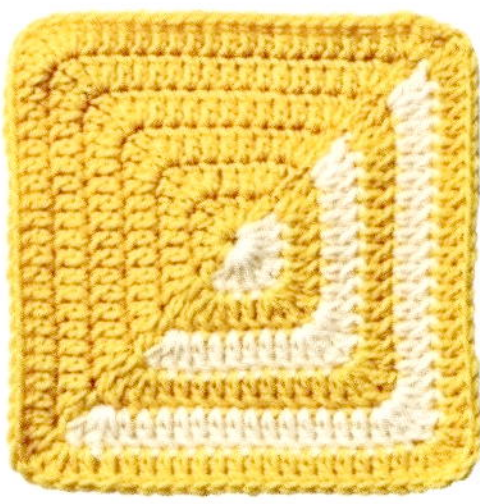

Main Block Colorway 4

Worked in two colors this block gives you some lovely layout options, but with all the colorways used you can create a truly vibrant layout.

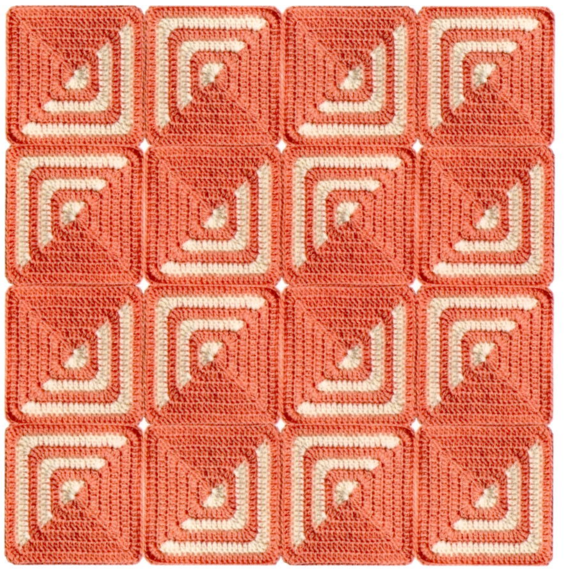

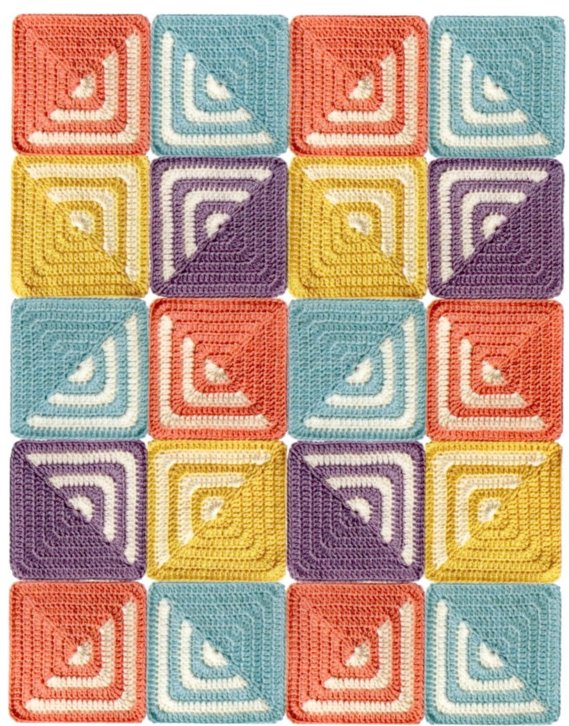

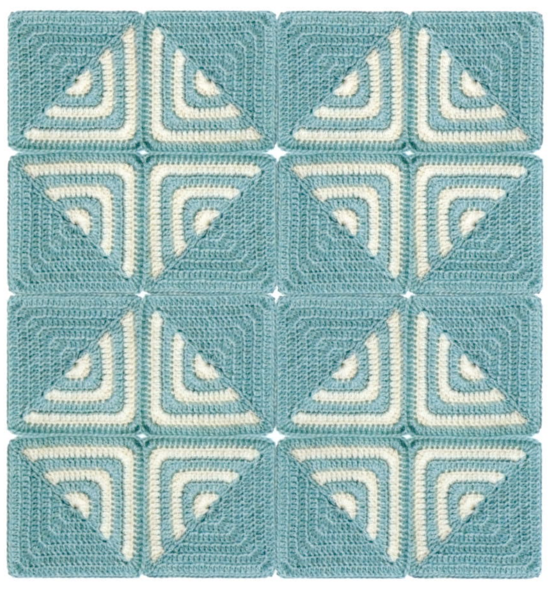

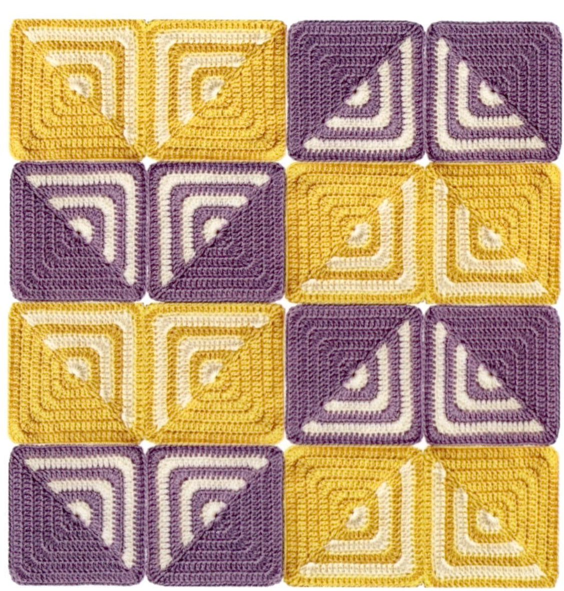

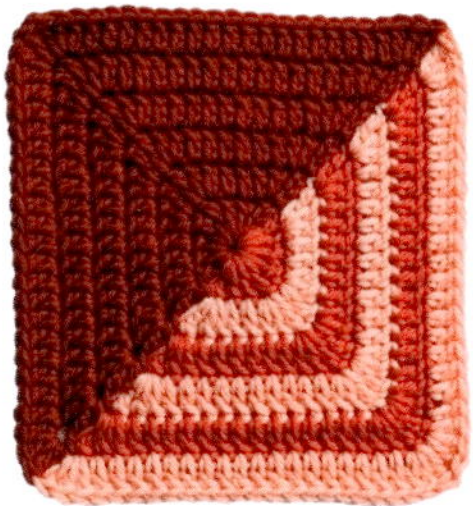
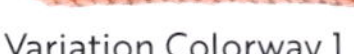
Variation Colorway 1

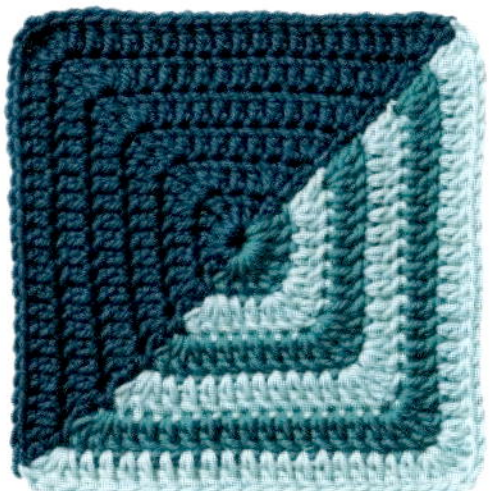
Variation Colorway 2

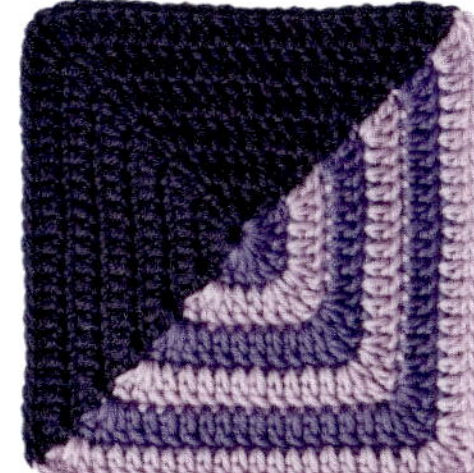
Variation Colorway 3

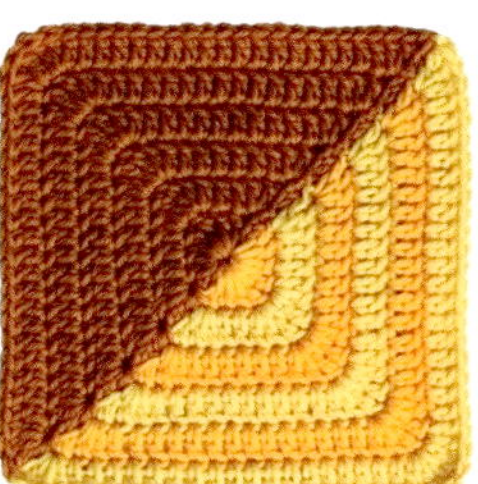
Variation Colorway 4

Still using a square color palette, I've used a dark shade for the main color and lighter shades for the stripes here. When combined it gives a calmer and more graduated look.

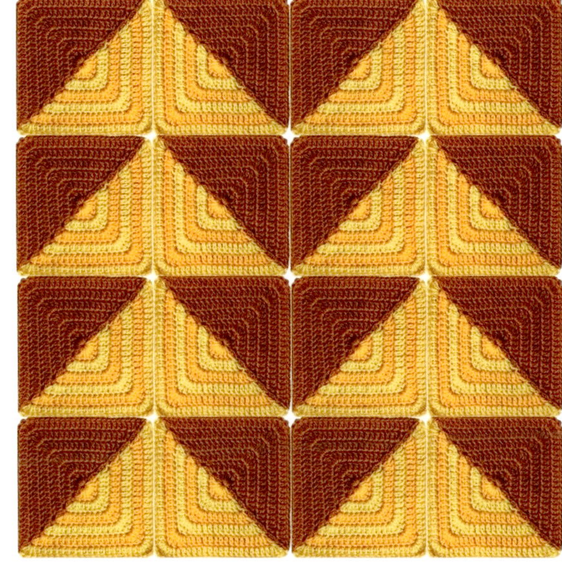

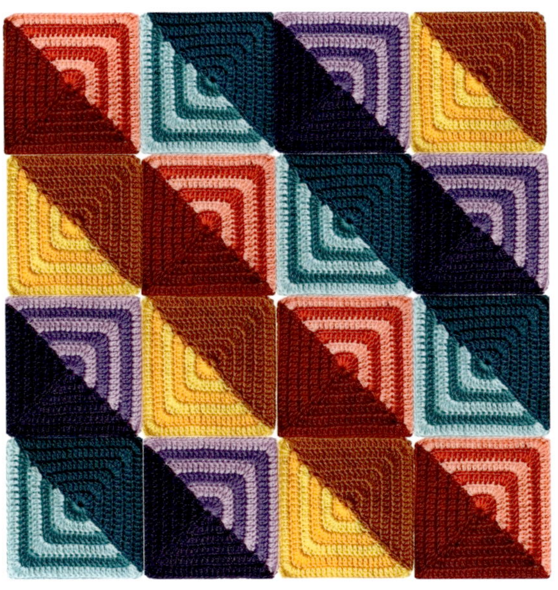

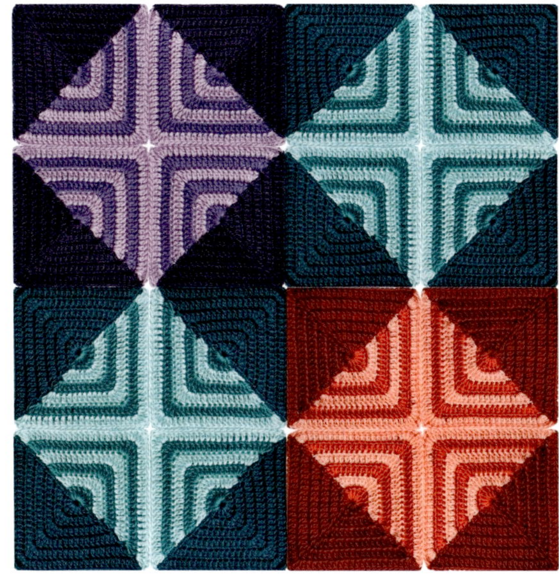

ARROW

Arrow is a lovely geometric design and one of my favorites. I've used two colors in the main samples, which can be used to create a chevron design. In the alternative colorway I've used different colors for each section of the arrow block, which, when joined, creates arrows in a rainbow of colors.

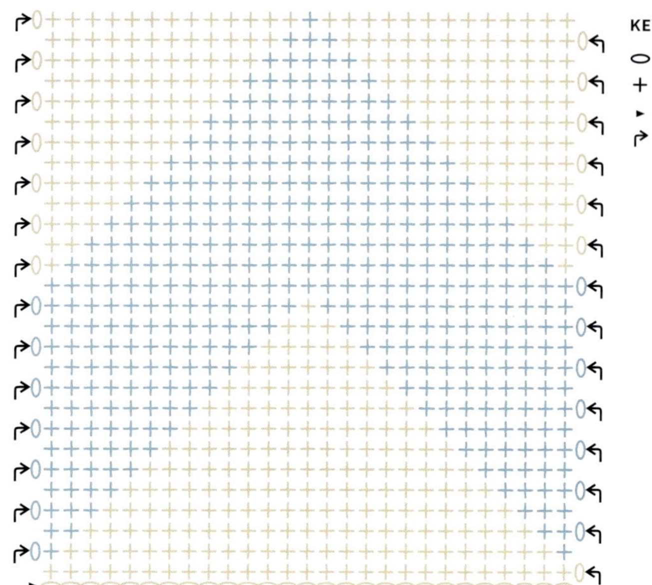

SKILL LEVEL: Intermediate

BLOCK SIZE: 6" x 6" (15 x 15 cm)

HOOK SIZE: G/6 (4 mm)

YARN WEIGHT: DK

YARN: Cascade 220 Superwash®

Main Block

Yarn Requirements

Color A: 36 yd (33 m)

Color B: 36 yd (33 m)

Colorway 1

A: 228 (Frosted Almond)

B: 351 (Pale Jade)

Colorway 2

A: 228 (Frosted Almond)

B: 210 (Deep Ocean)

Variations

Use yarn C instead of yarn A from Row 15 onward.

Yarn Requirements

Color A: 18½ yd (17 m)

Color B: 36 yd (33 m)

Color C: 17½ yd (16 m)

Colorway 1

A: 344 (Cherry Tomato)

B: 822 (Pumpkin)

C: 820 (Lemon)

Colorway 2

A: 820 (Lemon)

B: 851 (Lime)

C: 288 (Green Spruce)

Colorway 3

A: 288 (Green Spruce)

B: 1973 (Seafoam Heather)

C: 344 (Cherry Tomato)

Abbreviations and Stitches

ch	chain
sc	single crochet
st(s)	stitch(es)

Note

- You can choose to work over the unused yarn throughout. If so, try to pick colors that don't have too much contrast to one another since the carried yarn will show through in some places.

Crochet Pattern

Foundation Row: Using A, ch 28.

Row 1 (RS): sc in second ch from hook and each of next 26 ch changing to B when working last st, turn—27 sts.

Row 2 (WS): Ch 1 (does not count as a st here and throughout), sc in first st changing to A, sc in next 25 sts changing to a new strand of B when working last st, sc in last st, turn.

Row 3: Ch 1, sc in first 2 sts changing to A when working last st, sc in next 23 sts changing to B when working last st, sc in last 2 sts, turn.

Row 4: Ch 1, sc in first 3 sts changing to A when working last st, sc in next 21 sts changing to B when working last st, sc in last 3 sts, turn.

Row 5: Ch 1, sc in first 4 sts changing to A when working last st, sc in next 19 sts changing to B when working last st, sc in last 4 sts, turn.

Row 6: Ch 1, sc in first 5 sts changing to A when working last st, sc in next 17 sts changing to B when working last st, sc in last 5 sts, turn.

Row 7: Ch 1, sc in first 6 sts changing to A when working last st, sc in next 15 sts changing to B when working last st, sc in last 6 sts, turn.

Row 8: Ch 1, sc in first 7 sts changing to A when working last st, sc in next 13 sts changing to B when working last st, sc in last 7 sts, turn.

Row 9: Ch 1, sc in first 8 sts changing to A when working last st, sc in next 11 sts changing to B when working last st, sc in last 8 sts, turn.

Row 10: Ch 1, sc in first 9 sts changing to A when working last st, sc in next 9 sts changing to B when working last st, sc in last 9 sts, turn.

Row 11: Ch 1, sc in first 10 sts changing to A when working last st, sc in next 7 sts changing to B when working last st, sc in last 10 sts, turn.

Row 12: Ch 1, sc in first 11 sts changing to A when working last st, sc in next 5 sts changing to B when working last st, sc in last 11 sts, turn.

Row 13: Ch 1, sc in first 12 sts changing to A when working last st, sc in next 3 sts changing to B when working last st, sc in last 12 sts, turn.

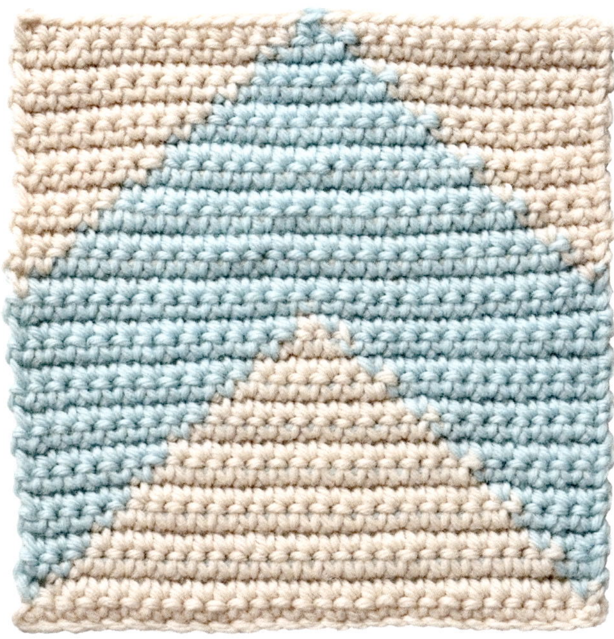

Main Block Colorway 1

Row 14: Ch 1, sc in first 13 sts changing to A when working last st, sc in next st changing to B, sc in last 13 sts, turn.

Row 15: Ch 1, sc in each st across changing to A when working last st, turn.

Row 16: Ch 1, sc in first st changing to B, sc in next 25 sts changing to A when working last st, sc in last st, turn.

Row 17: Ch 1, sc in first 2 sts changing to B when working last st, sc in next 23 sts changing to A when working last st, sc in last 2 sts, turn.

Row 18: Ch 1, sc in first 3 sts changing to B when working last st, sc in next 21 sts changing to A when working last st, sc in 3 sts, turn.

Row 19: Ch 1, sc in first 4 sts changing to B when working last st, sc in next 19 sts changing to A when working last st, sc in 4 sts, turn.

Row 20: Ch 1, sc in first 5 sts changing to B when working last st, sc in next 17 sts changing to A when working last st, sc in 5 sts, turn.

Row 21: Ch 1, sc in first 6 sts changing to B when working last st, sc in next 15 sts changing to A when working last st, sc in 6 sts, turn.

Row 22: Ch 1, sc in first 7 sts changing to B when working last st, sc in next 13 sts changing to A when working last st, sc in 7 sts, turn.

Row 23: Ch 1, sc in first 8 sts changing to B when working last st, sc in next 11 sts changing to A when working last st, sc in 8 sts, turn.

Row 24: Ch 1, sc in first 9 sts changing to B when working last st, sc in next 9 sts changing to A when working last st, sc in 9 sts, turn.

Row 25: Ch 1, sc in first 10 sts changing to B when working last st, sc in next 7 sts changing to A when working last st, sc in 10 sts, turn.

Row 26: Ch 1, sc in first 11 sts changing to B when working last st, sc in next 5 sts changing to A when working last st, sc in 11 sts, turn.

Row 27: Ch 1, sc in first 12 sts changing to B when working last st, sc in next 3 sts changing to A when working last st, sc in 12 sts, turn.

Row 28: Ch 1, sc in first 13 sts changing to B when working last st, sc in next st changing to A, sc in 13 sts.

Weave in all ends and block to measure 6" x 6" (15 x 15 cm).

This block can be used to create some lovely chevron layouts. When both colorways are used, you can boost the contrast to make the layouts a little more vibrant.

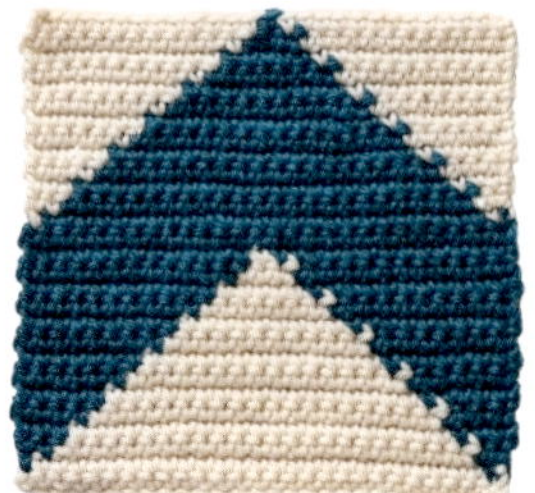

Main Block Colorway 2

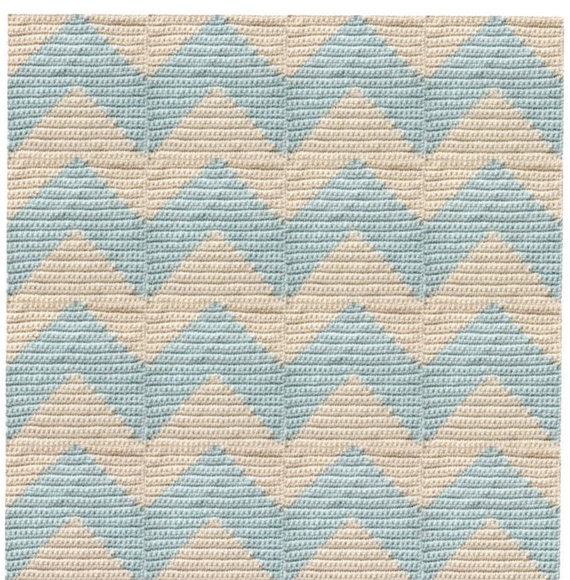

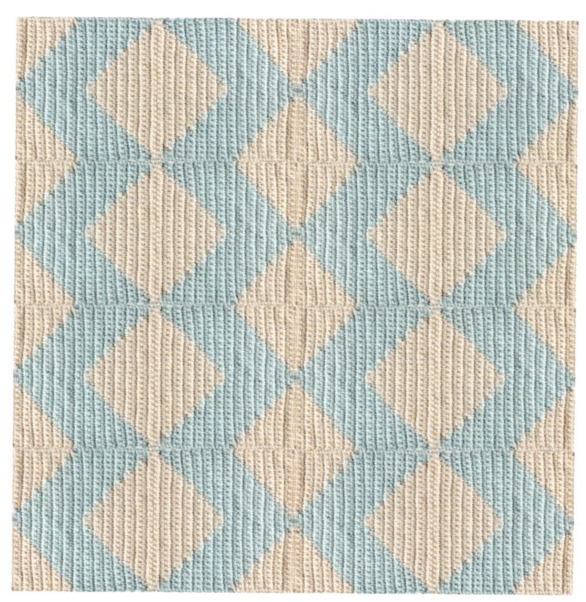

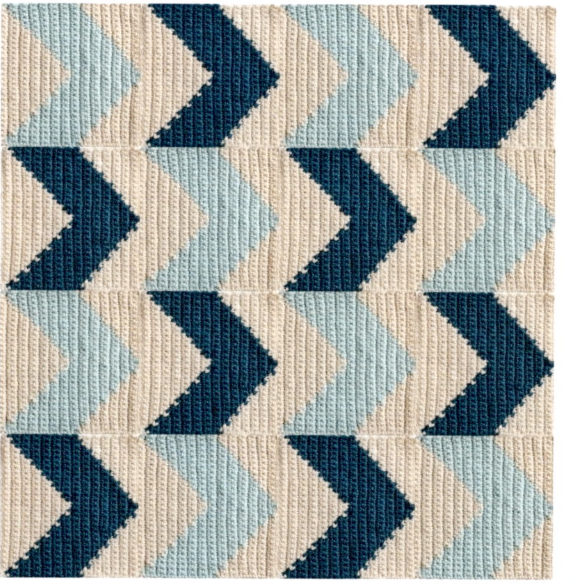

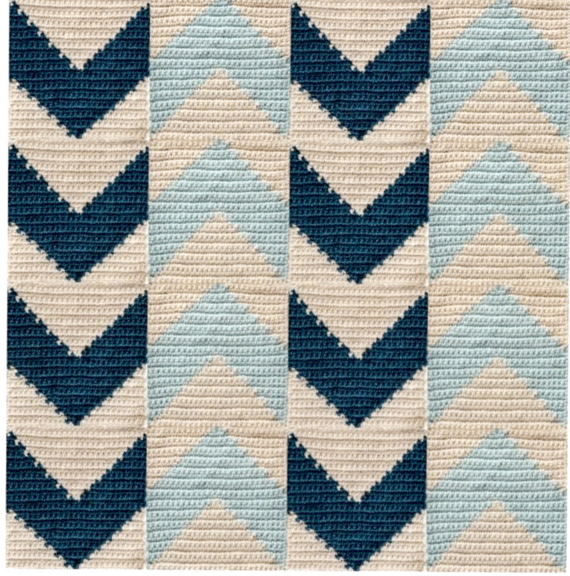

Using all three colorway variations gives you lots of layout options. This is perfect for using rainbow colors, but it would also look wonderful in more subtle colors and shades.

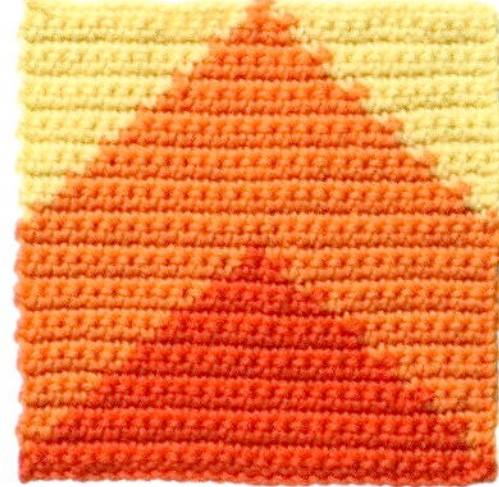

Variation Colorway 1

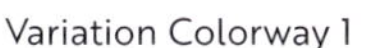

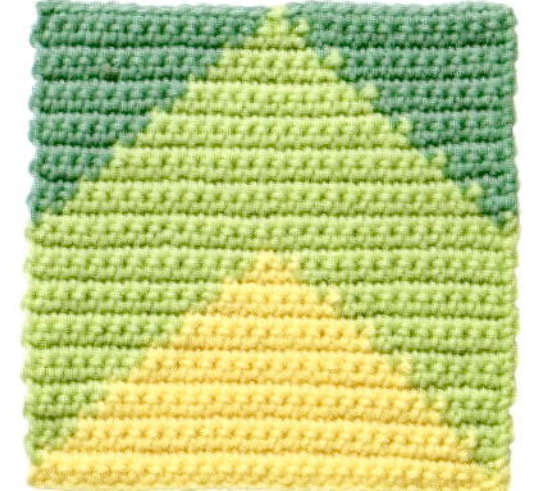

Variation Colorway 2

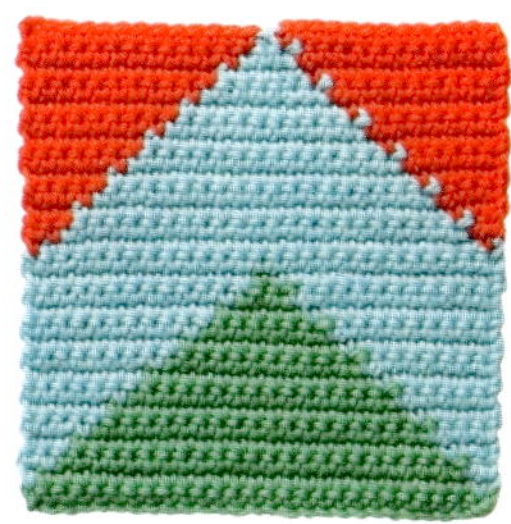

Variation Colorway 3

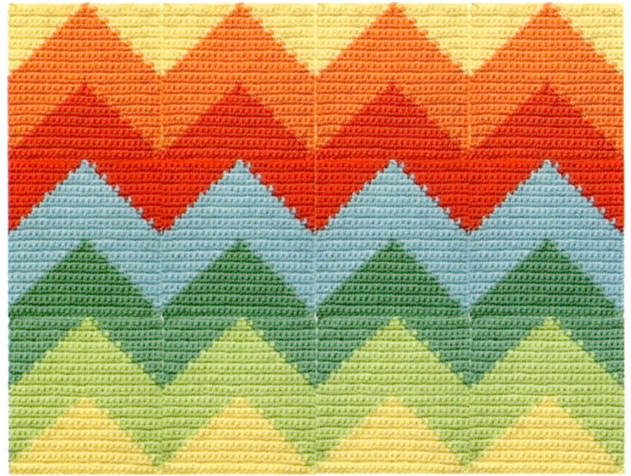

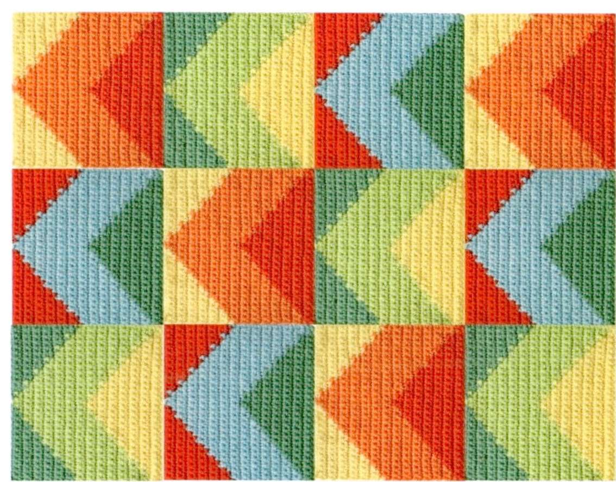

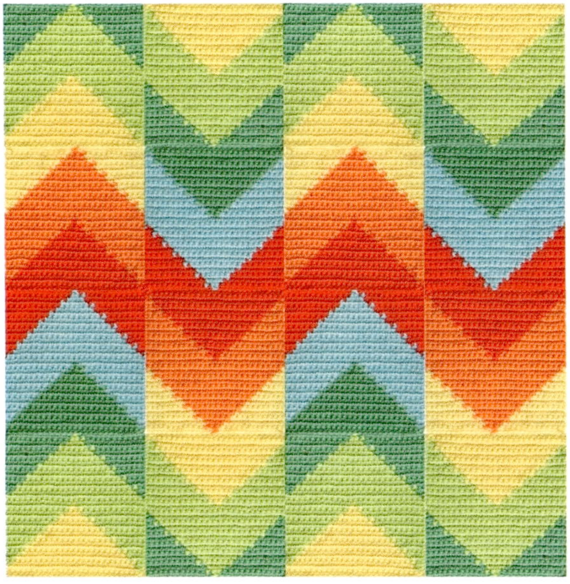

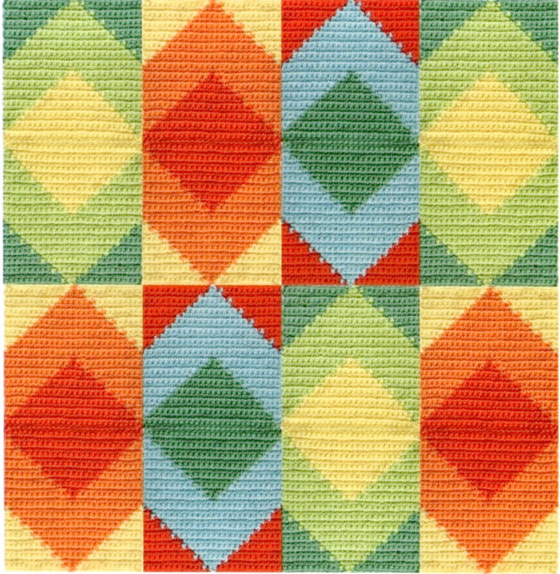

RAINBOW EDGE

This block features a rainbow of color along one edge. By reversing the order of the colors you can create even more color patterns. Try working in a variety of shades of your favorite color instead of a rainbow for a different look.

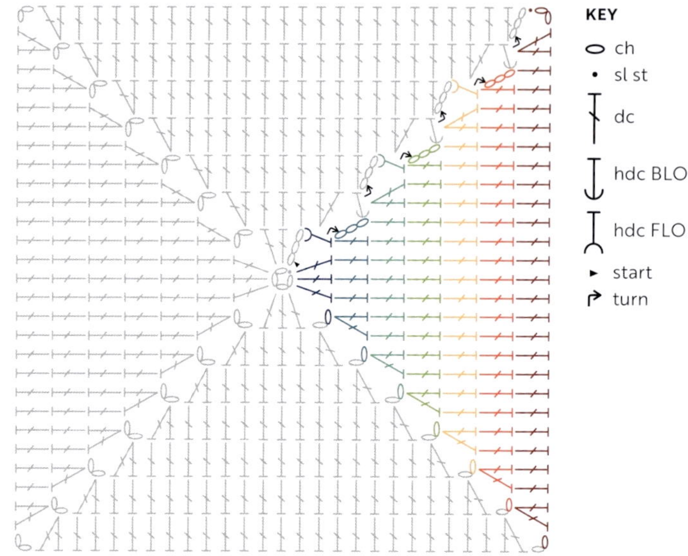

SKILL LEVEL: Intermediate

BLOCK SIZE: 6" x 6" (15 x 15 cm)

HOOK SIZE: E/4 (3.5 mm)

YARN WEIGHT: DK

YARN: Cascade 220 Superwash®

Main Block

Yarn Requirements

Color A: 28½ yd (26 m)

Color B: 1¼ yd (1 m)

Color C: 1¼ yd (1 m)

Color D: 1¼ yd (1 m)

Color E: 1¼ yd (1 m)

Color F: 1¼ yd (1 m)

Color G: 2¼ yd (2 m)

Color H: 3¼ yd (3 m)

Colorway 1

A: 871 (White)

B: 811 (Como Blue)

C: 259 (Blue Turquoise)

D: 288 (Green Spruce)

E: 370 (Sulfur)

F: 263 (Gold Fusion)

G: 822 (Pumpkin)

H: 809 (Really Red)

Colorway 2

A: 809 (Really Red); **B:** 822 (Pumpkin); **C:** 263 (Gold Fusion); **D:** 370 (Sulfur); **E:** 288 (Green Spruce); **F:** 259 (Blue Turquoise); **G:** 811 (Como Blue); **H:** 871 (White)

Variations

Yarn Requirements

Color A: 28½ yd (26 m)

Color B: 1¼ yd (1 m)

Color C: 1¼ yd (1 m)

Color D: 1¼ yd (1 m)

Color E: 1¼ yd (1 m)

Color F: 1¼ yd (1 m)

Color G: 2¼ yd (2 m)

Color H: 3¼ yd (3 m)

Colorway 1

A: 281 (Frost Grey)

B: 210 (Deep Ocean)

C: 371 (Chinois Green)

D: 338 (Harbor Mist)

E: 349 (Irish Cream)

F: 1941 (Salmon)

G: 1940 (Peach)

H: 364 (Faded Rose)

Colorway 2

A: 364 (Faded Rose); **B:** 1940 (Peach); **C:** 1941 (Salmon); **D:** 349 (Irish Cream); **E:** 338 (Harbor Mist); **F:** 371 (Chinois Green); **G:** 210 (Deep Ocean); **H:** 281 (Frost Grey)

Abbreviations and Stitches

ch	chain
sp	space
sl st	slip stitch
dc	double crochet
hdc	half-double crochet
beg	beginning
st(s)	stitch(es)
yo	yarn over
BLO	back loop only
FLO	front loop only
[ ]	repeat instructions within brackets the stated number of times
( )	work instructions within brackets in place indicated

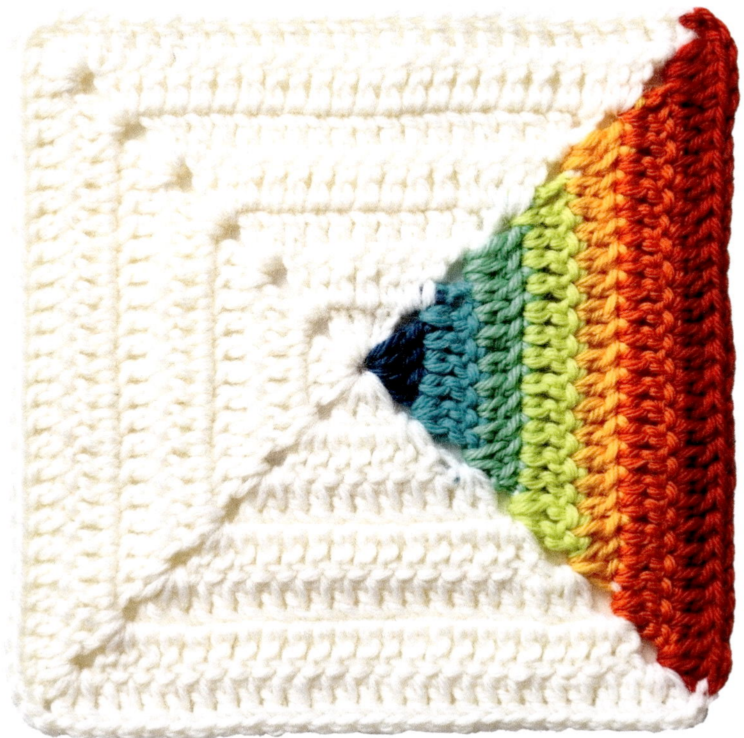

Main Block Colorway 1

Main Block Colorway 2

Notes

- Change yarn colors at the last yo of a designated stitch.
- Leave unused yarn A hanging on the wrong side of the work throughout and pick up from there when needed.
- When working into a stitch that already contains an hdc BLO or hdc FLO, make sure to work through both loops of that stitch. This helps to hide the join.

Crochet Pattern

Foundation Ring: Using A, ch 4, join with sl st to first ch made to form a ring.

Rnd 1 (RS): Ch 3 (counts as dc here and throughout), 2 dc, [ch 2, 3 dc] twice, ch 1, change to B, ch 1, 3 dc changing to C when working last dc, join with hdc BLO to top of beg ch-3 (hdc counts as ch 2), fasten off B, turn—12 sts.

Rnd 2 (WS): Ch 3, dc in sp, dc in 3 sts, 2 dc in sp, ch 1, change to A, ch 1, 2 dc in sp, [dc in 3 sts, (2 dc, ch 2, 2 dc) in sp] twice, dc in 3 sts, 2 dc in sp, join with hdc FLO to top of beg ch-3 (hdc counts as ch 2), fasten off C, turn—28 sts.

Rnd 3: Ch 3, dc in sp, [dc in 7 sts, (2 dc, ch 2, 2 dc) in sp] twice, dc in 7 sts, 2 dc in sp, ch 1, change to D, ch 1, 2 dc in same sp, dc in 7 sts, 2 dc in sp changing to E when working last st, join with hdc BLO to top of beg ch-3, fasten off D, turn—44 sts.

Rnd 4: Ch 3, dc in sp, dc in 11 sts, 2 dc in sp, ch 1, change to A, ch 1, 2 dc in same sp, [dc in 11 sts, (2 dc, ch 2, 2 dc) in sp] twice, dc in 11 sts, 2 dc in sp, join with hdc FLO to top of beg ch-3, fasten off E, turn—60 sts.

Rnd 5: Ch 3, dc in sp, [dc in 15 sts, (2 dc, ch 2, 2 dc) in sp] twice, dc in 15 sts, 2 dc in sp, ch 1, change to F, ch 1, 2 dc in same sp, dc in 15 sts, 2 dc in sp changing to G when working last st, join with hdc BLO to top of beg ch-3, fasten off F, turn—76 sts.

Rnd 6: Ch 3, dc in sp, dc in 19 sts, 2 dc in sp, ch 1, change to A, ch 1, 2 dc in same sp, [dc in 19 sts, (2 dc, ch 2, 2 dc) in sp] twice, dc in 19 sts, 2 dc in sp, join with hdc FLO to top of beg ch-3, fasten off G, turn—92 sts.

Rnd 7: Ch 3, dc in sp, [dc in 23 sts, (2 dc, ch 2, 2 dc) in sp] twice, dc in 23 sts, 2 dc in sp, ch 1, change to H, ch 1, 2 dc in same sp, dc in 23 sts, 2 dc in sp, ch 2, join with sl st to top of beg ch-3, fasten off H and A—108 sts.

Weave in all ends and block to measure 6" x 6" (15 x 15 cm).

Working with just one colorway you can create a trellis or twist design with the white parts of the blocks.

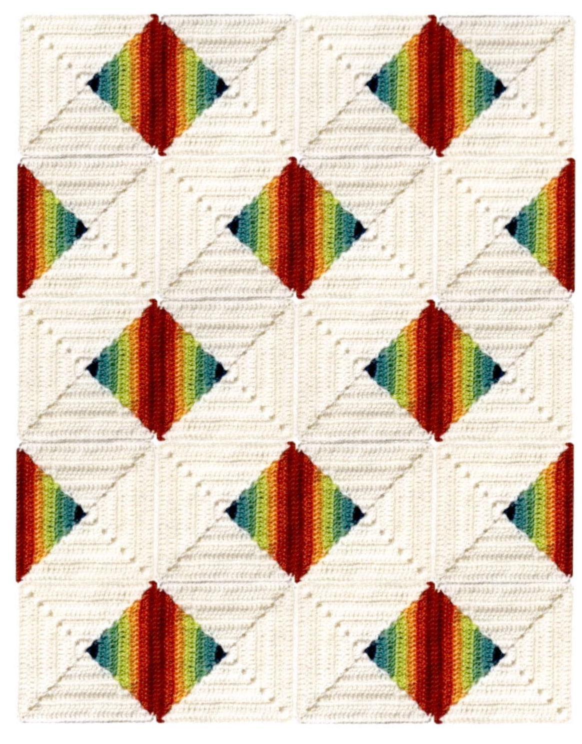

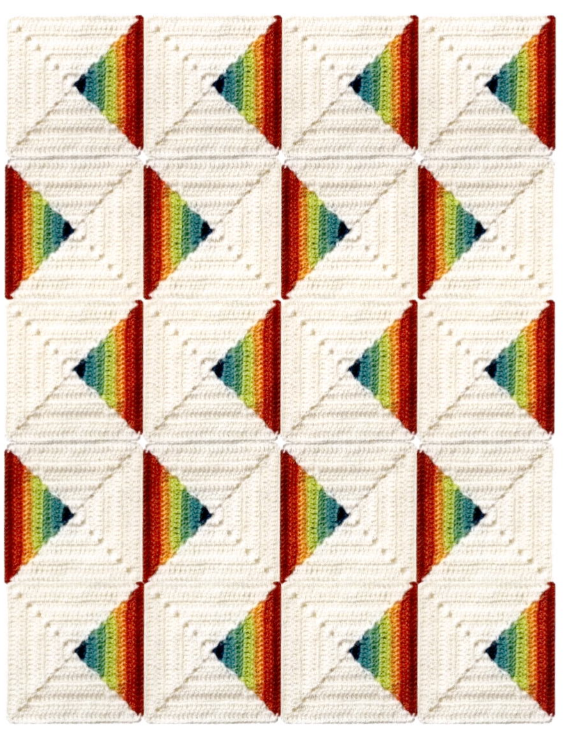

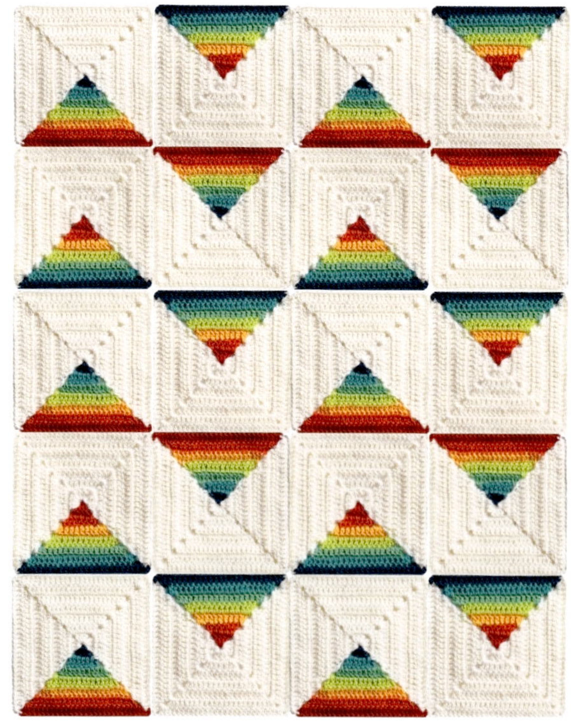

This colorway uses a more subtle color palette. When both colorways are joined together they can be used to create a stripy diamond shape.

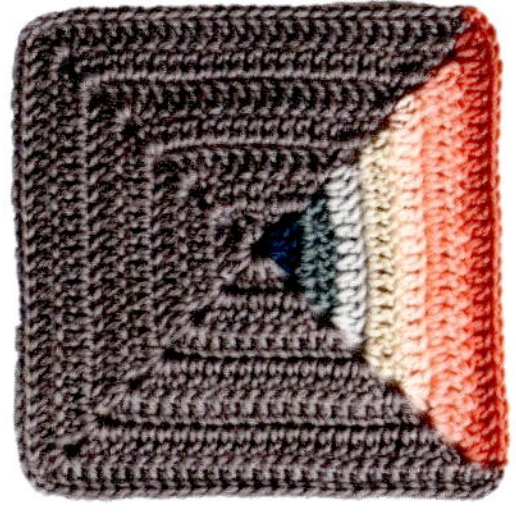

Variation Colorway 1

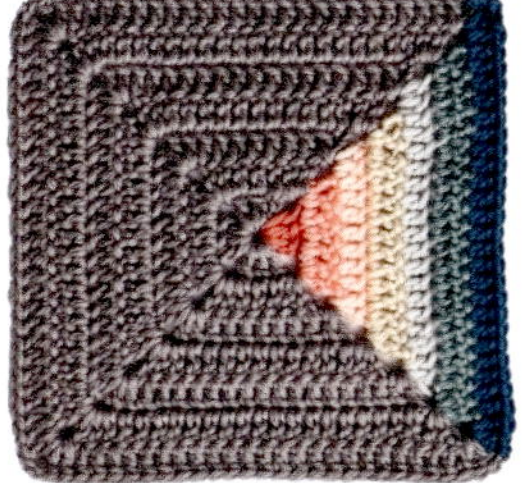

Variation Colorway 2

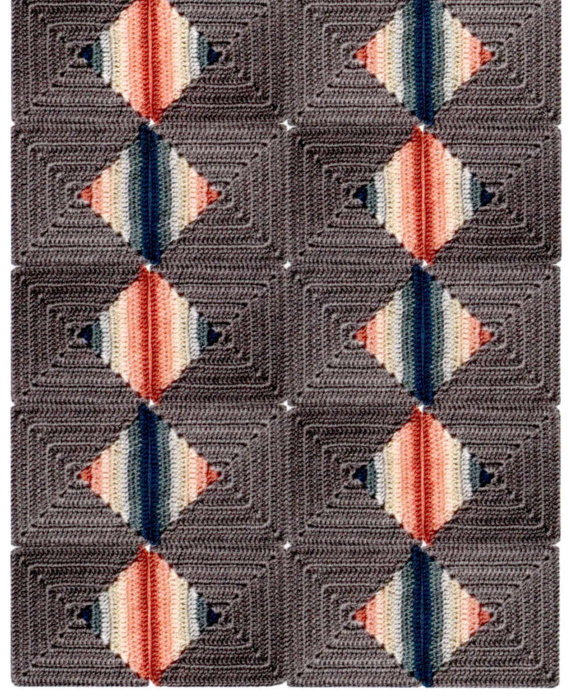

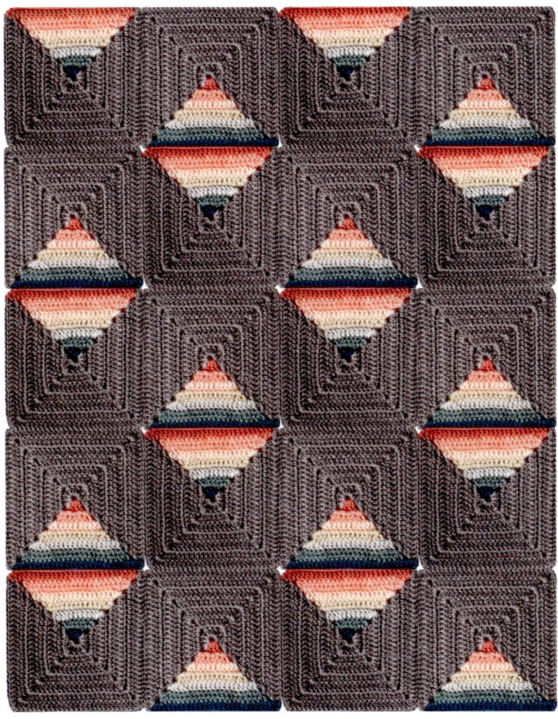

BOBBLE DIAGONAL

This design is worked in rows, with a row of bobbles across the center. When joined you can create a lovely trellis pattern. By working two corners at the beginning and end in a slightly different color, you can create diamonds. The stitch diagram may look like a diamond, but when worked, it makes a perfect square when blocked.

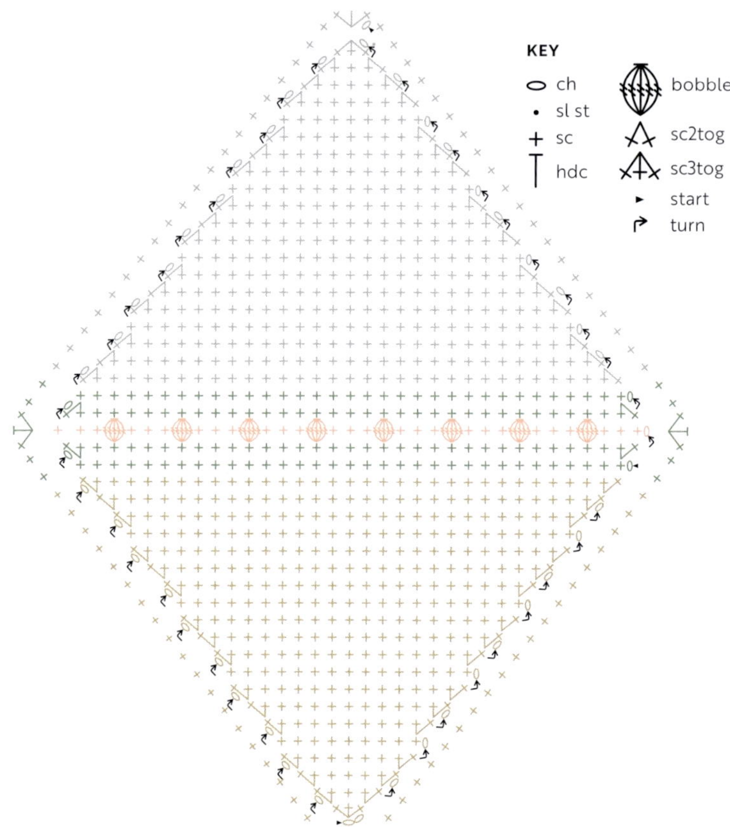

SKILL LEVEL: Intermediate

BLOCK SIZE: 6" x 6" (15 x 15 cm)

HOOK SIZE: E/4 (3.5 mm)

YARN WEIGHT: DK

YARN: Cascade 220 Superwash®

Main Block

Yarn Requirements

Color A: 19¾ yd (18 m)

Color B: 8¾ yd (8 m)

Color C: 7¾ yd (7 m)

Color D: 19¾ yd (18 m)

Colorway 1

- **A:** 289 (Creampuff)
- **B:** 250 (Laurel Green)
- **C:** 1941 (Salmon)
- **D:** 871 (White)

Colorway 2

- **A:** 1941 (Salmon)
- **B:** 250 (Laurel Green)
- **C:** 289 (Creampuff)
- **D:** 875 (Feather Grey)

Variations

Yarn Requirements

Color A: 19¾ yd (18 m)

Color B: 8¾ yd (8 m)

Color C: 7¾ yd (7 m)

Color D: 19¾ yd (18 m)

Colorway 1

- **A:** 355 (Stormy Weather)
- **B:** 349 (Irish Cream)
- **C:** 876 (Sandalwood)
- **D:** 204 (Smoke Blue)

Colorway 2

Work Rows 1–10 in yarn A, Rows 11–20 in yarn B, Rows 21 and 22 in yarn C, Row 23 in yarn D, Rows 24 and 25 in yarn C, Rows 26–35 in yarn A and Rows 36–45 in yarn B.

- **A:** 204 (Smoke Blue)
- **B:** 355 (Stormy Weather)
- **C:** 349 (Irish Cream)
- **D:** 876 (Sandalwood)

Abbreviations and Stitches

ch	chain
sl st	slip stitch
sc	single crochet
hdc	half-double crochet
st(s)	stitch(es)
bobble	5 tr worked into the same st and closed at the top
sc2tog	single crochet 2 together
sc3tog	single crochet 3 together

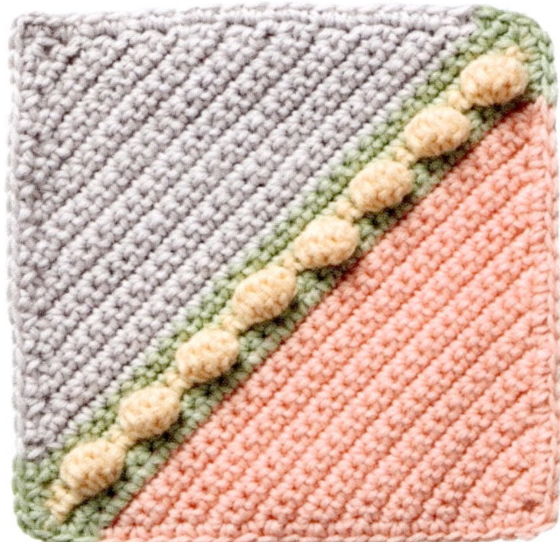
Main Block Colorway 2

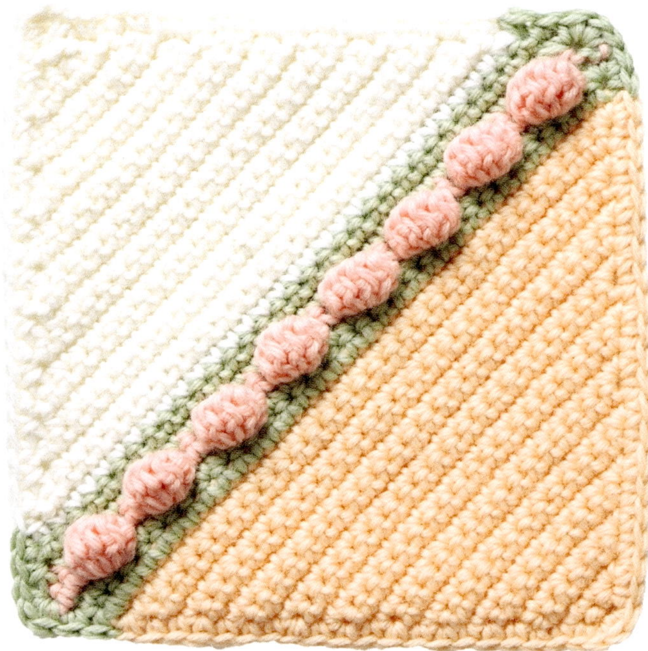
Main Block Colorway 1

Crochet Pattern

Foundation Row: Using A, ch 2.
Row 1 (RS): 3 sc in second ch from hook, turn—3 sts.
Row 2 (WS): Ch 1 (does not count as a st here and throughout), 2 sc in first st, sc in 1 st, 2 sc in last st, turn—5 sts.
Row 3: Ch 1, 2 sc in first st, sc in each st to last st, 2 sc in last st, turn—7 sts.
Row 4: Repeat Row 3—9 sts.
Row 5: Ch 1, sc in each st across, turn.
Rows 6–8: Repeat Row 3—15 sts.
Row 9: Repeat Row 5.
Rows 10–17: Repeat Rows 6–9 twice—27 sts.
Rows 18–20: Repeat Rows 6–8, fasten off A—33 sts.
Row 21: Join in B and repeat Row 9.
Row 22: Repeat Row 3, fasten off B—35 sts.
Row 23: Join in C, ch 1, [sc in 3 sts, bobble in next st] eight times, sc in 3 sts, fasten off C, turn.
Row 24: Join in B, ch 1, sc2tog over first 2 sts, sc in each st until 2 sts remain, sc2tog over last 2 sts, turn—33 sts.
Row 25: Repeat Row 9, fasten off B.
Rows 26–28: Join in C, repeat Row 24—27 sts.
Row 29: Ch 1, sc in each st to end, turn.
Rows 30–41: Repeat Rows 26–29 three times—9 sts.
Rows 42–44: Repeat Rows 26–28—3 sts.
Row 45: Ch 1, sc3tog—1 st.
Edging: Using D and continuing to work around the edge, ch 1, (sc, hdc, sc) in top of sc3tog, 20 sc over next 20 row ends, changing to C when working last st, sc in next 2 row ends, (sc, hdc, sc) in next row end, sc in next 2 row ends, changing to A when working last st, 20 sc over next 20 row ends, (sc, hdc, sc) in foundation ch, 20 sc over next 20 row ends, changing to B when working last st, sc in next 2 row ends, (sc , hdc, sc) in next row end, sc in next 2 row ends, changing to D when working last st, 20 sc over next 20 row ends, join with sl st to first st made, fasten off all yarns—100 sts.

Weave in all ends and block to measure 6" x 6" (15 x 15 cm).

This block would look lovely worked all in one color with just the tactile bobble stitches in a different color. Use the bobble stitches to create lines, chevrons, and diamonds. By using both colorways, you can make even more shapes and interest with color.

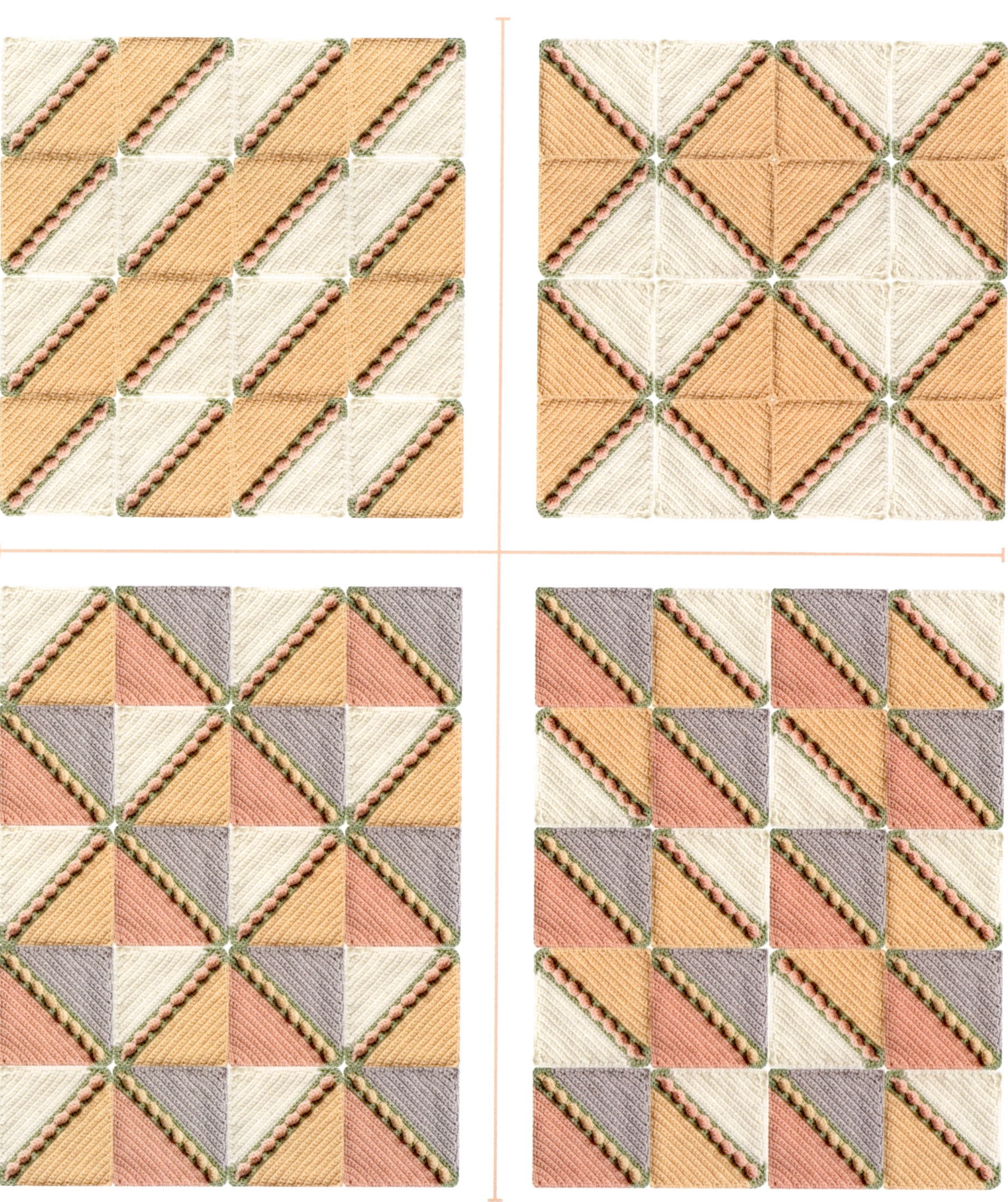

By switching the colors in the corners, as in variation colorway 2, you create even more layout options. This is also a chance to get creative with color choices. The second layout option below would look fabulous in punchy, vibrant colors.

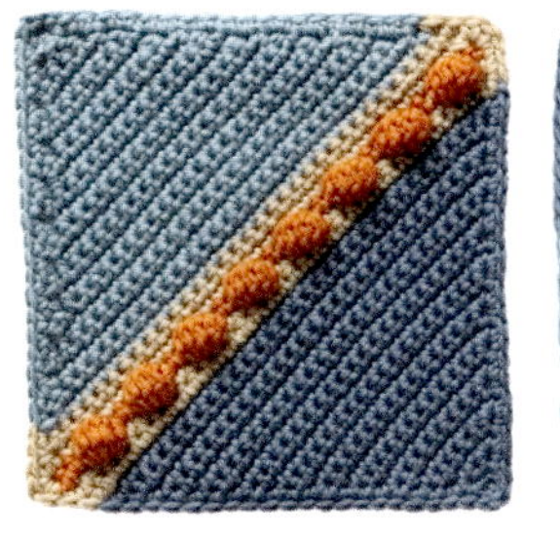

Variation Colorway 1

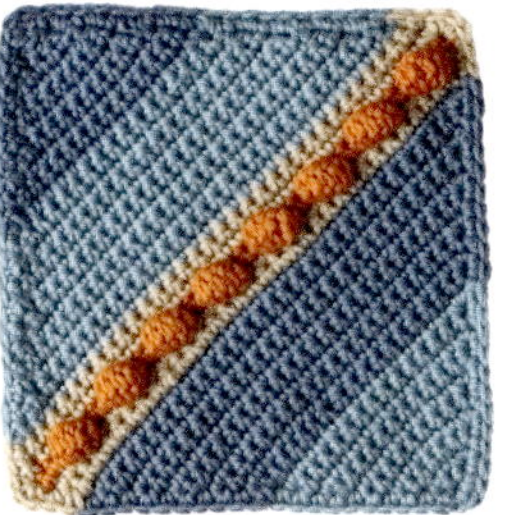

Variation Colorway 2

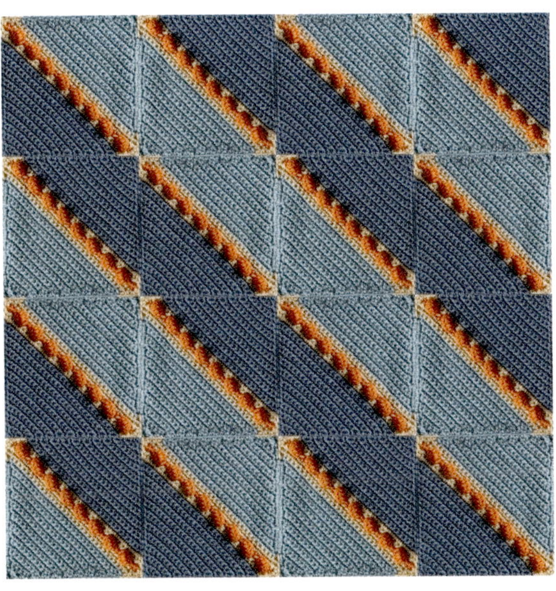

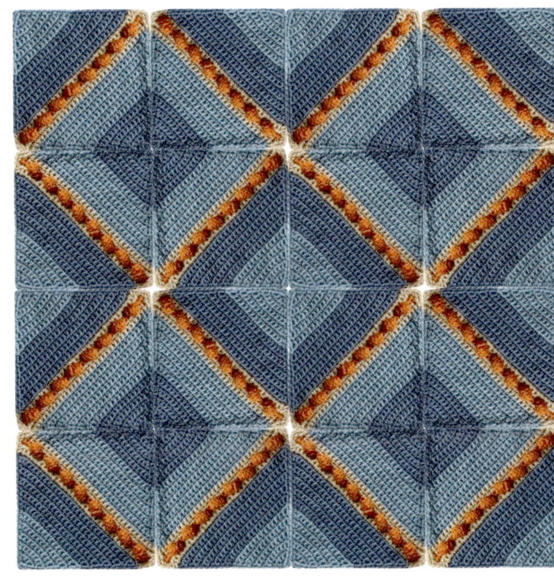

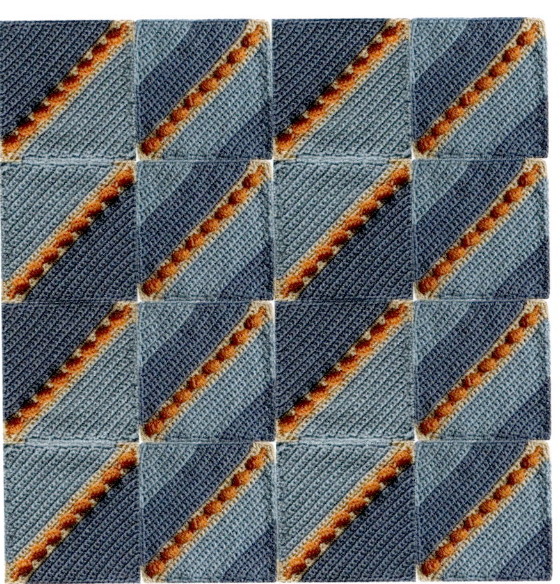

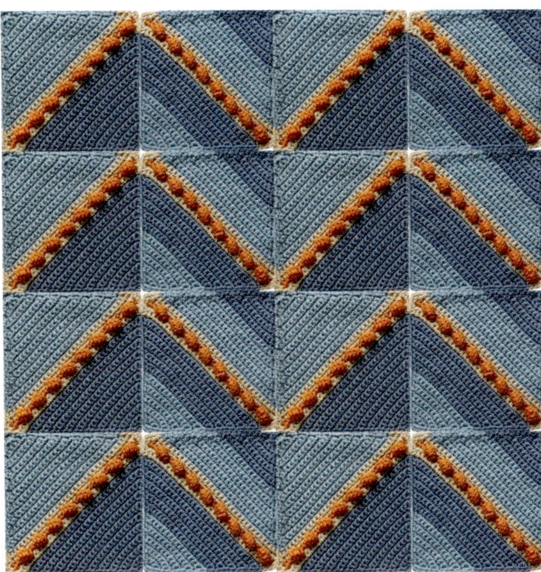

CIRCLE DIAGONALLY

A simple block that packs a punch. You can create some gorgeous color layouts with this block by working the background in a riot of colors. Or keep it simple by using the same diagonal background but changing the colors of the circle. See the Wall Hanging on page 118 and the Pillow on page 115, which both use this block.

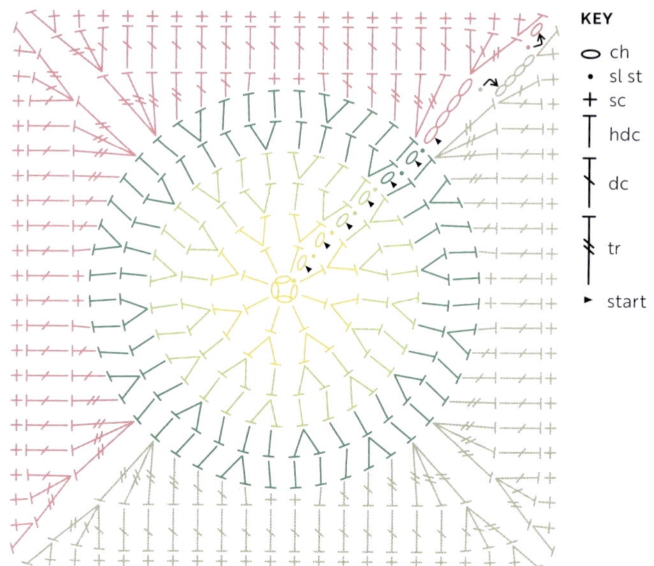

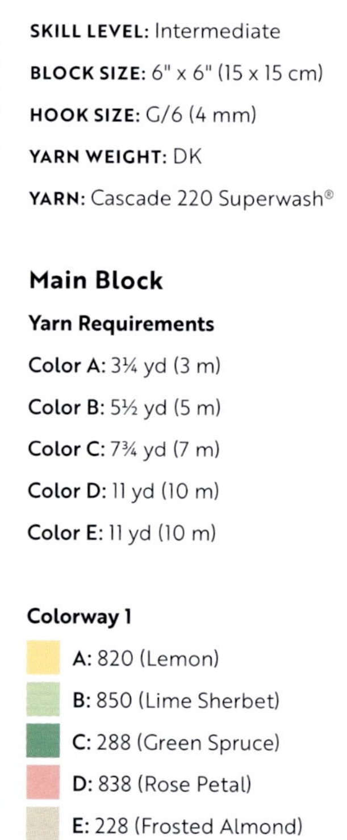

SKILL LEVEL: Intermediate

BLOCK SIZE: 6" x 6" (15 x 15 cm)

HOOK SIZE: G/6 (4 mm)

YARN WEIGHT: DK

YARN: Cascade 220 Superwash®

Main Block

Yarn Requirements

Color A: 3¼ yd (3 m)

Color B: 5½ yd (5 m)

Color C: 7¾ yd (7 m)

Color D: 11 yd (10 m)

Color E: 11 yd (10 m)

Colorway 1

A: 820 (Lemon)

B: 850 (Lime Sherbet)

C: 288 (Green Spruce)

D: 838 (Rose Petal)

E: 228 (Frosted Almond)

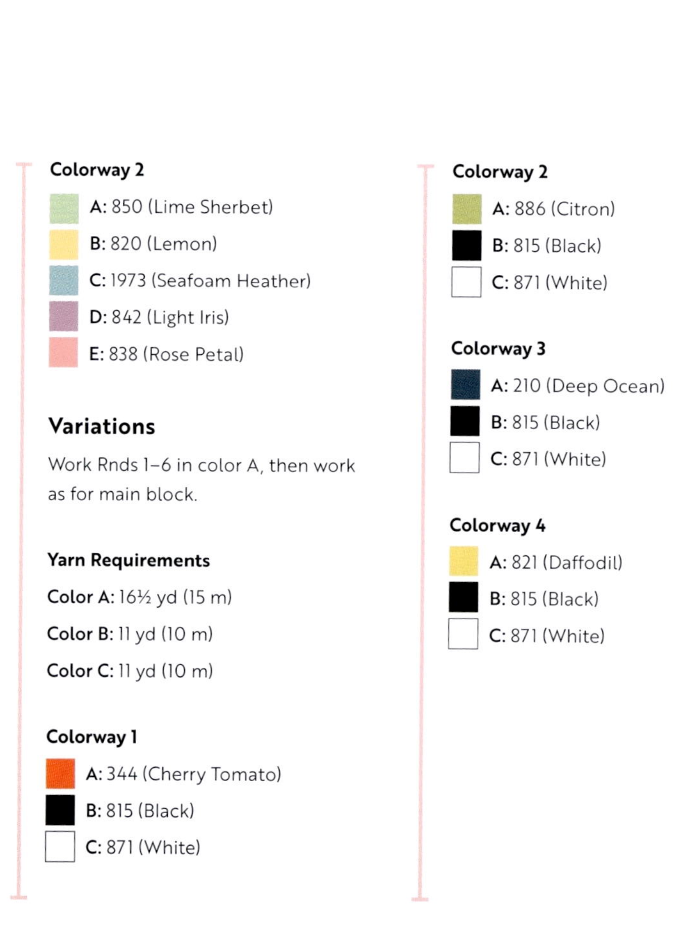

Colorway 2

A: 850 (Lime Sherbet)

B: 820 (Lemon)

C: 1973 (Seafoam Heather)

D: 842 (Light Iris)

E: 838 (Rose Petal)

Variations

Work Rnds 1–6 in color A, then work as for main block.

Yarn Requirements

Color A: 16½ yd (15 m)

Color B: 11 yd (10 m)

Color C: 11 yd (10 m)

Colorway 1

A: 344 (Cherry Tomato)

B: 815 (Black)

C: 871 (White)

Colorway 2

A: 886 (Citron)

B: 815 (Black)

C: 871 (White)

Colorway 3

A: 210 (Deep Ocean)

B: 815 (Black)

C: 871 (White)

Colorway 4

A: 821 (Daffodil)

B: 815 (Black)

C: 871 (White)

Crochet Pattern

Foundation Ring: Using A, ch 4, join with sl st in first ch made to form a ring.

Rnd 1 (RS): Ch 1 (does not count as a st here and throughout), 8 hdc into ring, join with sl st to top of first hdc made—8 sts.

Rnd 2: Ch 1, 2 hdc in each st, join with sl st in top of first hdc made, fasten off A—16 sts.

Rnd 3: Join in B, ch 1, [2 hdc in 1 st, hdc in 1 st] eight times, join with sl st in top of first hdc made—24 sts.

Rnd 4: Ch 1, [hdc in 2 sts, 2 hdc in 1 st] eight times, join with sl st in top of first hdc made, fasten off B—32 sts.

Rnd 5: Join in C, ch 1, [2 hdc in 1 st, hdc in 3 sts] eight times, join with sl st to top of first hdc made—40 sts.

Rnd 6: Ch 1, hdc in 3 sts, [2 hdc in 1 st, hdc in 4 sts] seven times, 2 hdc in next st, hdc in last st, join with sl st in top of first hdc made, fasten off C—48 sts.

Rnd 7: Join in D, ch 4 (counts as tr), 2 tr in same place, tr in next st, dc in next 2 sts, hdc in next st, sc in next 2 sts, hdc in next st, dc in next 2 sts, tr in next st, 3 tr in next 2 sts, tr in next st, dc in next 2 sts, hdc in next st, sc in next 2 sts, hdc in next st, dc in next 2 sts, tr in next st, 3 tr in next st changing to E when working last tr, 3 tr in next st, tr in next st, dc in next 2 sts, hdc in next st, sc in next 2 sts, hdc in next st, dc in next 2 sts, tr in next st, 3 tr in next 2 sts, tr in next st, dc in next 2 sts, hdc in next st, sc in next 2 sts, hdc in next st, dc in next 2 sts, tr in next st, 3 tr in last st, join with sl st to top of beg ch-4, turn—64 sts.

Rnd 8 (WS): Ch 4 (counts as tr), 2 dc in same place, dc in each st to third tr of first 3-tr group, (2 dc, tr) in next st, (tr, 2 dc) in next st, dc in each st to third of next 3-tr group, (2 dc, tr) in next st changing to D when working last tr, (tr, 2 dc) in next st, dc in each st to third of next 3-tr group, (2 dc, tr) in next st, (tr, 2 dc) in next st, dc in each st to last st, (2 dc, tr) in last st, join with sl st to top of beg ch-4, turn—80 sts.

Rnd 9: Ch 1, [(hdc, sc) in tr, sc in each st to next tr, (sc, hdc) in tr] twice changing to E when working last hdc, [(hdc, sc) in tr, sc in each st to next tr, (sc, hdc) in tr] twice, join with sl st to first hdc made, fasten off both yarns—88 sts.

Weave in all ends and block to measure 6" x 6" (15 x 15 cm).

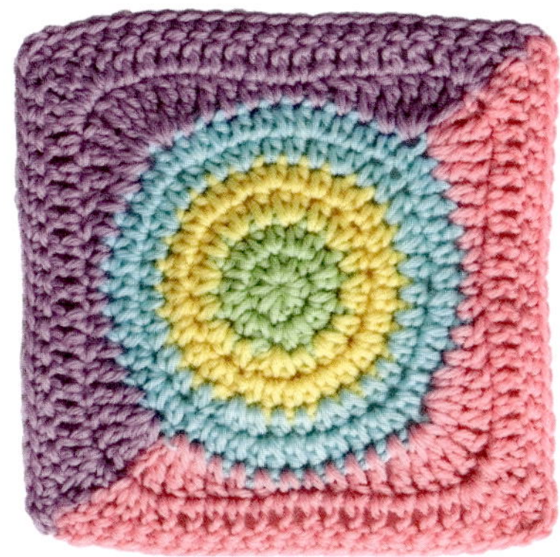

Main Block Colorway 2

Abbreviations and Stitches

ch	chain
sl st	slip stitch
sc	single crochet
hdc	half-double crochet
dc	double crochet
tr	treble crochet
beg	beginning
st(s)	stitch(es)
[ ]	repeat instructions within brackets the stated number of times
( )	work instructions within brackets in place indicated

Note

- On Rounds 7 and 8 leave unused yarn dangling at the back of the work for picking up on later rounds.

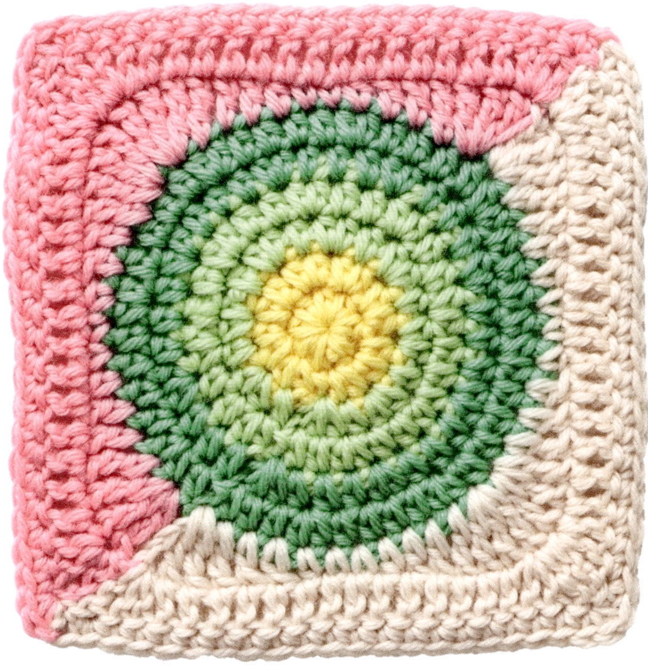

Main Block Colorway 1

Choose diagonal background colors to create shapes and lines, or just use any colors you fancy for a more patchwork feel.

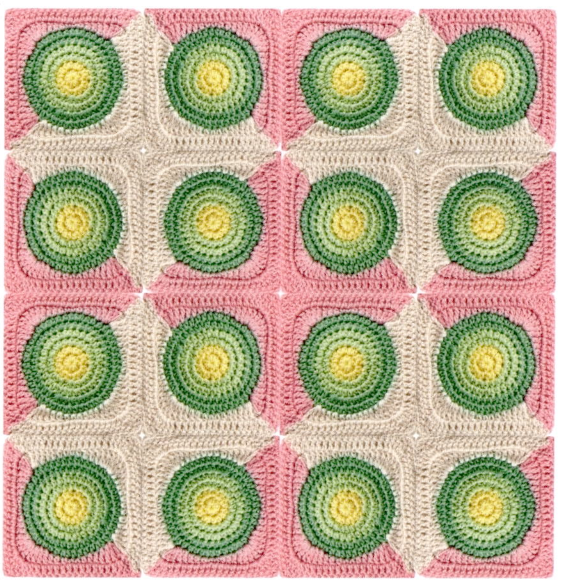

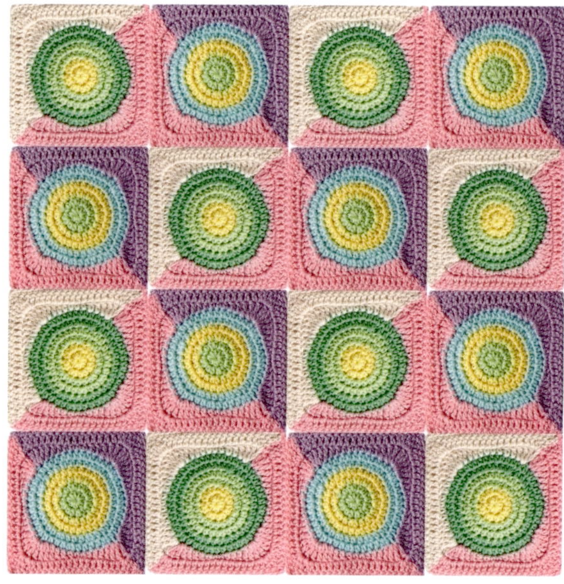

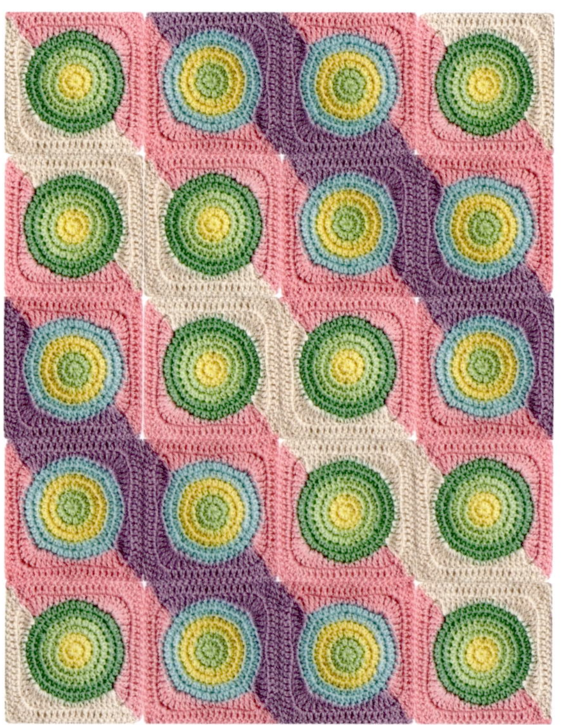

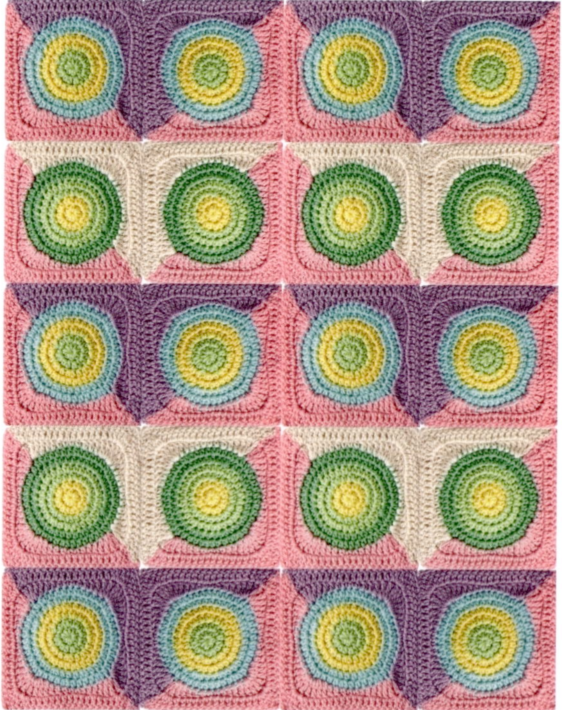

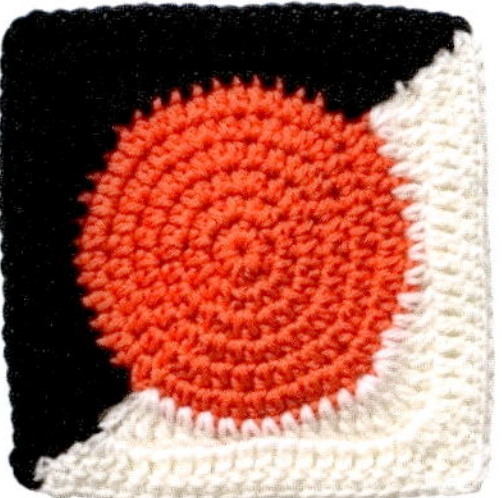
Variation Colorway 1

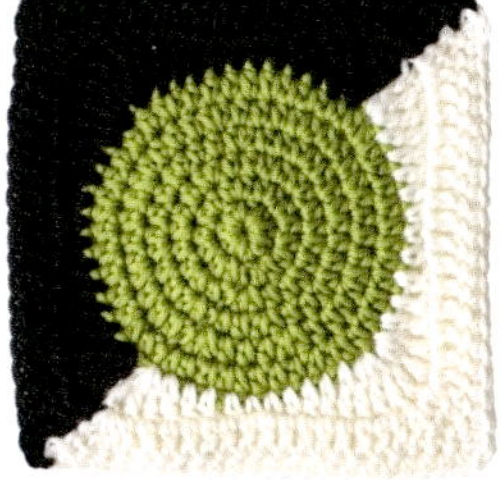
Variation Colorway 2

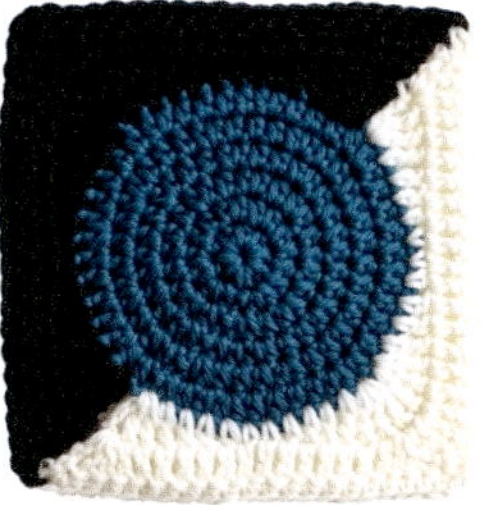
Variation Colorway 3

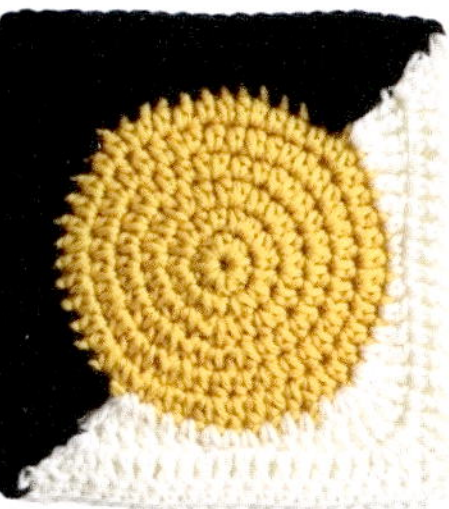
Variation Colorway 4

Well, this may be my favorite color combination of the whole book! These blocks give bold and vibrant layout options to create chevrons, lines, and diamonds. Softer colors would also look great.

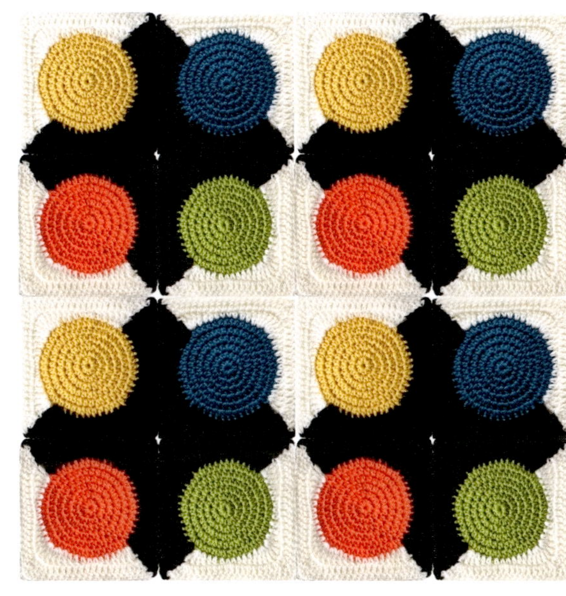

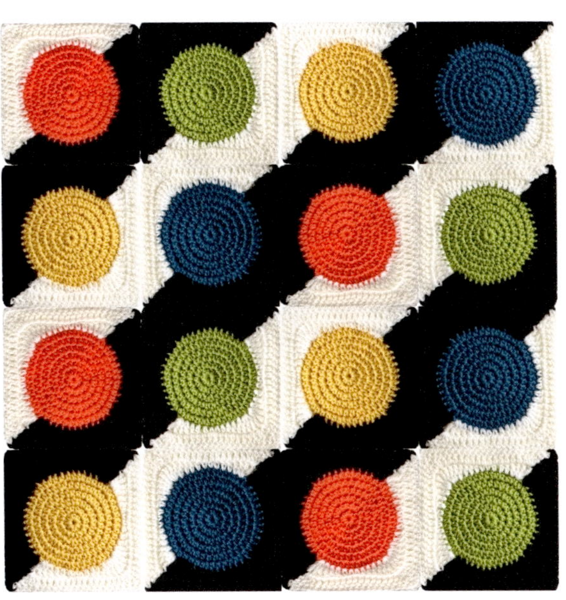

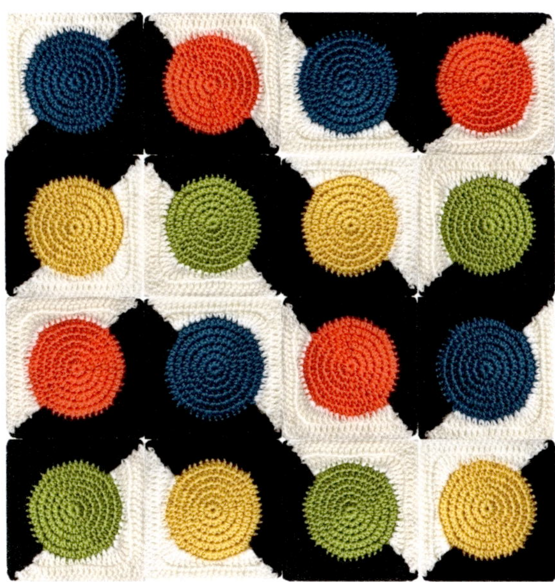

ECHO

This block has a simple, ever-increasing corner color change. When joined you can create a pretty pattern where the blocks connect. I've worked the contrasting colors into the horizontal bar here, but you can also work the stitches in the usual way if you prefer.

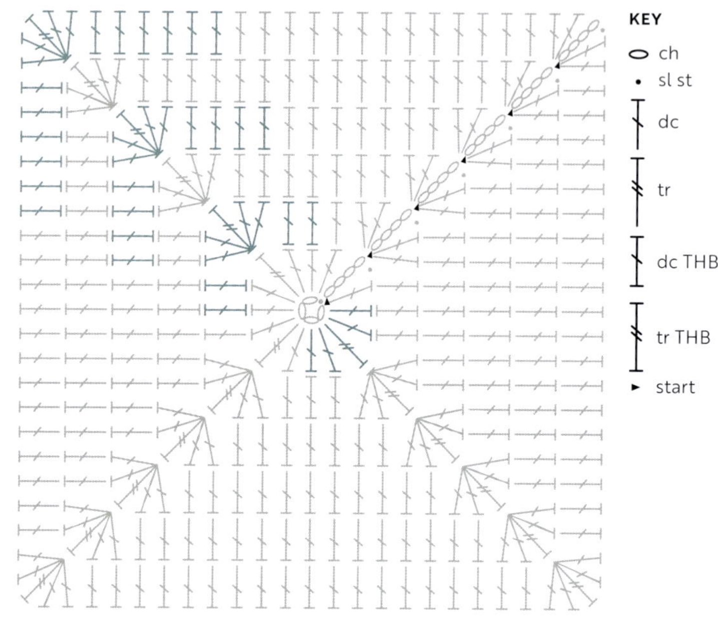

SKILL LEVEL: Intermediate

BLOCK SIZE: 6" x 6" (15 x 15 cm)

HOOK SIZE: G/6 (4 mm)

YARN WEIGHT: DK

YARN: Cascade 220 Superwash®

Main Block

Yarn Requirements

Color A: 29½ yd (27 m)

Color B: 6½ yd (6 m)

Colorway 1

A: 871 (White)

B: 1942 (Mint)

Colorway 2

A: 809 (Really Red)

B: 871 (White)

Variations

Yarn Requirements

Color A: 29½ yd (27 m)

Color B: 1¼ yd (1 m)

Color C: 1¼ yd (1 m)

Color D: 2¼ yd (2m)

Color E: 2¼ yd (2m)

Colorway 1

Use the colors B–E listed below where yarn B is specified on Rnds 1, 2, 4, and 6.

A: 349 (Irish Cream)

B: 314 (Garnet)

C: 364 (Faded Rose)

D: 1940 (Peach)

E: 1941 (Salmon)

Colorway 2

A: 349 (Irish Cream); **B:** 1941 (Salmon); **C:** 1940 (Peach); **D:** 364 (Faded Rose); **E:** 314 (Garnet)

Abbreviations and Stitches

ch	chain
sl st	slip stitch
dc	double crochet
tr	treble crochet
beg	beginning
st(s)	stitch(es)
THB	through horizontal bar
[ ]	repeat instructions within brackets the stated number of times
( )	work instructions within brackets in place indicated

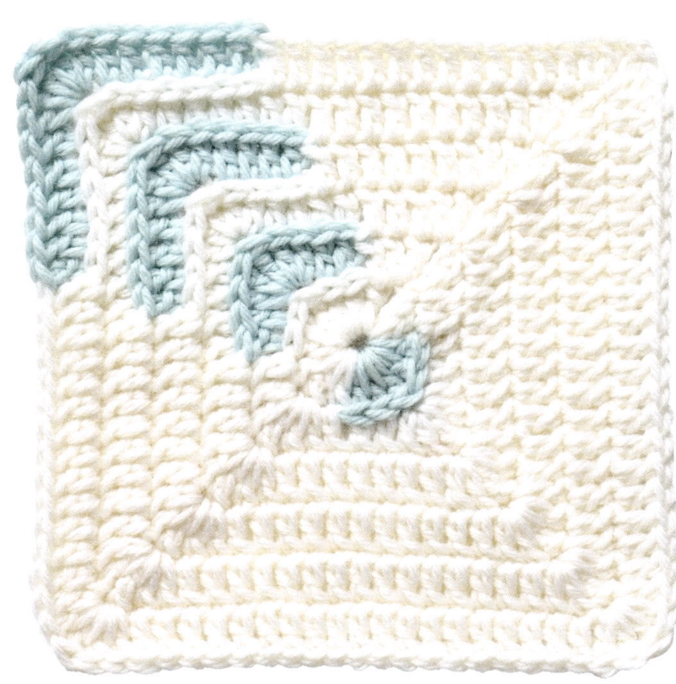

Main Block Colorway 1

Crochet Pattern

Foundation Ring: Using A, ch 4 and join with sl st to first ch made to form a ring.
Rnd 1: Ch 4 (counts as tr here and throughout), [3 dc, tr] twice, dc changing to B, 2 dc, tr, 2 dc changing to A, dc, join with sl st to top of beg ch-4—16 sts.
Rnd 2: Ch 4, 2 dc in same place, dc in next st changing to B, dc THB in next 2 sts, (2 dc, tr, 2 dc) THB in next st, dc THB in next 2 sts changing to A, dc in next st, (2 dc, tr, 2 dc) in next st, dc in next st, dc THB in next 2 sts, (2 dc, tr, 2 dc) THB in next st, dc THB in next 2 sts, dc in next st, 2 dc in same place as beg ch-4, join with sl st to top of beg ch-4—32 sts.
Rnd 3: Ch 4, 2 dc in same place, dc in 3 sts, dc THB in next 4 sts (2 dc, tr, 2 dc) THB in next st, dc THB in next 4 sts, dc in next 3 sts, [(2 dc, tr, 2 dc) in next st, dc in each st to next tr] twice, 2 dc in same place as beg ch-4, join with sl st to top of beg ch-4—48 sts.
Rnd 4: Ch 4, 2 dc in same place, dc in next 7 sts changing to B when working last st, dc THB in next 4 sts, (2 dc, tr, 2 dc) THB in next st, dc THB in next 4 sts changing to A, [dc in each st to next tr, (2 dc, tr, 2 dc) in tr] twice, dc in each st to next tr, 2 dc in same place as beg ch-4, join by sl st to top of beg ch-4—64 sts.
Rnd 5: Ch 4, 2 dc in same place, dc in next 9 sts, dc THB in next 6 sts, (2 dc, tr, 2 dc) THB in next st, dc THB in next 6 sts, dc in next 9 sts, [(2 dc, tr, 2 dc) in next st, dc in each st to next tr] twice, 2 dc in same place as beg ch-4, join with sl st to top of beg ch-4—80 sts.
Rnd 6: Ch 4, 2 dc in same place, dc in next 13 sts changing to B when working last st, dc THB in next 6 sts, (2 dc, tr, 2 dc) THB in next st, dc THB in next 6 sts changing to A, [dc in each st to next tr, (2 dc, tr, 2 dc) in tr] twice, dc in each st to next tr, 2 dc in same place as beg ch-4, join with sl st to top of beg ch-4. Fasten off all yarns—96 sts.

Weave in all ends and block to measure 6" x 6" (15 x 15 cm).

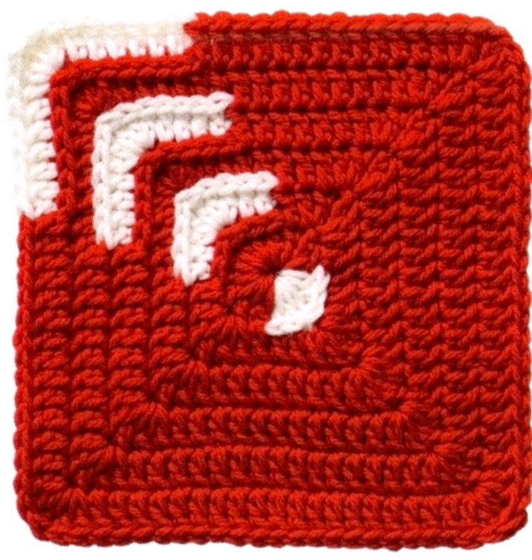

Main Block Colorway 2

This simple block reminds me of snowflakes and icicles, and when four are joined, you can create a snowflake-type shape. For the color variation a nice idea would be to use a range of red shades while keeping white for the corner highlights, creating a more patchwork feel.

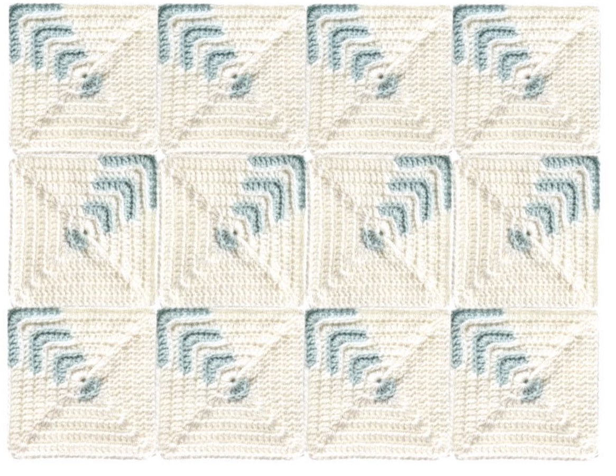

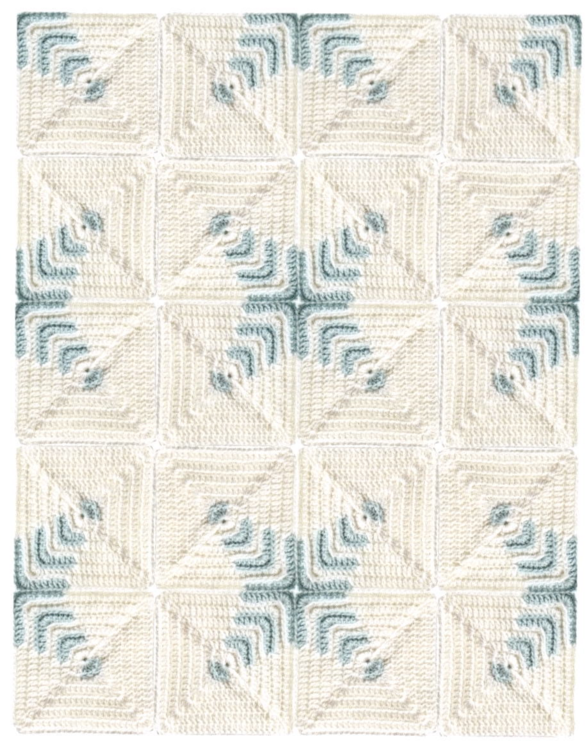

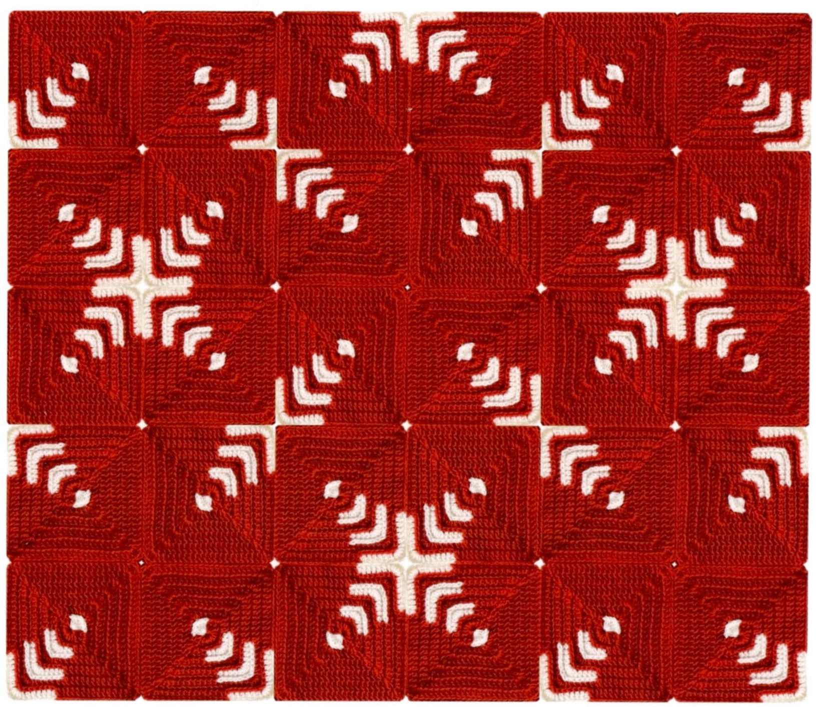

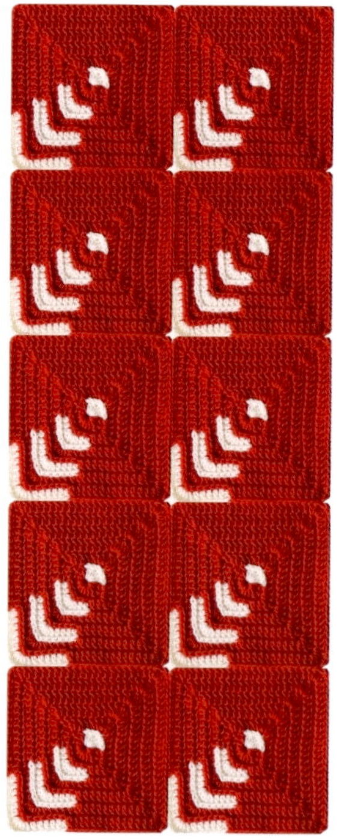

By changing the corner color on each round, you can create a fade which looks great when joined. Combining the two colorways gives you more color layout choices. For your own project, try picking four shades of your favorite color and a neutral background color.

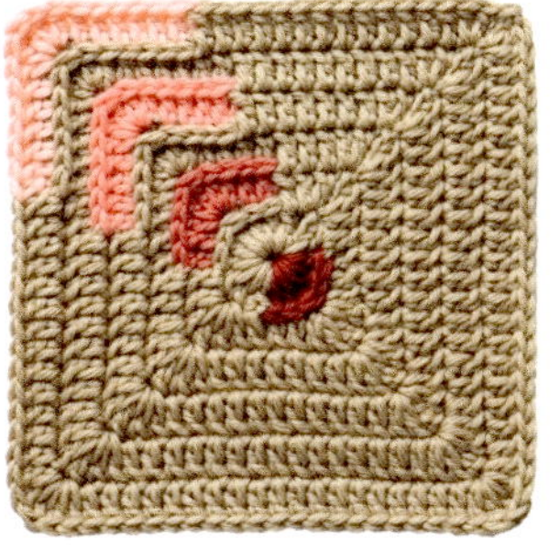
Variation Colorway 1

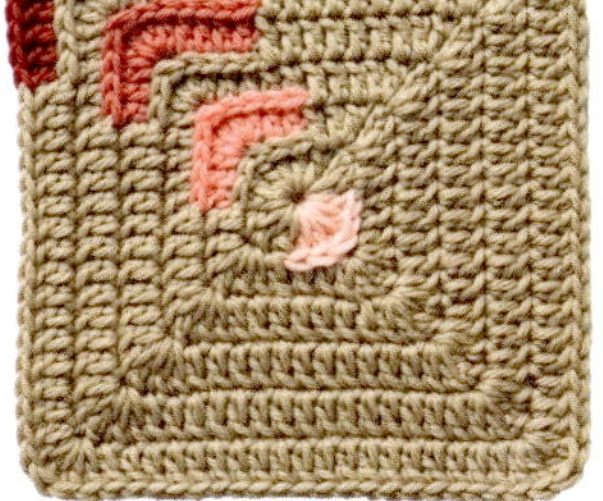
Variation Colorway 2

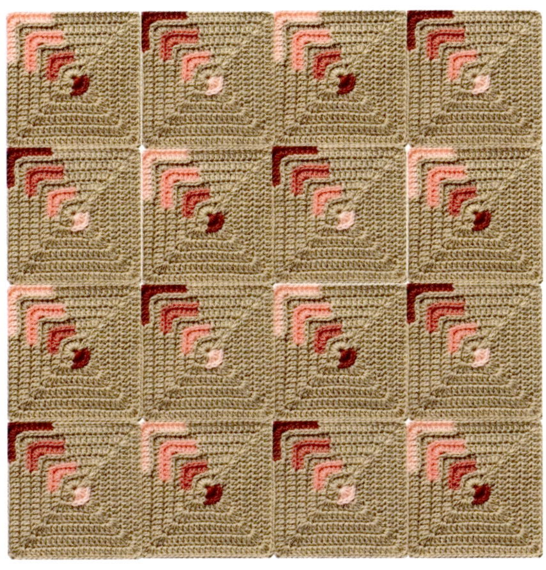

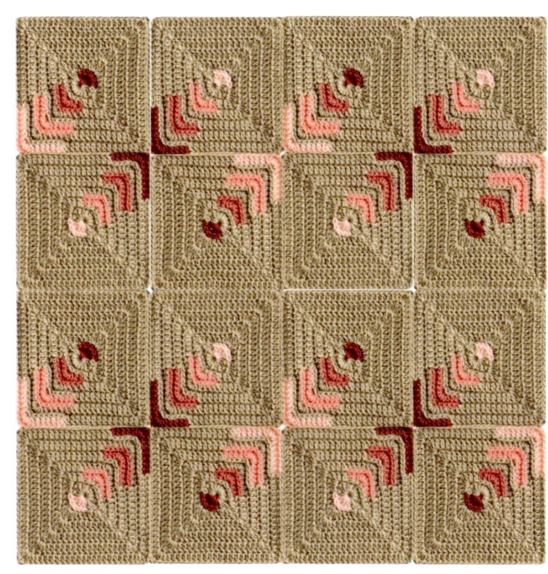

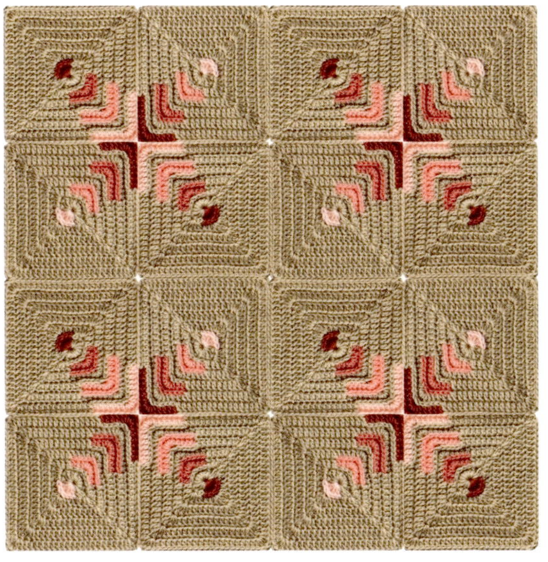

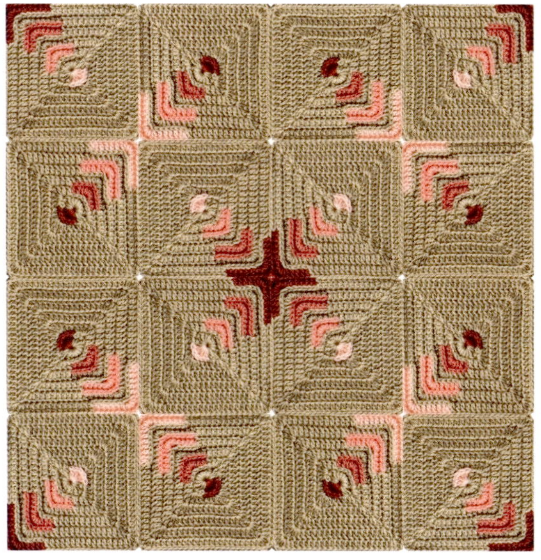

GRANNY'S POPCORN

Worked in the same way as the traditional granny square but with the addition of popcorn stitches in different colors, this block pairs well with the Diamond Granny square on page 44.

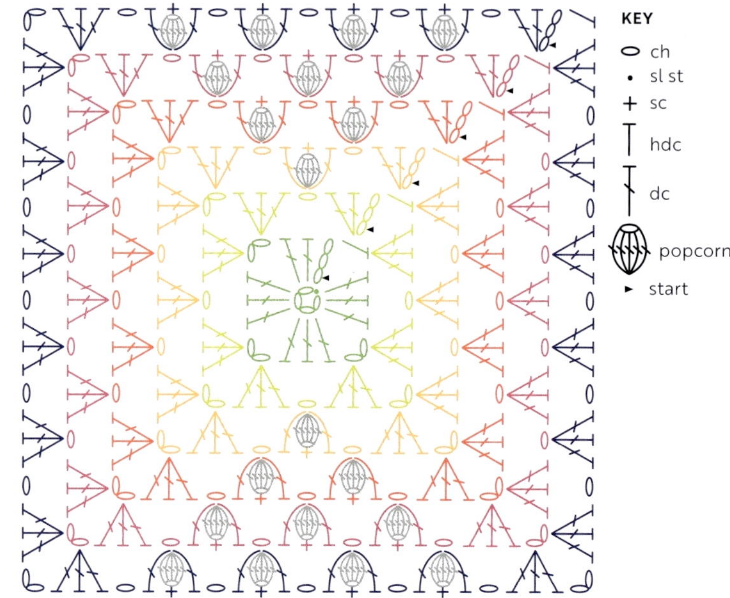

SKILL LEVEL: Intermediate

BLOCK SIZE: 6" x 6" (15 x 15 cm)

HOOK SIZE: G/6 (4mm)

YARN WEIGHT: DK

YARN: Cascade 220 Superwash®

Main Block

Yarn Requirements

Color A: 2¼ yd (2m)

Color B: 3¼ yd (3 m)

Color C: 11 yd (10 m)

Color D: 6½ yd (6 m)

Color E: 8¾ yd (8 m)

Color F: 10 yd (9 m)

Color G: 11 yd (10 m)

A: 887 (Wasabi)

B: 346 (Daisy Yellow)

C: 871 (White)

D: 263 (Gold Fusion)

E: 344 (Cherry Tomato)

F: 837 (Berry Pink)

G: 310 (Dark Violet)

Variations

Work the main block without changing color at the end of each round. Work each round of popcorns in sequence using yarns B–E.

Yarn Requirements

Color A: 41½ yd (38 m)

Color B: 1¼ yd (1 m)

Color C: 2¼ yd (2 m)

Color D: 3¼ yd (3 m)

Color E: 4½ yd (4 m)

Colorway 1

A: 871 (White)

B: 837 (Berry Pink)

C: 344 (Cherry Tomato)

D: 263 (Gold Fusion)

E: 346 (Daisy Yellow)

Colorway 2

A: 871 (White)

B: 346 (Daisy Yellow)

C: 887 (Wasabi)

D: 288 (Green Spruce)

E: 812 (Turquoise)

Abbreviations and Stitches

ch	chain
sp	space
sl st	slip stitch
sc	single crochet
hdc	half-double crochet
dc	double crochet
beg	beginning
st(s)	stitch(es)
rep	repeat
popcorn	5 dc worked into the same place and joined at the top. (The first popcorn should be worked as 3 ch, 4 dc)
[ ]	repeat instructions within brackets the stated number of times
( )	work instructions within brackets in place indicated

Note

- **Changing color when joining:** Begin working the joining hdc in the color used throughout the round, insert hook into third of beg ch-3, drop current color and pick up the next color, and complete the stitch. Continue in the new color.

Crochet Pattern

Foundation Ring: Using A, ch 4 and join with sl st in first ch made to form a ring.

Rnd 1: Ch 3 (counts as dc here and throughout), 2 dc, [ch 2, 3 dc] three times, join with hdc to top of beg ch-3, changing to B, fasten off A—12 sts.

Rnd 2: Ch 3, 2 dc in same place, [ch 1, (3 dc, ch 2, 3 dc) in next ch-2 sp] three times, ch 1, 3 dc in joining hdc, join with hdc to top of beg ch-3, changing to D, fasten off B—24 sts.

Rnd 3: Using D, ch 3, 2 dc in same place, [ch 1, dc in next ch sp, join C, popcorn in same ch sp, fasten off C, pick up D, sc in top of popcorn, dc in same ch sp, ch 1, (3 dc, ch 2, 3 dc) in next ch-2 sp, ch 1, 3 dc in next ch sp, ch 1, (3 dc, ch 2, 3 dc) in next ch-2 sp] twice omitting last (3 dc, ch 2, 3 dc) on final rep, 3 dc in hdc, join with hdc to top of beg ch-3, changing to E, fasten off D—36 sts.

Rnd 4: Using E, ch 3, 2 dc in same place, [[ch 1, dc in next ch sp, join C, popcorn in same ch sp, fasten off C, pick up D, sc in top of popcorn, dc in same ch sp] twice, ch 1, (3 dc, ch 2, 3 dc) in next ch-2 sp, [ch 1, 3 dc in next ch sp] twice, ch 1, (3 dc, ch 2, 3 dc) in next ch-2 sp] twice omitting last (3 dc, ch 2, 3dc) on final rep, 3 dc in hdc, join with hdc to top of beg ch-3, changing to F, fasten off E—48 sts.

Rnd 5: Using F, ch 3, 2 dc in same place, [[ch 1, dc in next ch sp, join C, popcorn in same ch sp, fasten off C, pick up D, sc in top of popcorn, dc in same ch sp] three times, ch 1, (3 dc, ch 2, 3 dc) in next ch-2 sp, [ch 1, 3 dc in next ch sp] three times, ch 1, (3 dc, ch 2, 3 dc) in next ch-2 sp] twice omitting last (3 dc, ch 2, 3 dc) on final rep, 3 dc in hdc, join with hdc to top of beg ch-3, changing to G, fasten off F—60 sts.

Rnd 6: Using G, ch 3, 2 dc in same place, [[ch 1, dc in next ch sp, join C, popcorn in same ch sp, fasten off C, pick up D, sc in top of popcorn, dc in same ch sp] four times, ch 1, (3 dc, ch 2, 3 dc) in next ch-2 sp, [ch 1, 3 dc in next ch sp] four times, ch 1, (3 dc, ch 2, 3 dc) in next ch-2 sp] twice omitting last (3 dc, ch 2, 3dc) on final rep, 3 dc in hdc, join with hdc to top of beg ch-3, fasten off G—72 sts.

Weave in all ends and block to measure 6" x 6" (15 x 15 cm).

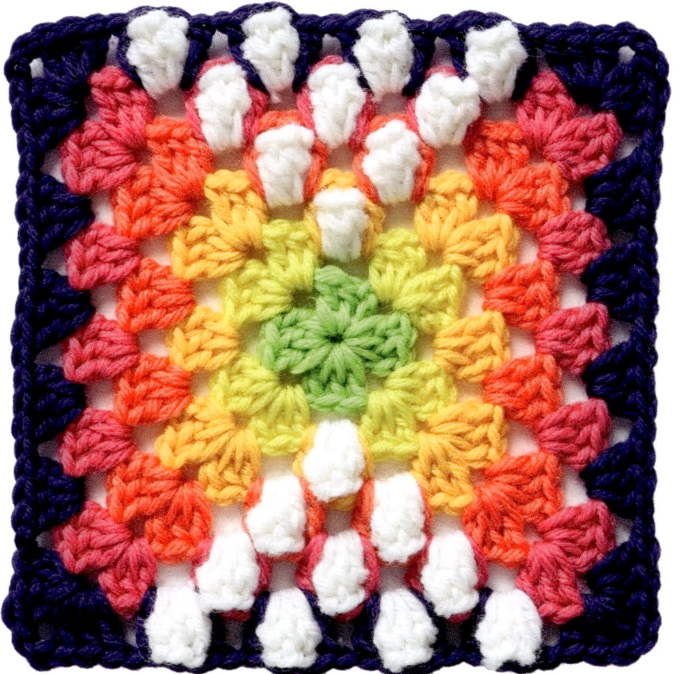

Main Block

With just one block you can create three different layouts. Here I've used one colorway for the blocks, but this would look fabulous if each block had a different colorway.

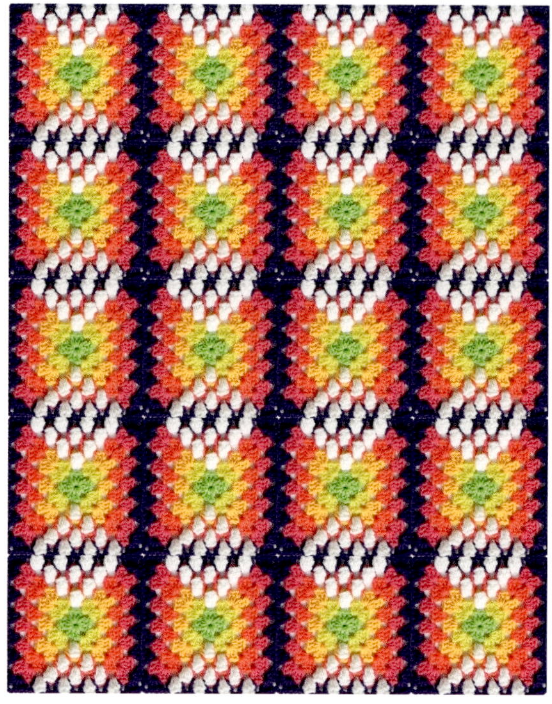

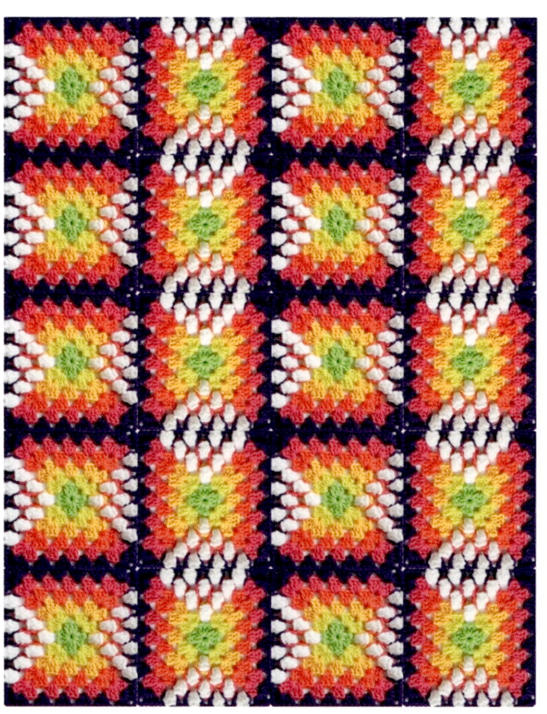

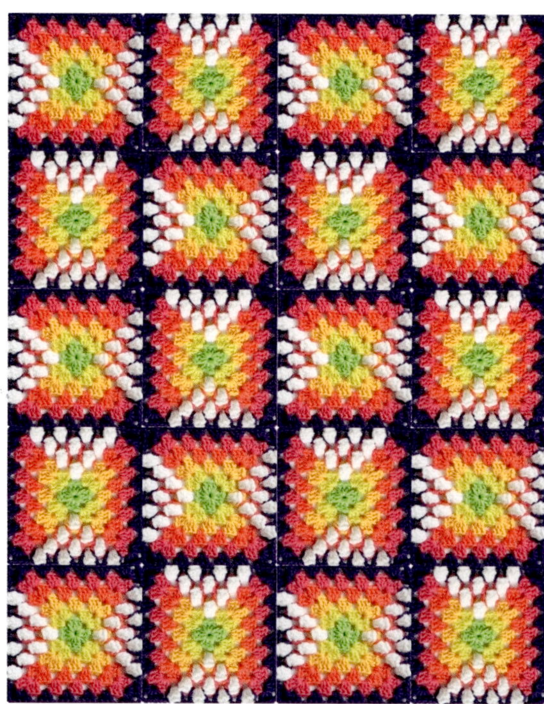

Using the same pattern but swapping where the colors are used gives a completely different vibe. You could also try working the popcorns in just one color, as in the main block, while keeping the background all one color.

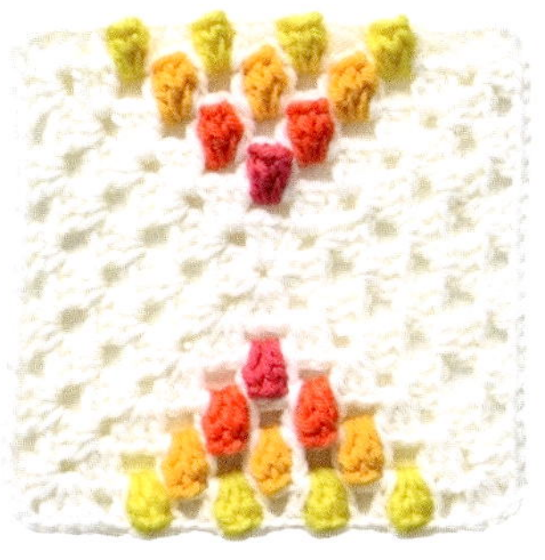

Variation Colorway 1

Variation Colorway 2

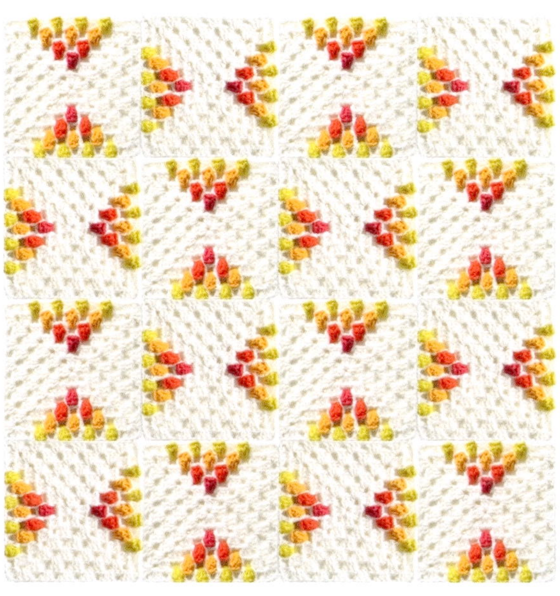

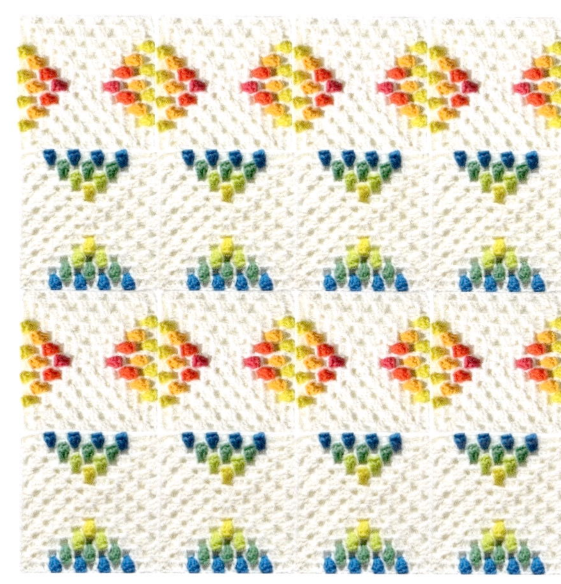

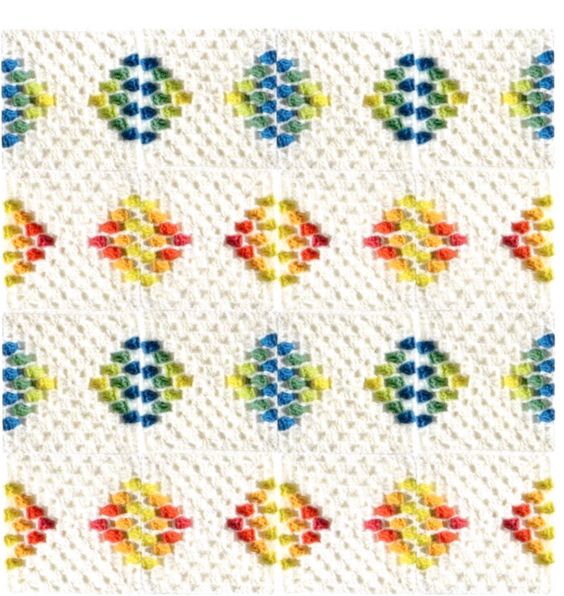

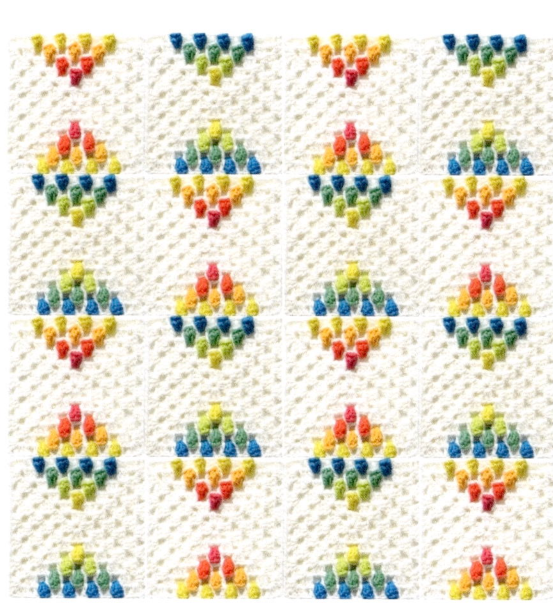

MIRROR REPEAT

Mirror Repeat is a great block for hue-shift afghans. By switching the order of colors on Row 3, you create a mirrored effect. Try working the blocks in shades of the same color for a subtle look, or use a bright color and white for a bolder effect. In the alternative colorway I've used two shades of green and two shades of blue.

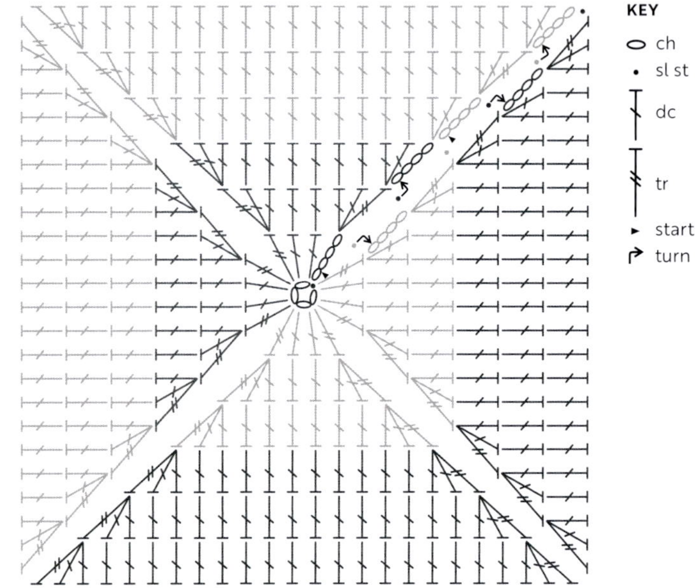

SKILL LEVEL: Intermediate

BLOCK SIZE: 6" x 6" (15 x 15 cm)

HOOK SIZE: G/6 (4mm)

YARN WEIGHT: DK

YARN: Cascade 220 Superwash®

Main Block

Colorway 1

Yarn Requirements

Color A: 22 yd (20 m)

Color B: 22 yd (20 m)

A: 339 (Sleet)

B: 875 (Feather Grey)

Colorways 2 and 3

For Colorway 2, use yarn C instead of yarn B on Rnds 4–6. For Colorway 3, use yarn C instead of yarn A for Foundation Ring & Rnds 1–3.

Yarn Requirements

Color A: 5½ yd (5 m)

Color B: 22 yd (20 m)

Color C: 16½ yd (15 m)

Colorways 2 and 3

A: 339 (Sleet)

B: 875 (Feather Grey)

C: 344 (Cherry Tomato)

Variation

Use yarns A and B for Rnds 1–3 and yarns C and D on Rnds 4–6.

Yarn Requirements

Color A: 5½ yd (5 m)

Color B: 5½ yd (5 m)

Color C: 16½ yd (15 m)

Color D: 16½ yd (15 m)

A: 1973 (Seafoam Heather)

B: 851 (Lime)

C: 227 (Bachelor Button)

D: 288 (Green Spruce)

Abbreviations and Stitches

ch	chain
sl st	slip stitch
dc	double crochet
tr	treble crochet
beg	beginning
st(s)	stitch(es)
( )	work instructions within brackets in place indicated

Note

- Leave unused yarns hanging on the wrong side of the work ready for picking up on later rounds. You can also choose to work over the unused yarn throughout. If so, try to pick colors that don't have too much contrast to one another as the carried yarn will show through in some places.

Crochet Pattern

Foundation Ring: Using A, ch 4 and join with sl st to first ch made to form a ring.

Rnd 1 (RS): Ch 4 (counts as tr here and throughout), 2 dc, 2 tr, 2 dc, tr changing to B, tr, 2 dc, 2 tr, 2 dc, tr, join with sl st to top of beg ch-4, turn—16 sts.

Rnd 2 (WS): Ch 4, 2 dc in same place, dc in next 2 sts, (2 dc, tr) in next st, (tr, 2 dc) in next st, dc in next 2 sts, (2 dc, tr) in next st, changing to A, (tr, 2 dc) in next st, dc in next 2 sts, (2 dc, tr) in next st, (tr, 2 dc) in next st, dc in next 2 sts, (2 dc, tr) in next st, join with sl st to top of beg ch-4, turn—32 sts.

Rnd 3 (RS): Ch 4, 2 dc in same place, dc in next 6 sts, (2 dc, tr) in next st, (tr, 2 dc) in next st, dc in next 6 sts, (2 dc, tr) in next st, changing to B, (tr, 2 dc) in next st, dc in next 6 sts, (2 dc, tr) in next st, (tr, 2 dc) in next st, dc in next 6 sts, (2 dc, tr) in next st, join with sl st to top of beg ch-4, do not turn—48 sts.

Rnd 4 (RS): Ch 4, 2 dc in same place, dc in next 10 sts, (2 dc, tr) in next st, (tr, 2 dc) in next st, dc in next 10 sts, (2 dc, tr) in next st, changing to A, (tr, 2 dc) in next st, dc in next 10 sts, (2 dc, tr) in next st, (tr, 2 dc) in next st, dc in next 10 sts, (2 dc, tr) in next st, join with sl st to top of beg ch-4, turn—64 sts.

Rnd 5 (WS): Ch 4, 2 dc in same place, dc in next 14 sts, (2 dc, tr) in next st, (tr, 2 dc) in next st, dc in next 14 sts, (2 dc, tr) in next st, changing to B, (tr, 2 dc) in next st, dc in next 14 sts, (2 dc, tr) in next st, (tr, 2 dc) in next st, dc in next 14 sts, (2 dc, tr) in next st, join with sl st to top of beg ch-4, turn—80 sts.

Rnd 6 (RS): Ch 4, 2 dc in same place, dc in next 18 sts, (2 dc, tr) in next st, (tr, 2 dc) in next st, dc in next 18 sts, (2 dc, tr) in next st, changing to A, (tr, 2 dc) in next st, dc in next 18 sts, (2 dc, tr) in next st, (tr, 2 dc) in next st, dc in next 18 sts, (2 dc, tr) in next st, join with sl st to top of beg ch-4, fasten off both yarns—96 sts.

Weave in all ends and block to measure 6" x 6" (15 x 15 cm).

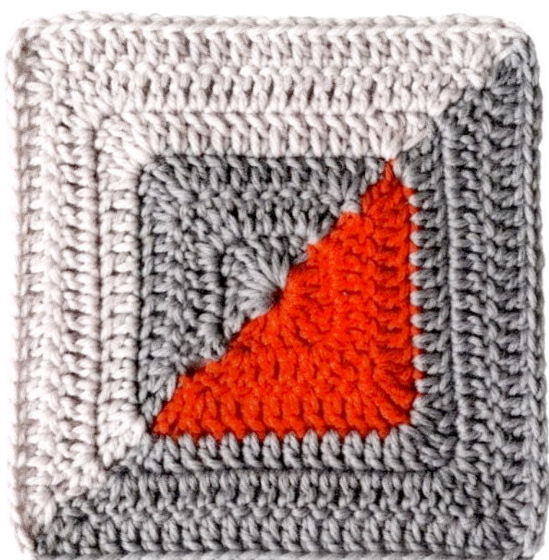

Main Block Colorway 3

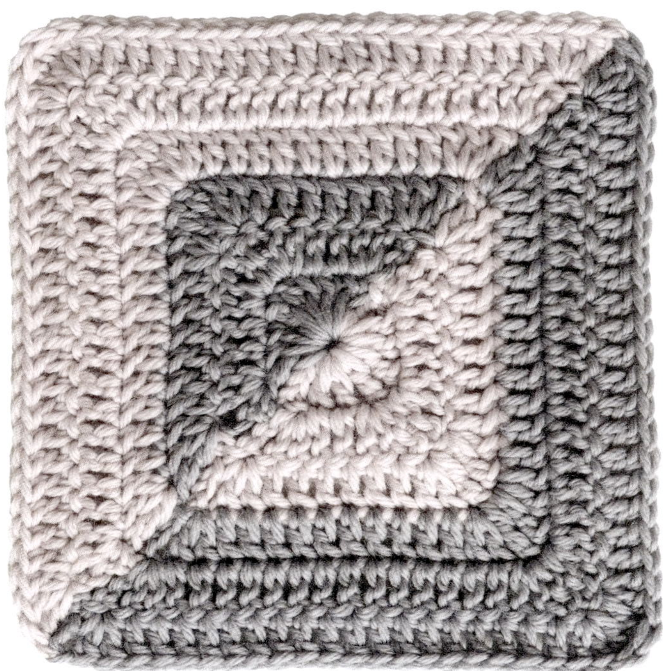

Main Block Colorway 1

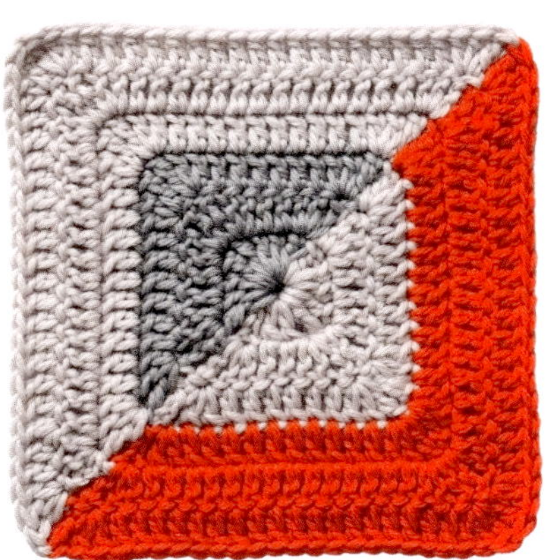

Main Block Colorway 2

Using one, two, or all three colorways offers some great layout choices. Using two neutral colors with a bright color gives you some bold designs. For a different look you could use two shades of the same color paired with one contrasting color.

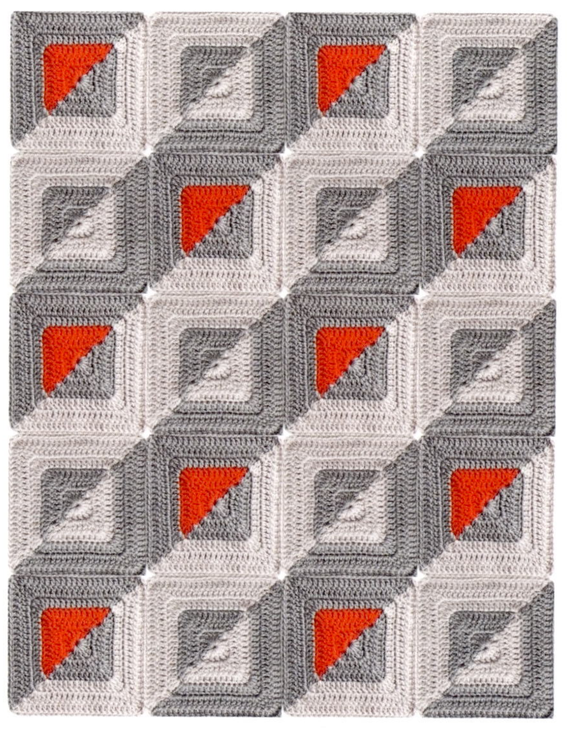

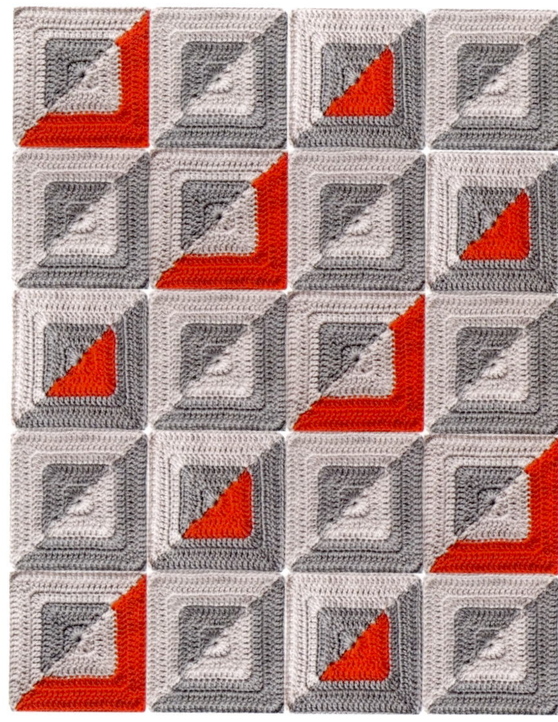

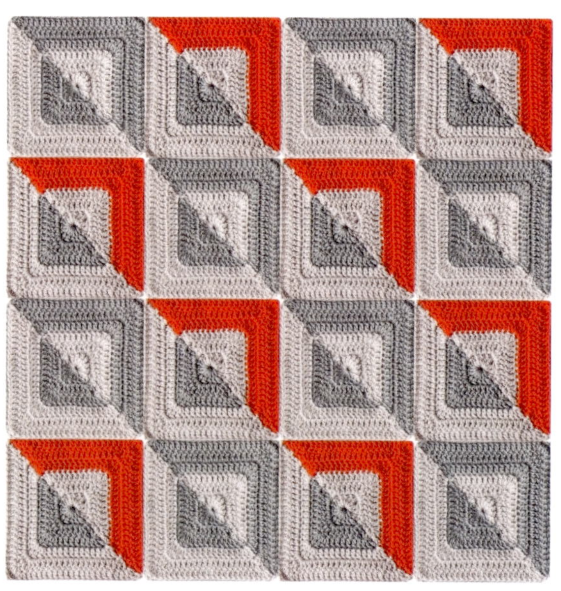

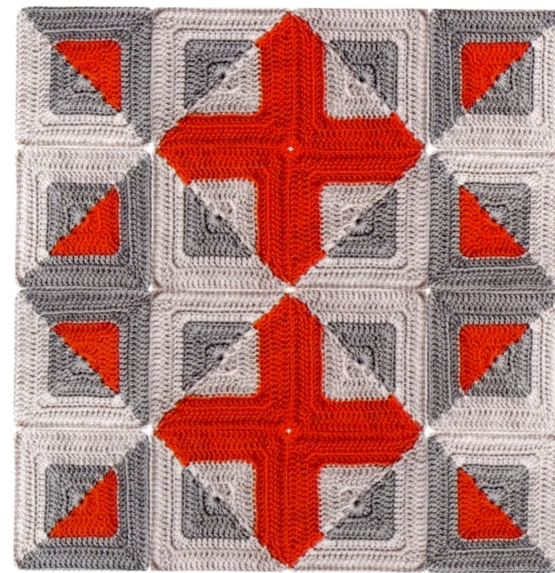

Here I've used four colors for each of the blocks. Use four shades of your favorite color, or two shades of one color and two of a contrasting color. Another possibility is to use warm colors on one half of the block and cool colors on the other, a bit like the Log Cabin block on page 48.

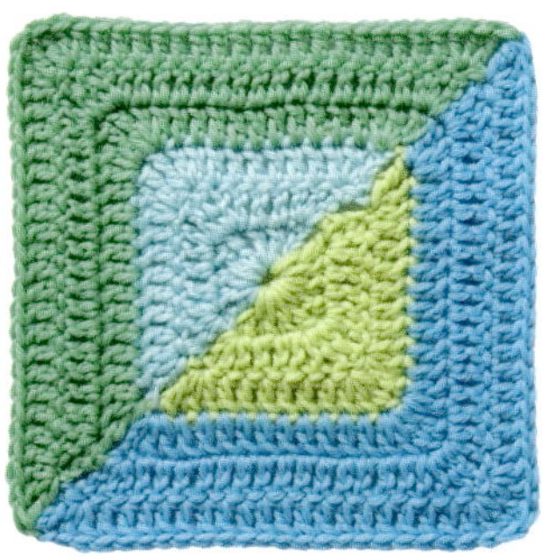

Variation

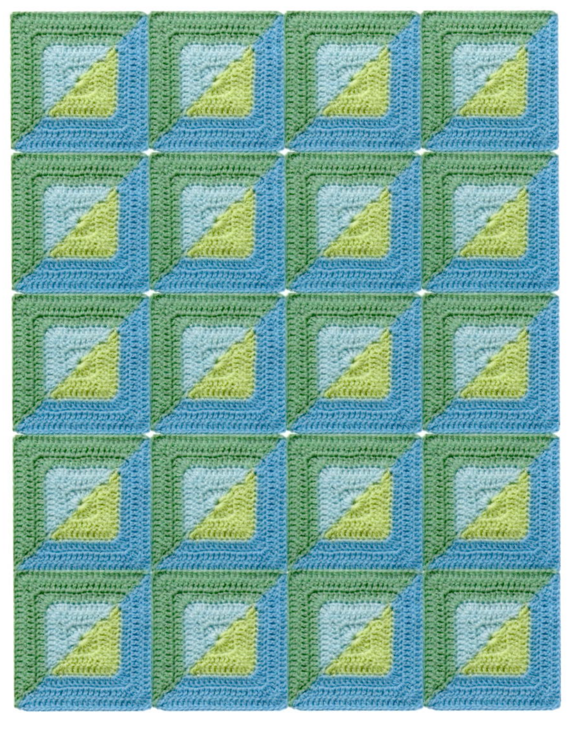

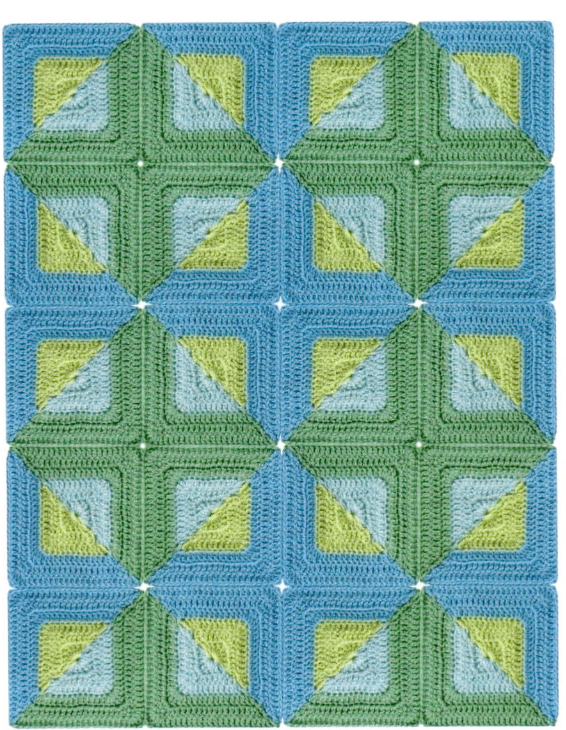

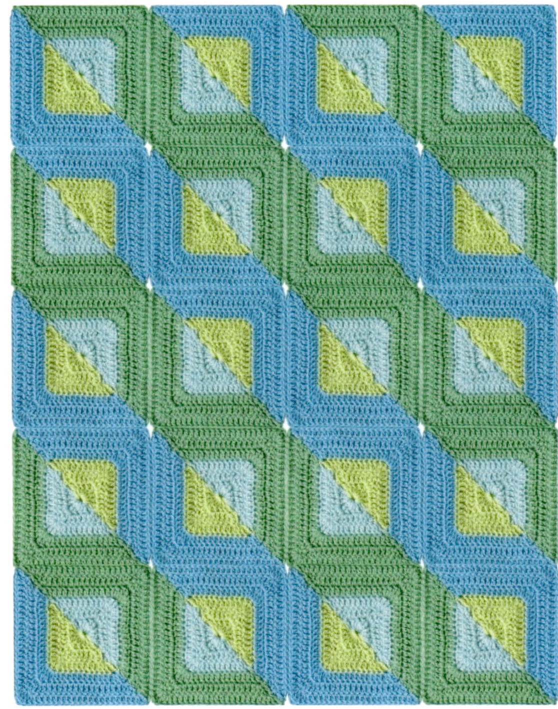

BLUE TILE

The main colorway I've used for the block is reminiscent of *azulejos*, the patterned Portuguese tiles. When they're joined, you can almost imagine you're in Portugal! You can also work the block in a rainbow of colors, as seen in the alternative colorway.

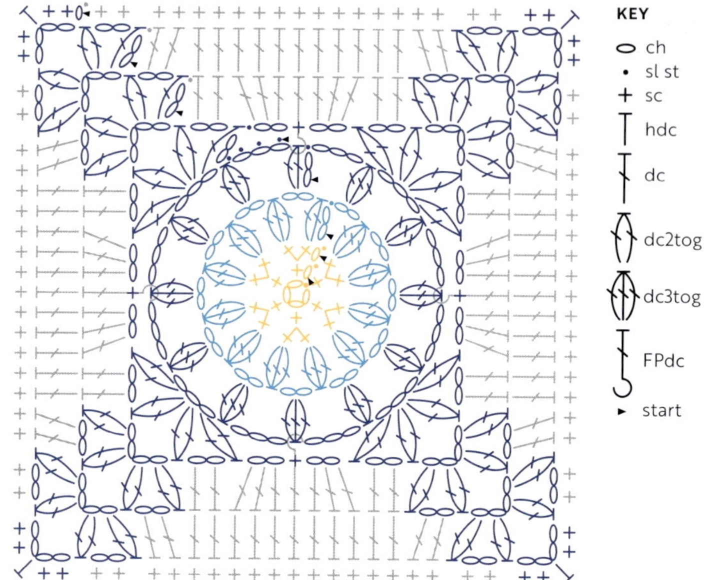

SKILL LEVEL: Advanced

BLOCK SIZE: 6" x 6" (15 x 15 cm)

HOOK SIZE: G/6 (4mm)

YARN WEIGHT: DK

YARN: Cascade 220 Superwash®

Main Block

Yarn Requirements

Color A: 1¼ yd (1 m)

Color B: 3¼ yd (3 m)

Color C: 19¼ yd (17.5 m)

Color D: 22 yd (20 m)

Colorway 1

- **A:** 821 (Daffodil)
- **B:** 227 (Bachelor Button)
- **C:** 311 (Blue Sapphire)
- **D:** 871 (White)

Colorway 2

Work as for colorway 1 using yarns A and D, but the following for yarns B and C.

- **B:** 876 (Sandalwood)
- **C:** 311 (Blue Sapphire)

Variations

Yarn Requirements

Color A: 1¼ yd (1 m)

Color B: 3¼ yd (3 m)

Color C: 7¼ yd (6.5 m)

Color D: 3¼ yd (3 m)

Color E: 3¼ yd (3 m)

Color F: 22 yd (20 m)

Color G: 3¼ yd (3 m)

Color H: 3¼ yd (3 m)

Colorway 1

From Rnd 5, change to the next color in the list when working the corner groups. Use yarn F instead of Main Colorway yarn D.

- **A:** 351 (Pale Jade)
- **B:** 1973 (Seafoam Heather)
- **C:** 850 (Lime Sherbet)
- **D:** 820 (Lemon)
- **E:** 827 (Coral)
- **F:** 338 (Harbor Mist)
- **G:** 835 (Pink Rose)
- **H:** 842 (Light Iris)

Colorway 2

A: 842 (Light Iris); **B:** 835 (Pink Rose); **C:** 827 (Coral); **D:** 820 (Lemon); **E:** 850 (Lime Sherbet); **F:** 338 (Harbor Mist); **G:** 1973 (Seafoam Heather); **H:** 351 (Pale Jade)

Abbreviations and Stitches

ch	chain
sp	space
sl st	slip stitch
sc	single crochet
hdc	half-double crochet
dc	double crochet
beg	beginning
st(s)	stitch(es)
rep	repeat
dc2 cluster	cluster made of double crochet 2 together
dc3 cluster	cluster made of double crochet 3 together
beg dc3 cluster	ch 2, double crochet 2 together
beg cg	beginning corner group: in ch sp indicated work (ch 2, dc, ch 2, dc2tog, ch 4, dc2tog, ch 2, dc2tog)

Crochet Pattern

Foundation Ring: Using A, ch 4 and join with sl st to first ch made to form a ring.
Rnd 1: Ch 1 (does not count as a st here and throughout), 6 sc into ring, join with sl st to first st made—6 sts.
Rnd 2: Ch 1, 2 sc in each st around, join with sl st to first st made, fasten off A —12 sts.
Rnd 3: Join in B, beg dc3 cluster in next st (counts as dc3 cluster), ch 2, [dc3 cluster in next st, ch 2] eleven times, join with sl st to top of beg dc3 cluster, fasten off B—12 sts, 12 ch-2 sp.
Rnd 4: Join in C in ch-2 sp, beg dc3 cluster, ch 3, [dc3 cluster in next ch-2 sp, ch 3] eleven times, join with sl st to top of beg dc3 cluster—12 sts, 12 ch-3 sp.
Rnd 5: Sl st across ch-3 sp, beg cg in next ch-3 sp, [ch 2, skip next st and ch sp, sc in next dc3 cluster, ch 2, skip next ch sp and st, cg in next ch sp] four times omitting last cg on final rep, join with sl st to top of first dc2 cluster of beg cg, fasten off C—4 cg, 4 sc, 8 ch-2 sp.
Rnd 6: Rejoin C in corner ch-4 sp, beg cg in same place, changing to D when working last dc2 cluster, [2 dc in next ch-2 sp, 3 dc in next ch-2 sp, FPdc around next dc3 cluster on Rnd 4, 3 dc in next ch-2 sp, 2 dc in next ch-2 sp, changing to C when working last st, cg in next ch sp, changing to D when working last dc2 cluster] four times omitting last yarn change and cg on final rep, join with sl st to top of first dc2 cluster of beg cg, fasten off C—4 cg, 40 dc, 4 FPdc.
Rnd 7: Rejoin C in corner ch-4 sp, beg cg in same place, changing to D when working last dc2 cluster, [2 dc in next ch-2 sp, skip next st, dc in next 11 sts, skip next st, 2 dc in ch-2 sp, changing to C when working last dc, cg in ch-4 sp changing to D when working last dc2 cluster] four times omitting last yarn change and cg, join with sl st to top of first dc2 cluster of beg cg, fasten off C—4 cg, 60 dc.
Rnd 8: Rejoin C in corner ch-4 sp, ch 1, [(2 sc, hdc, 2 sc) in ch-4 sp, changing to D when working last st, 2 sc in next ch-2 sp, skip next st, sc in next 15 sts, skip next st, 2 sc in next ch-2 sp, changing to C when working last st] four times, join with sl st to first st made, fasten off yarns C and D—96 sts.

Weave in all ends and block to measure 6" x 6" (15 x 15 cm).

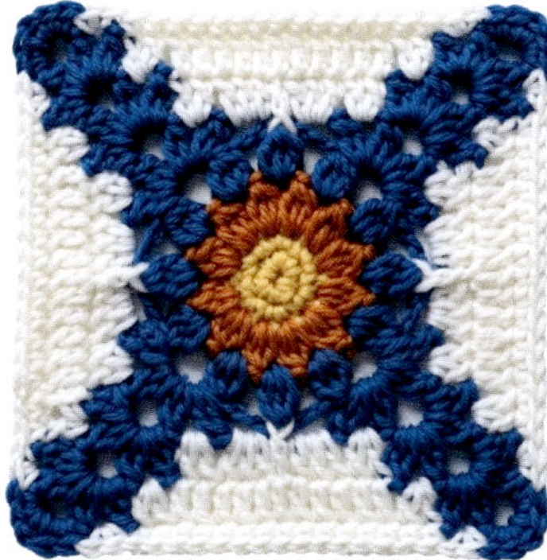
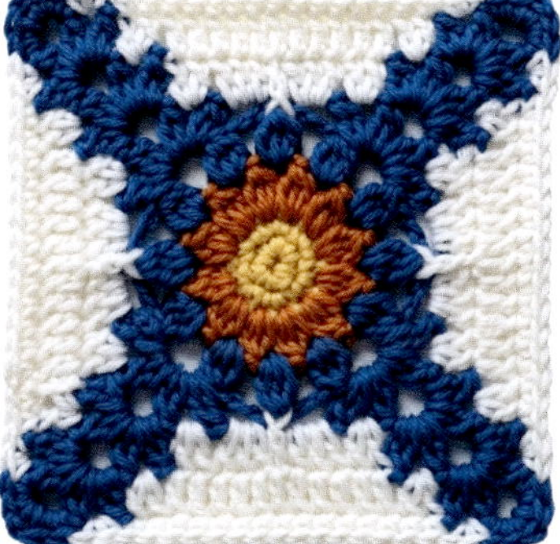

Main Block Colorway 2

cg	corner group: in ch sp indicated work (dc2tog, ch 2, dc2tog, ch 4, dc2tog, ch 2, dc2tog)
FPdc	front post double crochet
[ ]	repeat instructions within brackets the stated number of times
( )	work instructions within brackets in place indicated

Note

- You can choose to work over the unused yarn throughout. If so, try to pick colors that don't have too much contrast to one another since the carried yarn will show through in some places. In the sample shown, the yarn was fastened off after working the corner group, and a new strand joined for each corner group. This means there are more ends to weave in, but the finish is neater.

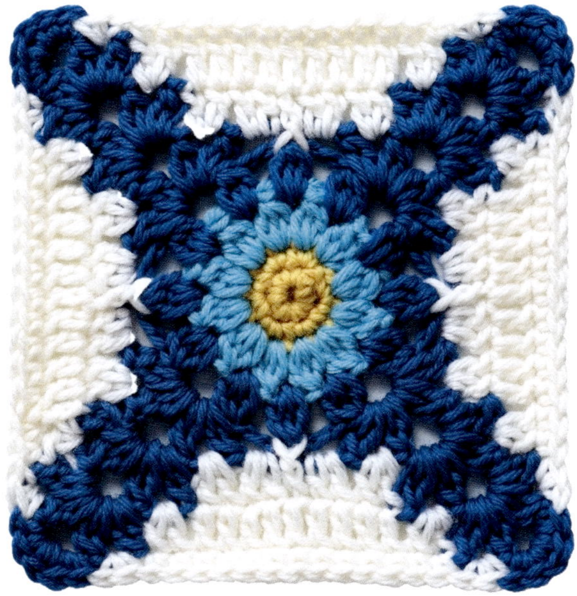

Main Block Colorway 1

When joined together these blocks create new shapes. Though the layout options are limited, the color options aren't. Try picking a background color you love and a contrasting color for the trellis section (color C) and then work the first two rounds in random colors, using up scrap yarn.

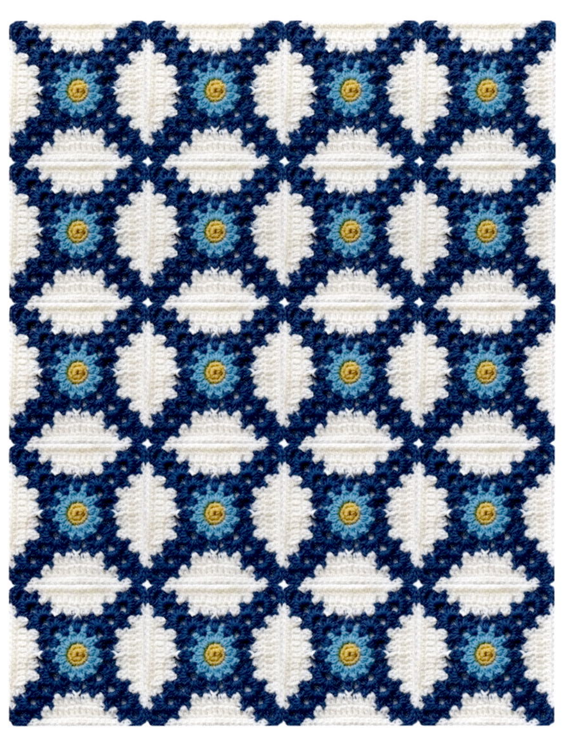

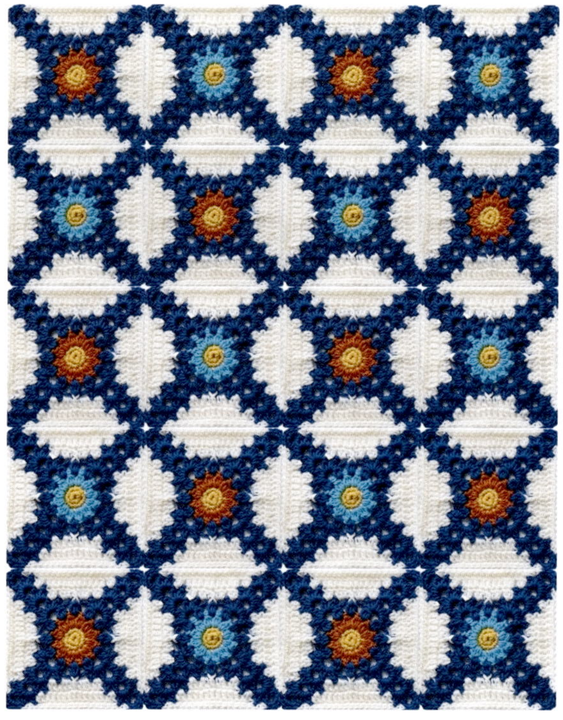

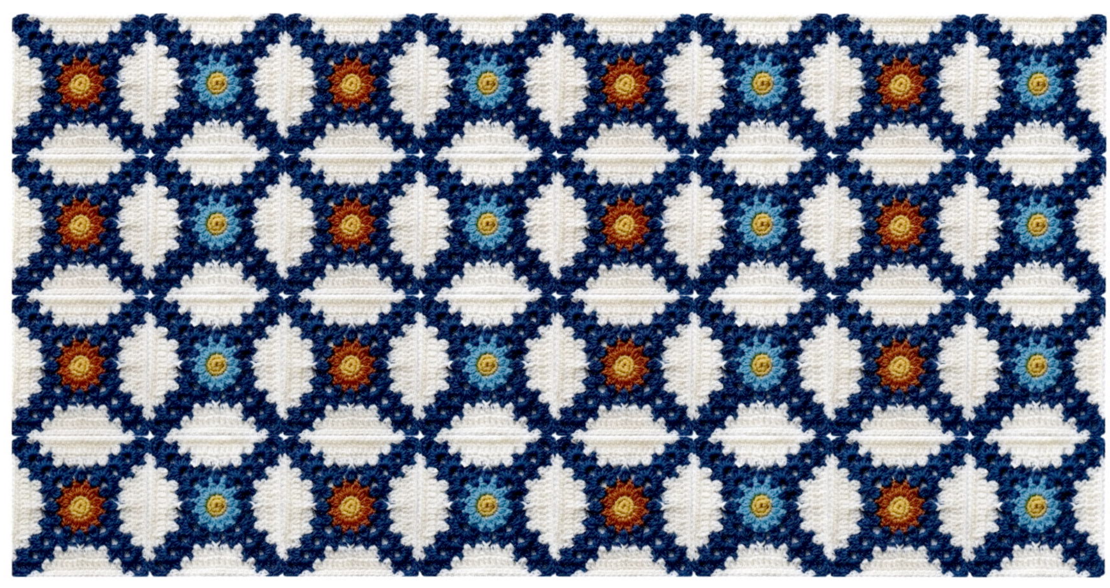

Here I've used a rainbow of colors for the trellis section on each round, which gives the block a quite different feel. Try working the blocks in the same way using an ombre of your favorite color with a neutral background.

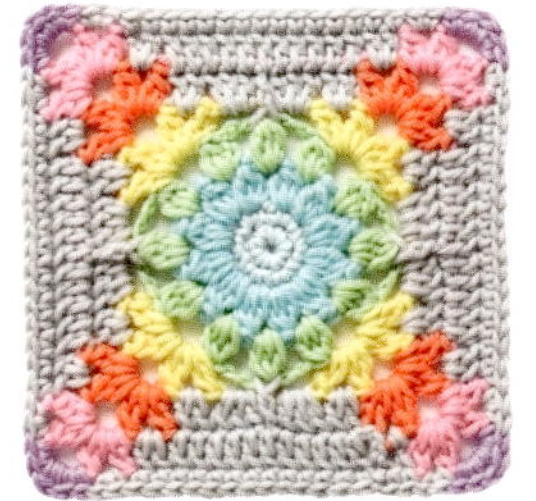
Variation Colorway 1

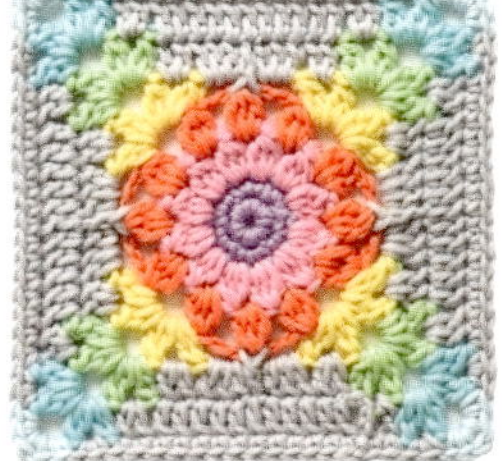
Variation Colorway 2

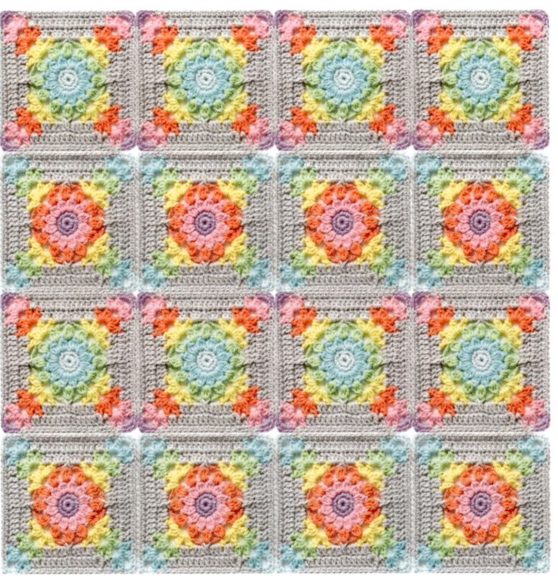

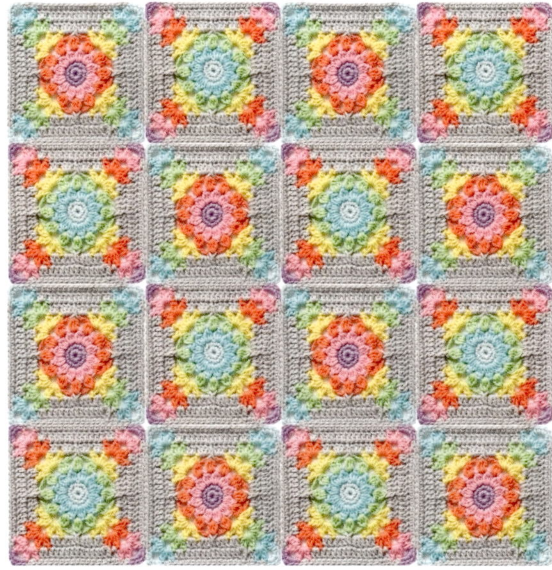

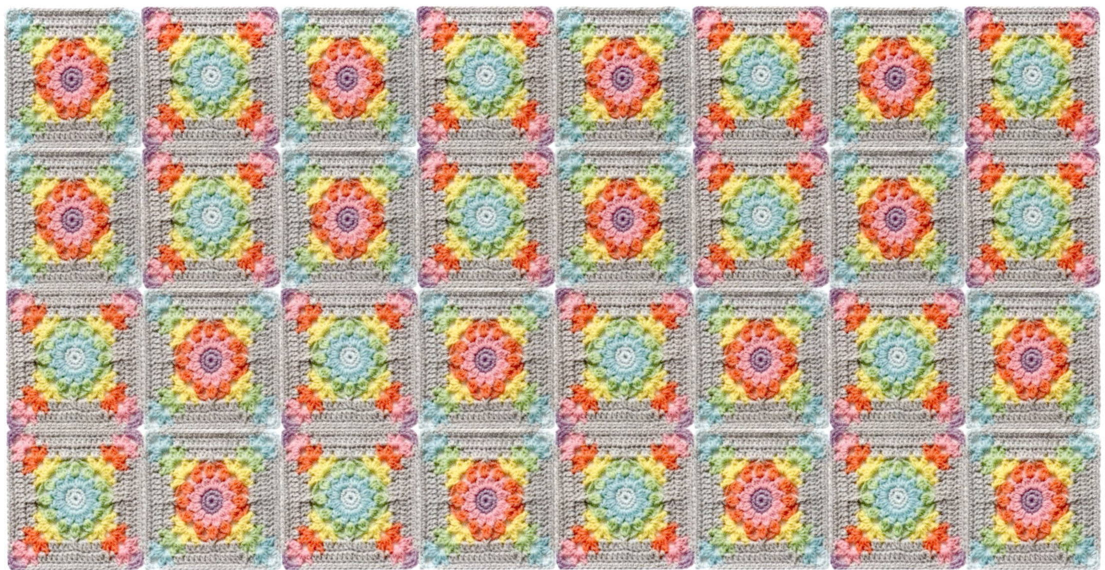

GEOMETRIC

Using two primary colors in two different combinations makes for a visually exciting pattern. I have also included a monochrome variation, as well as another variation where I include a pop of bright color. This really shows how effective just playing with color can be, the outcomes are so different but all use the same granny square design.

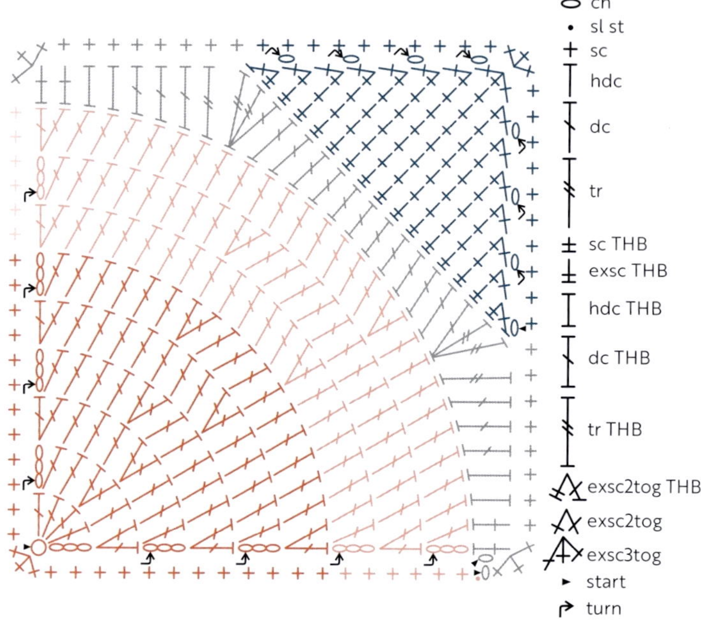

SKILL LEVEL: Advanced

BLOCK SIZE: 6" x 6" (15 x 15 cm)

HOOK SIZE: G/6 (4 mm)

YARN WEIGHT: DK

YARN: Cascade 220 Superwash®

Main Block

Yarn Requirements

Color A: 10 yd (9 m)

Color B: 8¾ yd (8 m)

Color C: 5 yd (4.5 m)

Color D: 7¾ yd (7 m)

Colorway 1

A: 290 (Chrysanthemum)

B: 1941 (Salmon)

C: 817 (Ecru)

D: 1960 (Pacific)

Colorway 2

A: 1960 (Pacific)

B: 1942 (Mint)

C: 817 (Ecru)

D: 290 (Chrysanthemum)

Variations

Work colorways 1 and 2 as for main block using color A instead of color D. For more variation, use color D randomly.

Yarn Requirements

Color A: 17½ yd (16 m)

Color B: 8¾ yd (8 m)

Color C: 5 yd (4.5 m)

Colorway 1

A: 871 (White)

B: 815 (Black)

C: 892 (Space Needle)

Colorway 2

A: 815 (Black)

B: 871 (White)

C: 892 (Space Needle)

Extra variation

D: 370 (Sulfur)

Abbreviations and Stitches

ch	chain
sl st	slip stitch
sc	single crochet
hdc	half-double crochet
dc	double crochet
tr	treble crochet
beg	beginning
st(s)	stitch(es)
THB	through horizontal bar
exsc	extended single crochet
exsc2tog	extended single crochet 2 together
exsc3tog	extended single crochet 3 together
( )	work instructions within brackets in place indicated

Crochet Pattern

Row 1 (RS): Using A, ch 4 (counts as 1 foundation ch and 1 dc), 4 dc in first ch made, turn—5 sts.

Row 2 (WS): Ch 3 (counts as dc throughout), dc in same place, dc in next st, 2 dc in next st, dc in next st, 2 dc in last st, turn —8 sts.

Row 3: Ch 3, dc in same place, dc in 2 sts, 2 dc in next st, dc in 3 sts, 2 dc in last st, turn—11 sts.

Row 4: Ch 3, dc in same place, dc in 3 sts, 2 dc in next st, dc in 5 sts, 2 dc in last st, turn—14 sts.

Row 5: Ch 3, dc in same place, dc in 4 sts, 2 dc in next st, dc in 7 sts, 2 dc in last st, turn—17 sts.

Row 6: Ch 3, dc in same place, dc in 5 sts, 2 dc in next st, dc in 9 sts, 2 dc in last st, changing to B when working last st, fasten off A, turn—20 sts.

Row 7: Ch 3, dc in same place, dc in 6 sts, 2 dc in next st, dc in 11 sts, 2 dc in last st, turn—23 sts.

Row 8: Ch 3, dc in same place, dc in 7 sts, 2 dc in next st, dc in 13 sts, 2 dc in last st, turn—26 sts.

Row 9: Ch 3, dc in same place, dc in 8 sts, 2 dc in next st, dc in 15 sts, 2 dc in last st, fasten off B, do not turn—29 sts.

Row 10 (RS): Join C THB in first st of last row, ch 1 (does not count as a st here and throughout), sc THB in same place, sc THB in next st, hdc THB in next 2 sts, dc THB in 3 sts, tr THB in next st, (2 tr THB, dc THB) in next st, dc THB in 11 sts, (dc THB, 2 tr THB) in next st, tr THB in next st, dc THB in 3 sts, hdc THB in 2 sts, sc THB in 2 sts, fasten off C, do not turn—33 sts.

Row 11: Join D THB in first tr of (2 tr, dc) group, ch 1, exsc2tog THB in first 2 sts, exsc THB in 13 sts, exsc2tog THB in next 2 sts, turn—15 sts.

Row 12: Ch 1, exsc2tog in first 2 sts, exsc in 11 sts, exsc2tog in last 2 sts, turn—13 sts.

Row 13: Ch 1, exsc2tog in first 2 sts, exsc in 9 sts, exsc2tog in last 2 sts, turn—11 sts.

Row 14: Ch 1, exsc2tog in first 2 sts, exsc in 7 sts, exsc2tog in last 2 sts, turn—9 sts.

Row 15: Ch 1, exsc2tog in first 2 sts, exsc in 5 sts, exsc2tog in last 2 sts, turn—7 sts.

Row 16: Ch 1, exsc2tog in first 2 sts, exsc in 3 sts, exsc2tog in last 2 sts, turn—5 sts.

Row 17: Ch 1, exsc2tog in first 2 sts, exsc in next st, exsc2tog in last 2 sts, turn—3 sts.

Row 18: Ch 1, exsc3tog over next 3 sts, ch 1 to close the st tightly, fasten off D—1 st.

Edging: Join C at beg of Row 10, ch 1 (does not count as a st), 3 sc in corner st, sc in 8 sts changing to D when working last st, 10 sc over next 7 row ends, 3 sc in corner st, 10 sc over next 7 row ends changing to C when working last st, sc in 8 sts, 3 sc in corner st changing to B when working last st, 6 sc over next 3 row ends changing to A when working last st, 12 sc over next 6 row ends, 3 sc in foundation ch, 12 sc over next 6 row ends changing to B when working last st, 6 sc over next 3 row ends, join with sl st to first st made, fasten off all yarns—84 sts.

Weave in all ends and block to measure 6" x 6" (15 x 15 cm).

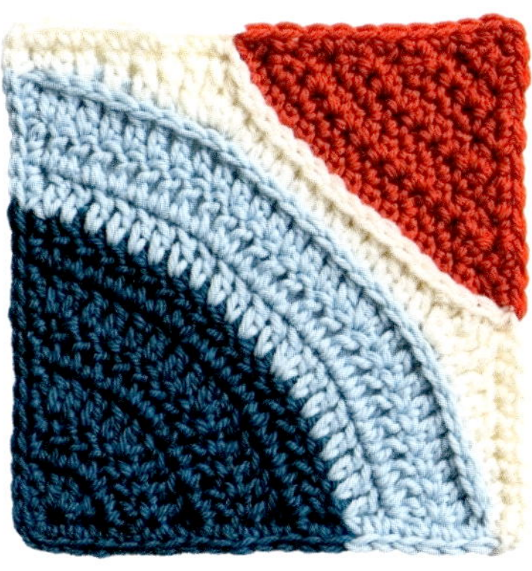

Main Block Colorway 2

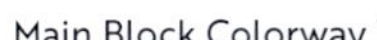

Main Block Colorway 1

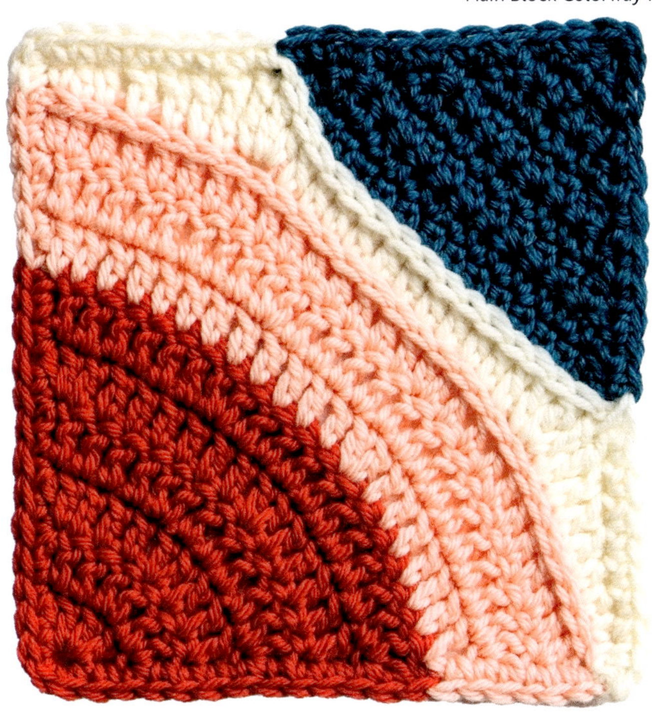

Two beautiful primary colors are paired in this palette. Red is a warm color and blue a cool color, so when they are combined they create a strong contrast. Adding in a lighter shade of each color, plus soft cream, helps to blend the blocks together so they do not contrast too strongly. Play with the blocks to see how many combinations you can make.

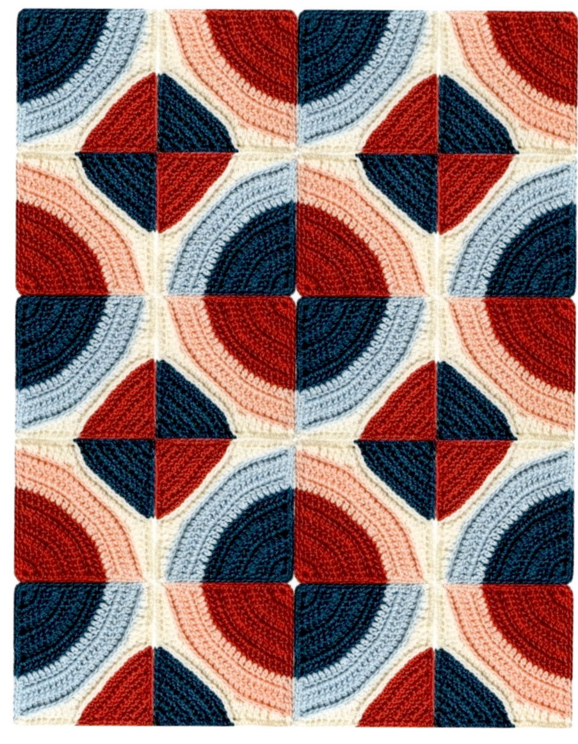

Scan the QR code for more information on the colorways used in the blocks on cover.

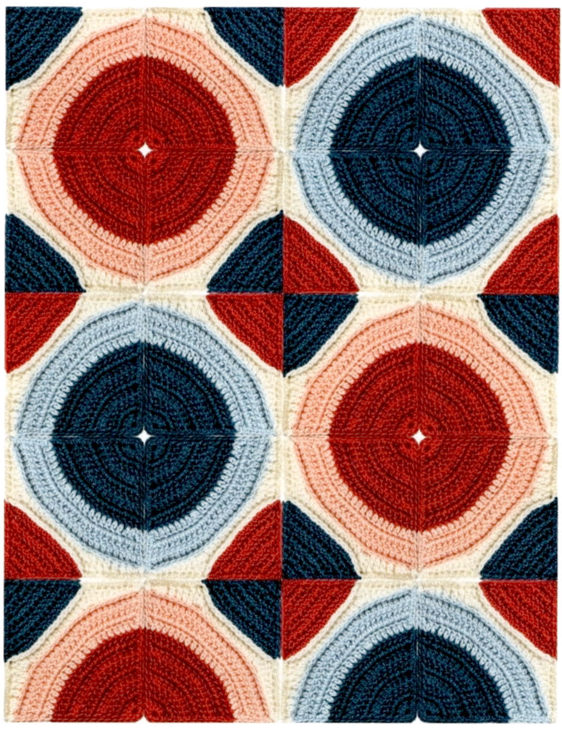

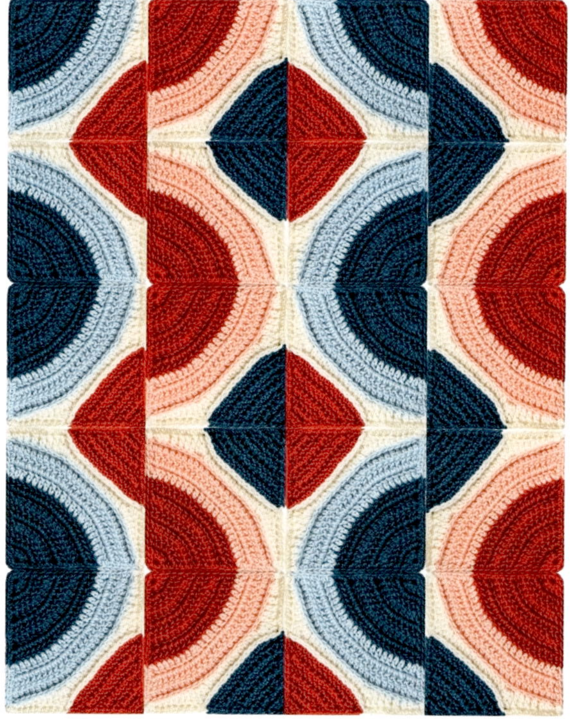

Neutrals such as black, gray, and off-white always look fantastic together. However, adding a well-placed splash of lime green really gives impact. You could use any bright or neon color as the "splash": hot pink, orange, neon blue, or a warm, saturated yellow.

Variation Colorways

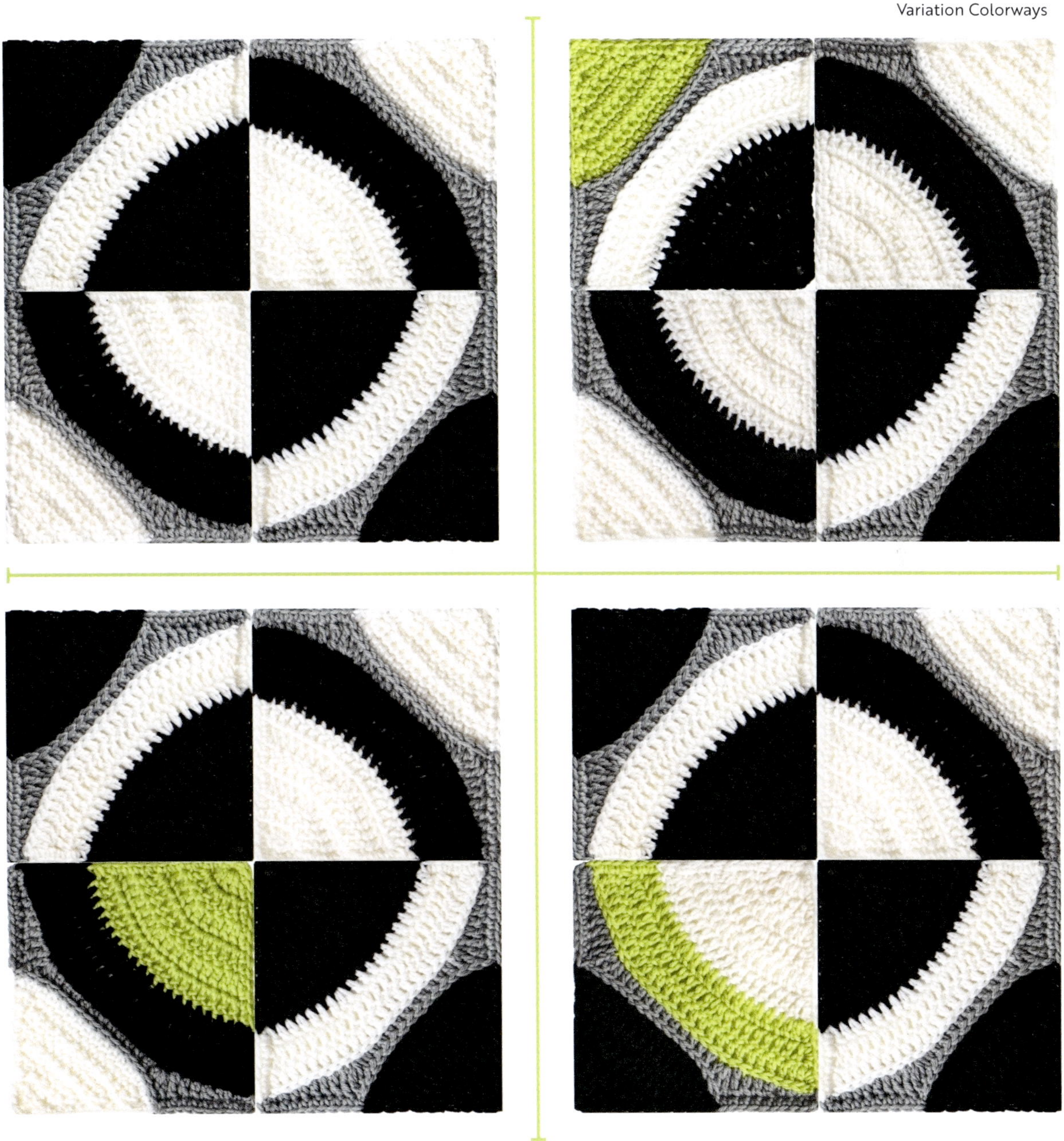

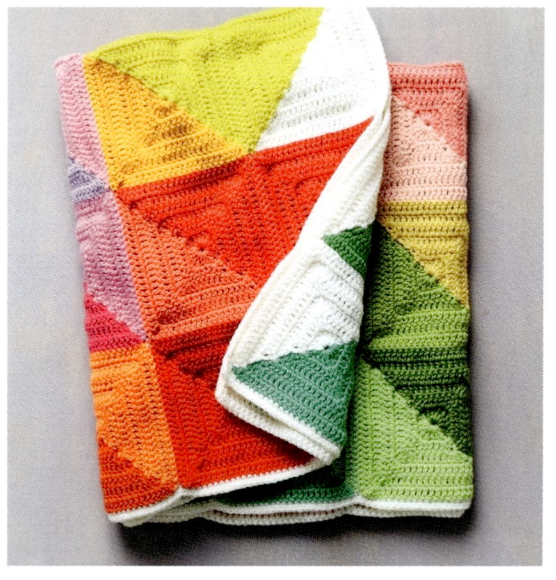

AFGHAN

This afghan project uses the Diagonal Split block (page 60), worked in lots of different color combinations—this is a great project for using up leftovers from the yarn stash!

SKILL LEVEL: Intermediate

SIZE: 36" x 48" (92 x 122 cm)

HOOK SIZE: G/6 (4 mm)

YARN WEIGHT: DK

YARN: Cascade 220 Superwash®

Yarn Requirements

Color A: 96¼ yd (88 m)
Color B: 382¾ yd (350 m)
Color C: 96¼ yd (88 m)
Color D: 96¼ yd (88 m)
Color E: 96¼ yd (88 m)
Color F: 96¼ yd (88 m)
Color G: 96¼ yd (88 m)
Color H: 48¼ yd (44 m)
Color I: 48¼ yd (44 m)
Color J: 48¼ yd (44 m)
Color K: 48¼ yd (44 m)
Color L: 48¼ yd (44 m)
Color M: 48¼ yd (44 m)
Color N: 48¼ yd (44 m)
Color O: 48¼ yd (44 m)
Color P: 48¼ yd (44 m)
Color Q: 48¼ yd (44 m)
Color R: 48¼ yd (44 m)
Color S: 48¼ yd (44 m)
Color T: 48¼ yd (44 m)
Color U: 48¼ yd (44 m)
Color V: 48¼ yd (44 m)
Color W: 48¼ yd (44 m)
Color X: 48¼ yd (44 m)
Color Y: 48¼ yd (44 m)
Color Z: 96¼ yd (88 m)
Color 1: 96¼ yd (88 m)
Color 2: 96¼ yd (88 m)
Color 3: 96¼ yd (88 m)
Color 4: 48¼ yd (44 m)
Color 5: 48¼ yd (44 m)
Color 6: 48¼ yd (44 m)
Color 7: 48¼ yd (44 m)

A: 809 (Really Red)
B: 871 (White)
C: 287 (Deep Sea Coral)
D: 346 (Daisy Yellow)
E: 370 (Sulfur)
F: 906 (Chartreuse)
G: 288 (Green Spruce)
H 344 (Cherry Tomato)
I: 827 (Coral)
J: 263 (Gold Fusion)
K: 820 (Lemon)
L: 887 (Wasabi)
M: 850 (Lime Sherbet)
N: 907 (Tangerine Heather)
O: 345 (Autumn Sunset)
P: 837 (Berry Pink)
Q: 901 (Cotton Candy)
R: 842 (Light Iris)
S: 835 (Pink Rose)
T: 1940 (Peach)
U: 1941 (Salmon)
V: 821 (Daffodil)
W: 886 (Citron)
X: 841 (Moss)
Y: 851 (Lime)
Z: 1973 (Seafoam Heather)
1: 259 (Blue Turquoise)
2: 227 (Bachelor Button)
3: 812 (Turquoise)
4: 847 (Caribbean)
5: 252 (Celestial)
6: 311 (Blue Sapphire)
7: 351 (Pale Jade)

Abbreviations and Stitches

ch	chain
sl st	slip stitch
sc	single crochet
hdc	half-double crochet
tr	treble crochet
st(s)	stitch(es)
[ ]	repeat instructions within brackets the stated number of times
( )	work instructions within brackets in place indicated

Note

- You can change the look of this afghan by angling the blocks in different directions. Alternatively, you could create an afghan using a more limited color palette but still following the assembly diagram.

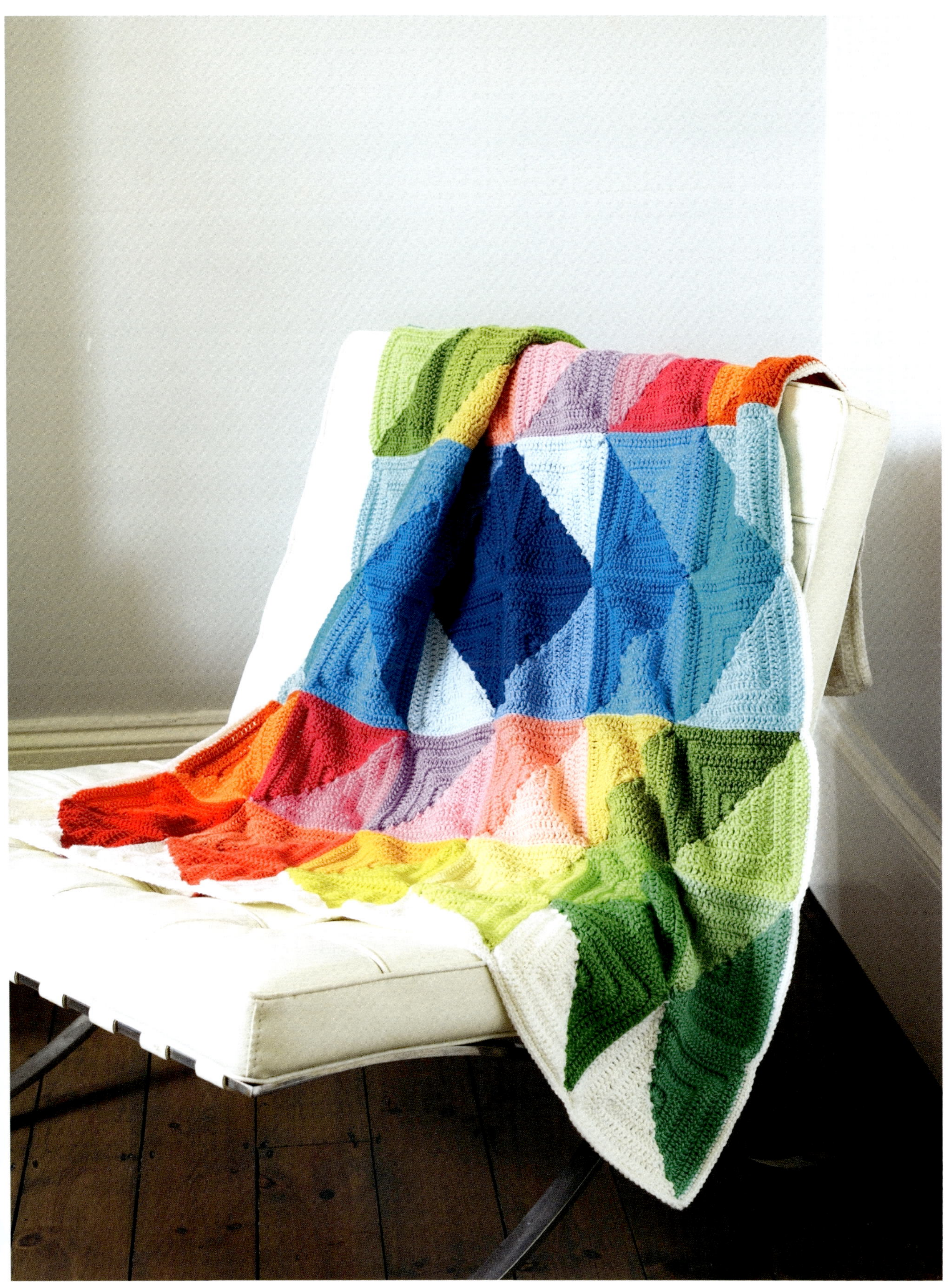

Instructions

Make 48 blocks following the Diagonal Split block pattern (page 60) using the following color combinations:

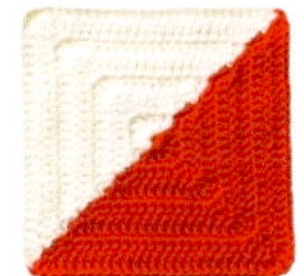

Diagonal Split

2 x yarn A and yarn B
2 x yarn C and yarn B
2 x yarn D and yarn B
2 x yarn E and yarn B
2 x yarn F and yarn B
2 x yarn G and yarn B
2 x yarn A and yarn H
2 x yarn I and yarn C
2 x yarn J and yarn D
2 x yarn K and yarn E
2 x yarn L and yarn F
2 x yarn M and yarn G
2 x yarn N and yarn O
2 x yarn P and yarn Q
2 x yarn R and yarn S
2 x yarn T and yarn U
2 x yarn V and yarn W
2 x yarn X and yarn Y
4 x yarn Z and yarn 1
4 x yarn 2 and yarn 3
2 x yarn 4 and yarn 5
2 x yarn 6 and yarn 7

Weave in all ends and block all squares to measure 6" x 6" (15 x 15 cm)

ASSEMBLY DIAGRAM

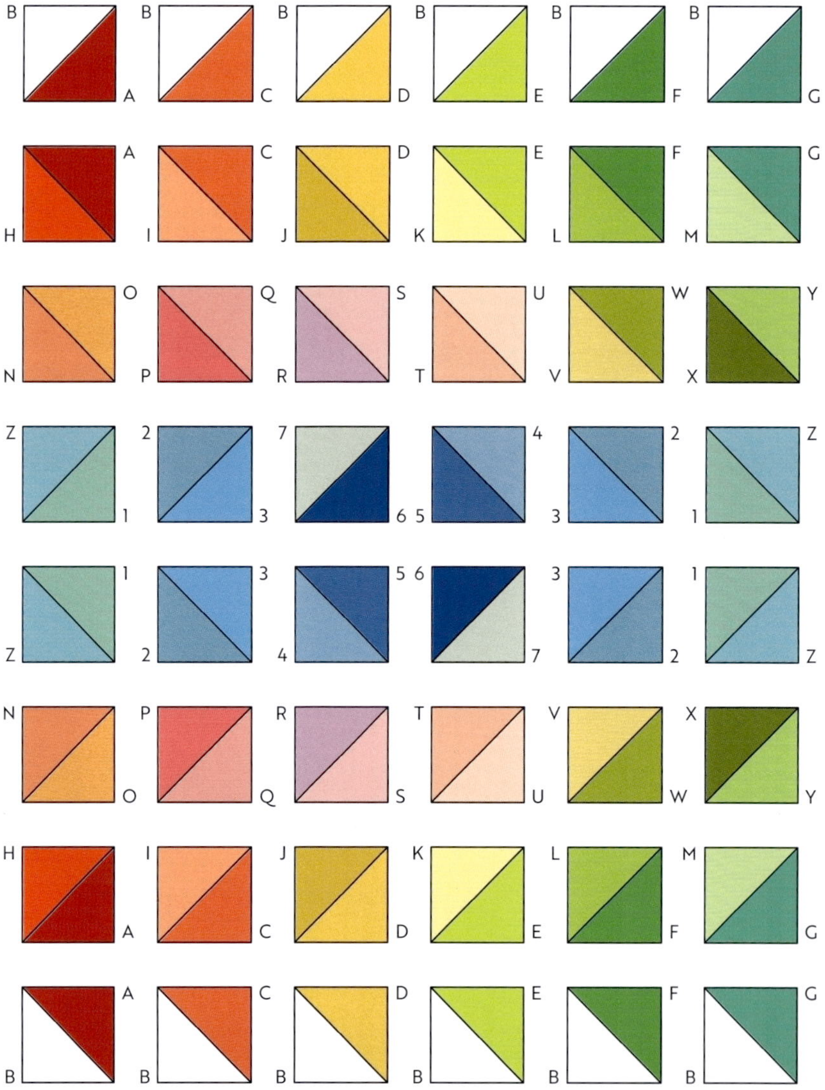

Assembly

Following the assembly diagram, join the blocks using the mattress stitch (see Crochet Seams on page 24) and working in a midtone yarn color.

Edging

Rnd 1: With RS facing, join B in any right-hand tr of 2 corner tr sts, ch 1, [(sc, hdc) in first corner tr, (hdc, sc) in next corner tr, sc in each st to next corner tr] four times, join with sl st to first st made.

Rnd 2: Ch 1, sc in same place, [(sc, hdc) in first corner hdc, (hdc, sc) in next corner hdc, sc in each st to next corner hdc] four times, join with sl st to first st made.

Rnd 3: Ch 1, sc in 2 sts, [(sc, hdc) in first corner hdc, (hdc, sc) in next corner hdc, sc in each st to next corner hdc] four times, join with sl st to first st made, fasten off B.

PILLOW

This pillow uses the Diagonal Split block (page 60) and Circle Diagonally block (page 88). Both sides of the pillow are the same. This project would also look nice in a monochrome colorway to match your home décor.

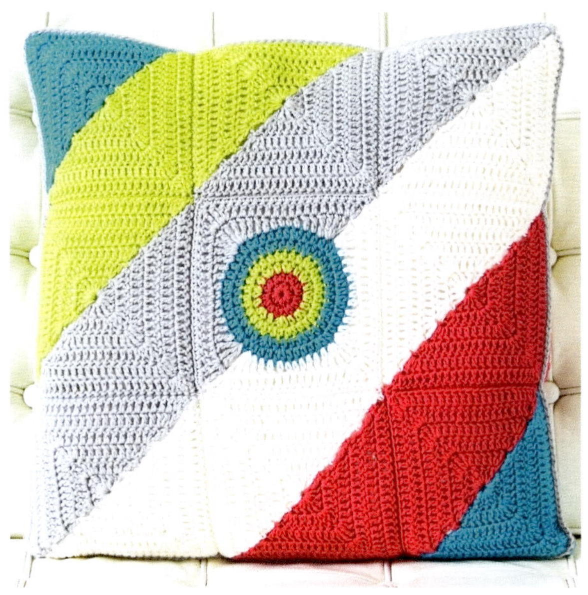

SKILL LEVEL: Intermediate

SIZE: 18" x 18" (46 x 46 cm)

HOOK SIZE: G/6 (4 mm)

YARN WEIGHT: DK

YARN: Cascade 220 Superwash®

Yarn Requirements

Color A: 151 yd (138 m)
Color B: 155½ yd (142 m)
Color C: 111½ yd (102 m)
Color D: 214½ yd (196 m)
Color E: 214½ yd (196 m)

A: 837 (Berry Pink)
B: 370 (Sulfur)
C: 259 (Blue Turquoise)
D: 338 (Harbor Mist)
E: 871 (White)

Abbreviations and Stitches

ch	chain
sl st	slip stitch
sc	single crochet
hdc	half-double crochet
tr	treble crochet
st(s)	stitch(es)
[ ]	repeat instructions within brackets the stated number of times
( )	work instructions within brackets in place indicated

Note

- You'll need an 18" x 18" (46 x 46 cm) pillow form insert.

Instructions

Make two blocks using the Circle Diagonally pattern (page 88). Work each in the colorway given on page 115.

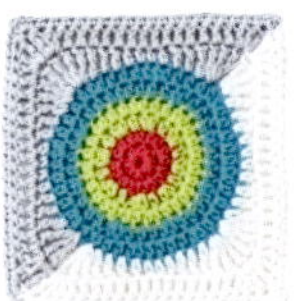

Circle Diagonally

To make the blocks easier to join a small change is needed on the final round. Work Rnd 9 as follows:

Rnd 9 (RS): Ch 1, [(hdc, 2 sc) in first tr, sc in each st to next tr, (2 sc, hdc) in tr] twice changing to E when working last hdc, [(hdc, 2 sc) in tr, sc in each st to next tr, (2 sc, hdc) in tr] twice, join with sl st to top of first hdc made, fasten off both colors—96 sts.

Make 16 blocks using the Diagonal Split pattern (page 60). Work each block to Rnd 6 only, in the following colorways:

2 x yarn A and yarn C
2 x yarn B and yarn C
4 x yarn A and yarn E
4 x yarn B and yarn D
4 x yarn D and yarn E

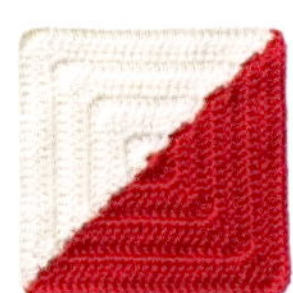

Diagonal Split

Weave in all ends and block all squares to measure 6" x 6" (15 x 15 cm)

Assembly

Make two panels by joining the blocks following the assembly diagram and with right sides facing, use a crochet sl st join (see Crochet Seams, page 24). Make sure to change color as you are joining to match the color of the stitches you are working into.

Block both panels to measure 18" x 18" (46 x 46 cm).

Join the two panels together either by using a crochet sl st join or by sewing with right sides facing. Once three edges have been joined, insert the pillow form insert, then continue to sew or crochet the last edge together.

ASSEMBLY DIAGRAM

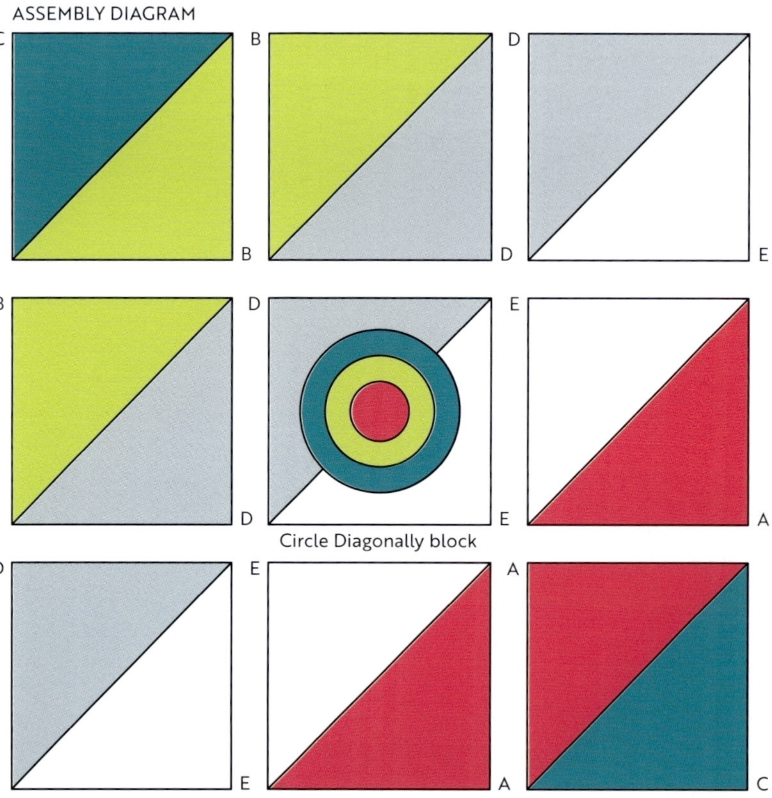

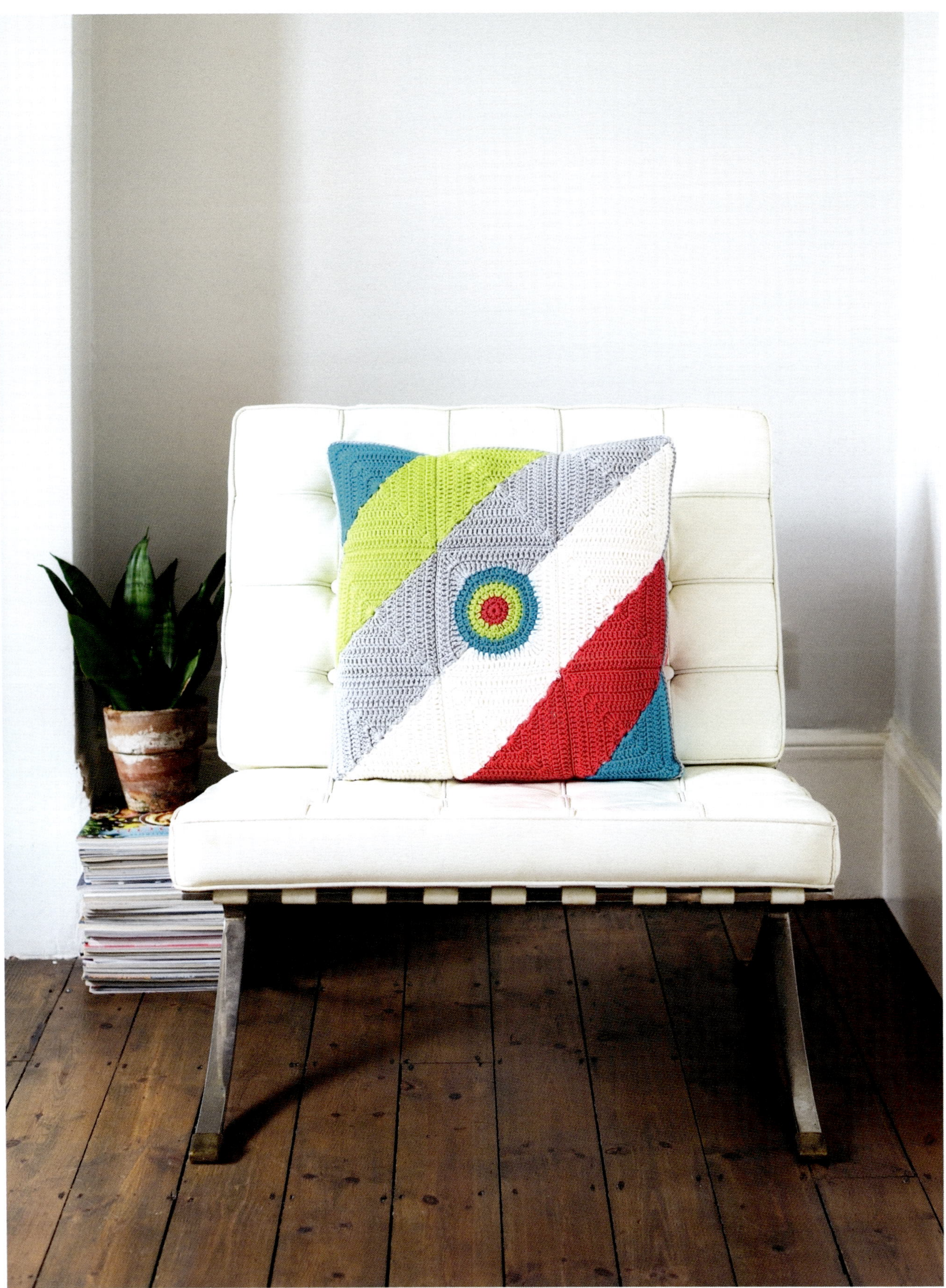

WALL HANGING

This wall hanging combines several squares from the book, plus an additional smaller square. Only four colors are used in this project, so it can easily be worked in colors to suit your décor. You can use a piece of dowel or forage for a suitably nice stick from outdoors to hang the finished piece.

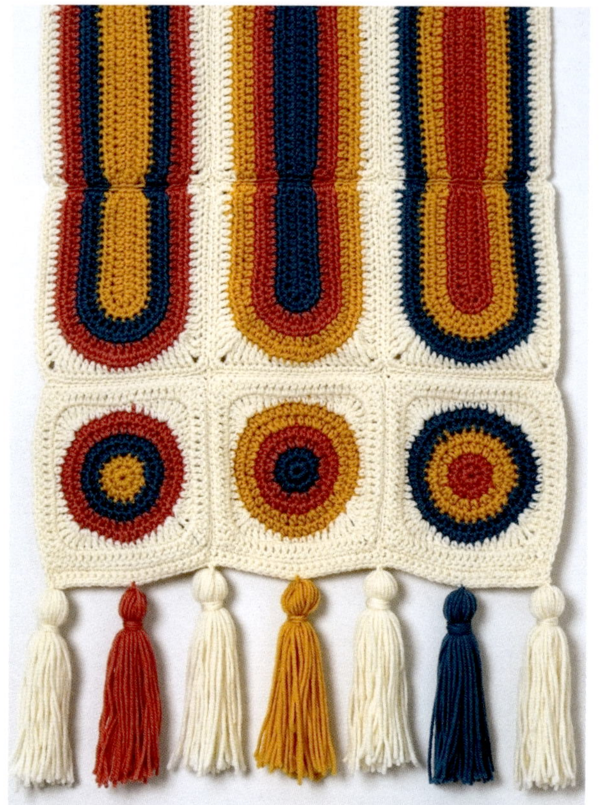

SKILL LEVEL: Intermediate

SIZE: 18" x 22" (46 x 56 cm)

HOOK SIZE: G/6 (4 mm)

YARN WEIGHT: DK

YARN: Cascade 220 Superwash®

Yarn Requirements

Color A: 93 yd (85 m)
Color B: 93 yd (85 m)
Color C: 93 yd (85 m)
Color D: 183¾ yd (168 m)

You'll need extra yarn if you are adding tassels.

A: 877 (Golden)
B: 354 (Mallard Blue)
C: 364 (Faded Rose)
D: 817 (Ecru)

Abbreviations and Stitches

ch	chain
sl st	slip stitch
sc	single crochet
hdc	half-double crochet
dc	double crochet
tr	treble crochet
beg	beginning
st(s)	stitch(es)
[ ]	repeat instructions within brackets the stated number of times
( )	work instructions within brackets in place indicated

Small Block Pattern

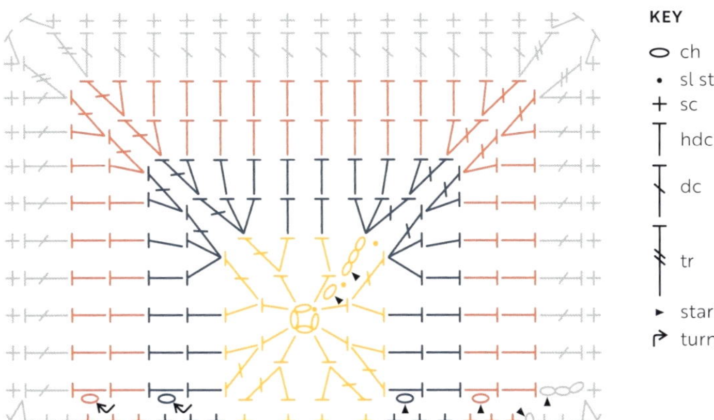

Foundation Ring: Using A, ch 4, join with sl st to first ch made to form a ring.

Rnd 1 (RS): Ch 1 (does not count as a st), 8 hdc into ring, join with sl st to top of first hdc made—8 sts.

Rnd 2: Ch 3 (counts as dc), hdc in same place, [(hdc, dc) in next st, (dc, hdc) in next st] three times, (hdc, dc) in last st, join with sl st to top of beg ch-3, fasten off A—16 sts.

Row 3 (RS): Join in B in any dc of (dc, hdc) group, ch 1, hdc in same place, [hdc in next 2 sts, (2 hdc, dc) in next st, (dc, 2 hdc) in next st] twice, hdc in next 3 sts, turn—20 sts.

Row 4 (WS): Ch 1, hdc in next 5 sts, (hdc, dc) in next st, (dc, hdc) in next st, hdc in next 6 sts, (hdc, dc) in next st, (dc, hdc) in next st, hdc in next 5 sts, fasten off B, turn—24 sts.

Row 5: Join in C, ch 1, hdc in next 6 sts, (hdc, dc) in next st, (dc, hdc) in next st, hdc in next 8 sts, (hdc, dc) in next st, (dc, hdc) in next st, hdc in next 6 sts, turn—28 sts.

Row 6: Ch 1, hdc in next 7 sts, (hdc, dc) in next st, (dc, hdc) in next st, hdc in next 10 sts, (hdc, dc) in next st, (dc, hdc) in next st, hdc in next 7 sts, fasten off C, turn—32 sts.

Row 7: Join in D, ch 3 (counts as dc), dc in next 7 sts, (dc, tr) in next st, (tr, dc) in next st, dc in next 12 sts, (dc, tr) in next st, (tr, dc) in next st, dc in 8 sts, fasten off D—36 sts.

Rnd 8: Join in D around post of first st of previous rnd, ch 1, 2 sc around post, (sc, hdc, sc) in next st, sc in next 8 sts, (sc, hdc) in next st, (hdc, sc) in next st, sc in next 14 sts, (sc, hdc) in next st, (hdc, sc) in next st, sc in next 8 sts, (sc, hdc, sc) in next st, 2 sc around post of same st changing to C when working last st, work 3 sc across next 2 row ends changing to B when working last st, work 3 sc across next 2 row ends changing to A when working last st, sc in next 4 sts changing to B when working last st, 3 sc across next 2 row ends changing to C when working last st, 3 sc across next 2 row ends, join with sl st to first st made, fasten off all yarns—64 sts.

Weave in ends and block to measure 6" x 3" (15 x 8 cm).

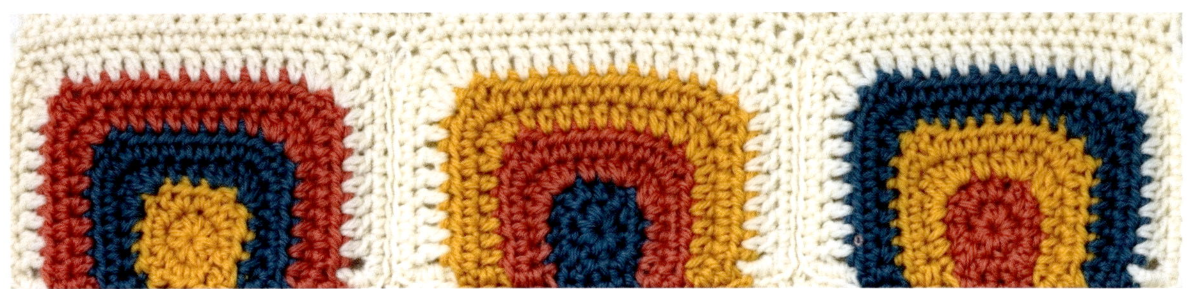

Instructions

Make three blocks using the Arch pattern (page 56) in the following colorways:

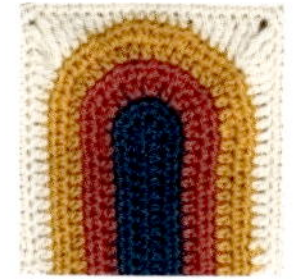

Arch

Block 1
A: 877 (Golden)
B: 354 (Mallard Blue)
C: 364 (Faded Rose)
D: 817 (Ecru)

Block 2
A: 354 (Mallard Blue)
B: 364 (Faded Rose)
C: 877 (Golden)
D: 817 (Ecru)

Block 3
A: 364 (Faded Rose)
B: 877 (Golden)
C: 354 (Mallard Blue)
D: 817 (Ecru)

Make three blocks using the Central Stripe pattern (page 40) in the following colorways:

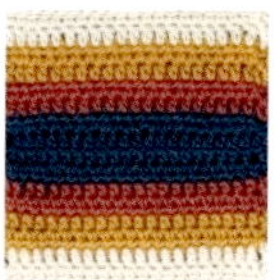

Central Stripe

Block 1
A: 877 (Golden)
B: 354 (Mallard Blue)
C: 364 (Faded Rose)
D: 817 (Ecru)

Block 2
A: 354 (Mallard Blue)
B: 364 (Faded Rose)
C: 877 (Golden)
D: 817 (Ecru)

Block 3
A: 364 (Faded Rose)
B: 877 (Golden)
C: 354 (Mallard Blue)
D: 817 (Ecru)

Make three blocks using the Circle Diagonally pattern (page 88) in the following colorways:

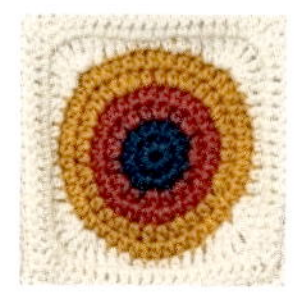

Circle Diagonally

Block 1
A: 877 (Golden)
B: 354 (Mallard Blue)
C: 364 (Faded Rose)
D: 817 (Ecru)

Block 2
A: 354 (Mallard Blue)
B: 364 (Faded Rose)
C: 877 (Golden)
D: 817 (Ecru)

Block 3
A: 364 (Faded Rose)
B: 877 (Golden)
C: 354 (Mallard Blue)
D: 817 (Ecru)

Make three Small Blocks using the pattern on page 119 in the following colorways:

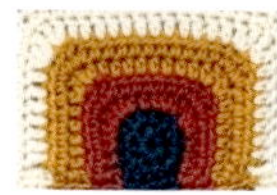

Small Block

Block 1
A: 877 (Golden)
B: 354 (Mallard Blue)
C: 364 (Faded Rose)
D: 817 (Ecru)

Block 2
A: 354 (Mallard Blue)
B: 364 (Faded Rose)
C: 877 (Golden)
D: 817 (Ecru)

Block 3
A: 364 (Faded Rose)
B: 877 (Golden)
C: 354 (Mallard Blue)
D: 817 (Ecru)

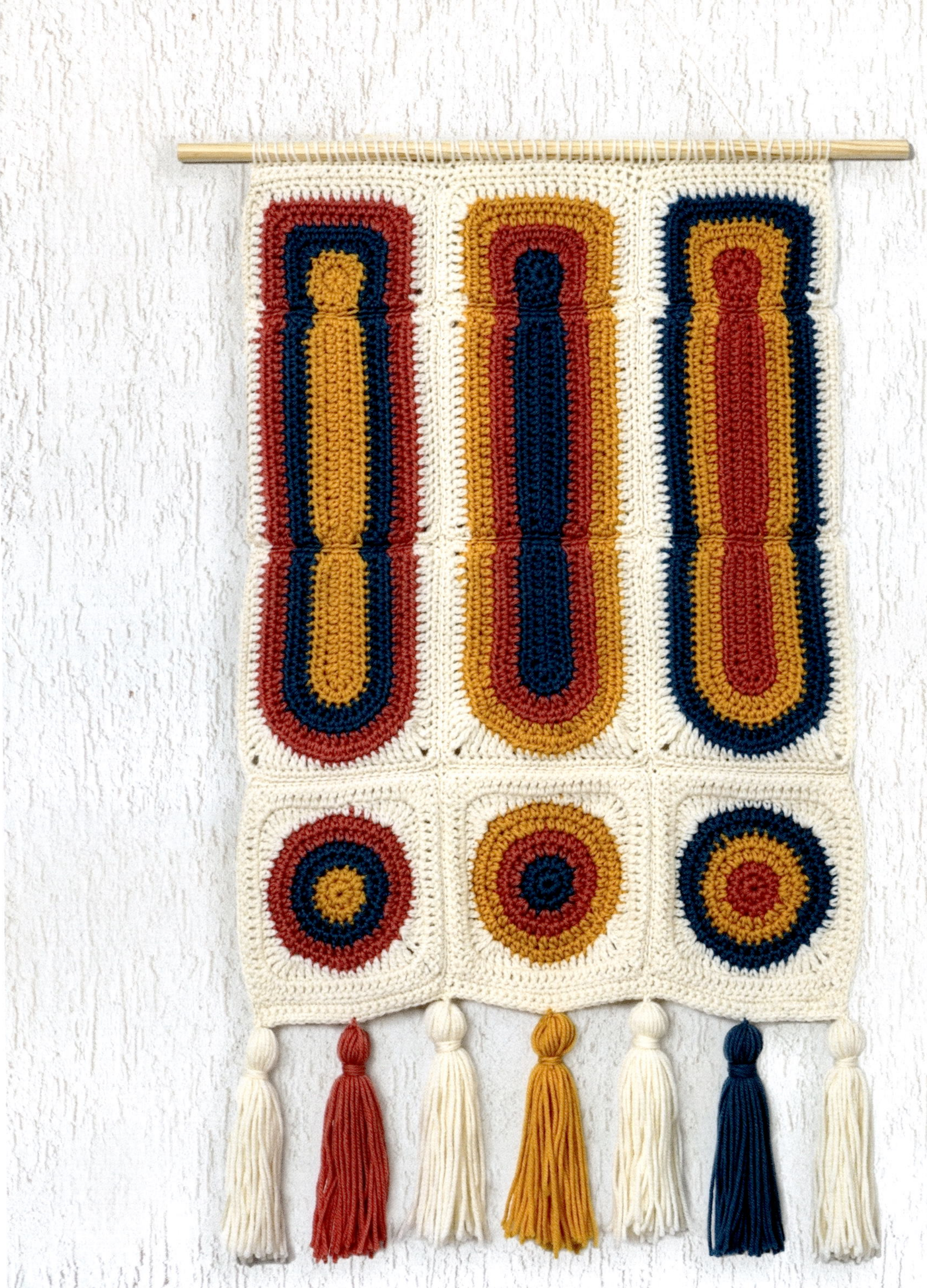

ASSEMBLY DIAGRAM

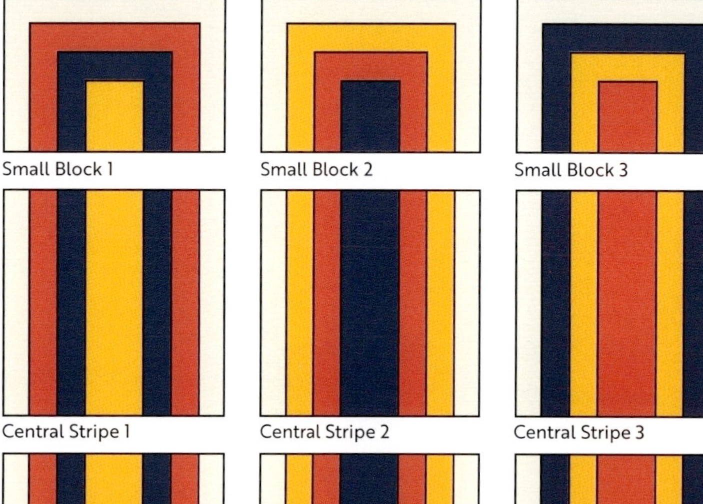

Small Block 1 | Small Block 2 | Small Block 3

Central Stripe 1 | Central Stripe 2 | Central Stripe 3

Arch 1 | Arch 2 | Arch 3

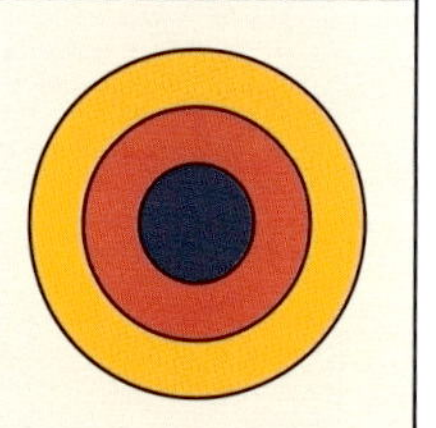

Circle Diagonally 1 | Circle Diagonally 2 | Circle Diagonally 3

Assembly

Join the blocks following the assembly diagram. With right sides together join by using crochet sl st join (see Crochet Seams, page 24). Make sure to change color as you are joining to match the color of the stitches you are working into.

Top Edging

Row 1 (WS): Using D, ch 1 (does not count as a st), work sc in each st across the top of the piece, turn—54 sts.
Row 2 (RS): Ch 1, sc in each st across, fasten off.
Weave in yarn ends.

Bottom Edging

Row 1 (WS): Using D, ch 1 (does not count as a st), work sc in each st across the bottom of the piece, turn—66 sts.
Row 2 (RS): Ch 1, sc in each st across, fasten off.
Weave in yarn ends.

Prepare to Hang

Attach the hanging to a suitable piece of dowel or branch by sewing. Begin by inserting the needle from back to front through the first st of the piece, bring the yarn over the dowel. Continue in the same way in each st across. You can also add some tassels to the bottom of the hanging if you have enough yarn to spare (see Making Tassels, page 25).

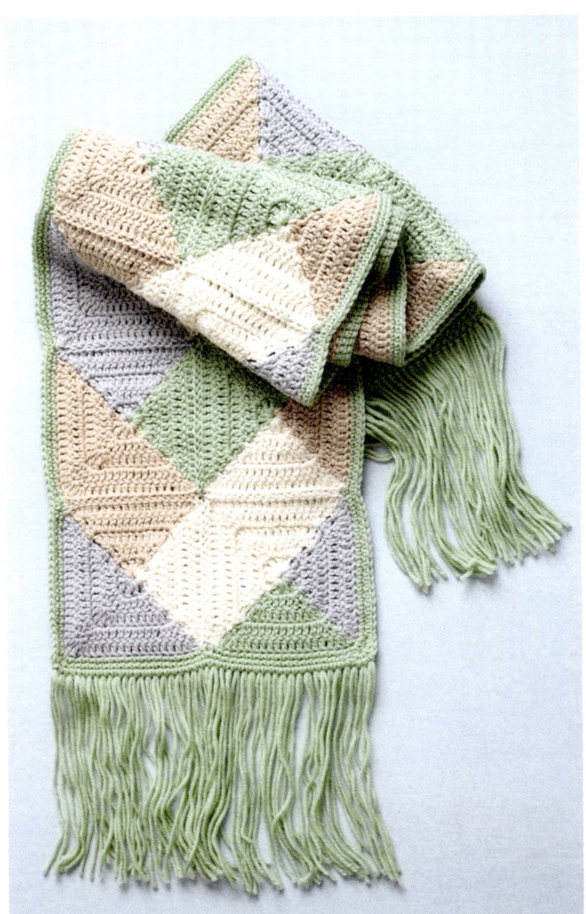

SCARF

This scarf is made using the Diagonal Double Split block (page 32), worked in four different colorways. Once joined, the blocks create a herringbone pattern. You could work this scarf in any four colors you fancy for a cozy geometric accessory.

SKILL LEVEL: Intermediate

SIZE: 10" x 60" (26 x 153 cm)

HOOK SIZE: E/4 (3.5 mm)

YARN WEIGHT: DK

YARN: Cascade 220 Superwash®

Yarn Requirements

Color A: 192½ yd (176 m)
Color B: 192½ yd (176 m)
Color C: 192½ yd (176 m)
Color D: 230 yd (210 m)

A: 338 (Harbor Mist)
B: 817 (Ecru)
C: 228 (Frosted Almond)
D: 250 (Laurel Green)

Abbreviations and Stitches

ch	chain
sl st	slip stitch
sc	single crochet
hdc	half-double crochet
tr	treble crochet
st(s)	stitch(es)
[ ]	repeat instructions within brackets the stated number of times
( )	work instructions within brackets in place indicated

Note

- To adjust the scarf width, you could work fewer or more rounds on each block. To increase the length, you can crochet more blocks, to decrease the length, crochet fewer blocks. For this scarf I've worked only up until Rnd 5 of the block, which creates a block measuring 5" x 5" (13 x 13 cm).

Instructions

Using the pattern for Diagonal Double Split (page 32), make 24 blocks. Work each block to Rnd 5 only and in the following colorways:

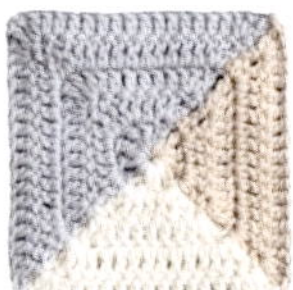

Diagonal Double Split

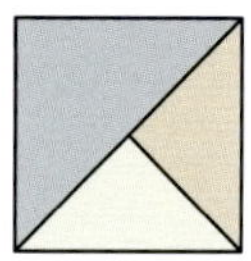

Block 1 (make 4)
A: 338 (Harbor Mist)
B: 817 (Ecru)
C: 228 (Frosted Almond)

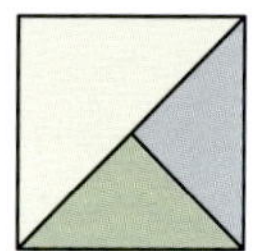

Block 2 (make 4)
A: 817 (Ecru)
B: 250 (Laurel Green)
C: 338 (Harbor Mist)

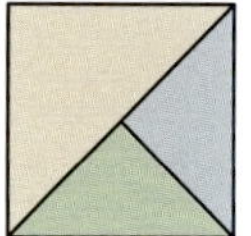

Block 3 (make 4)
A: 228 (Frosted Almond)
B: 250 (Laurel Green)
C: 338 (Harbor Mist)

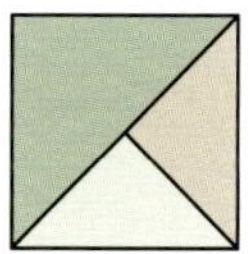

Block 4 (make 4)
A: 250 (Laurel Green)
B: 817 (Ecru)
C: 228 (Frosted Almond)

Weave in all ends and block all squares to measure 5" x 5" (13 x 13 cm).

Assembly

Following the assembly diagram, join the blocks using the mattress stitch method (see Crochet Seams, page 24) and yarn D.

Edging

Rnd 1: With RS facing, join D in any right-hand tr of 2 corner tr sts, ch 1, [(sc, hdc) in first corner tr, (hdc, sc) in next corner tr, sc in each st to next corner tr] four times, join with sl st to first st made.
Rnd 2: Ch 1, sc in same place, [(sc, hdc) in first corner hdc, (hdc, sc) in next corner hdc, sc in each st to next corner hdc] four times, join with sl st to first st made, fasten off D.

Fringe

If you have yarn to spare you can add a fringe along the short edges of the scarf. Add a fringe as follows: Cut 20" (51 cm) lengths of yarn D, one for each st along your short edges. Fold in half and, using a crochet hook, pull the folded loop through the stitch. Pick up the yarn tails and pull through the loop made. Pull on the yarn tails to tighten.

ASSEMBLY DIAGRAM

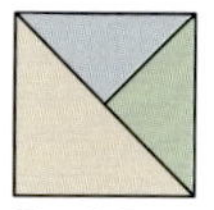
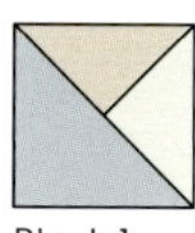
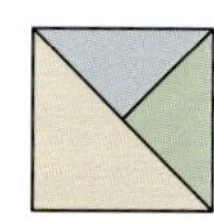
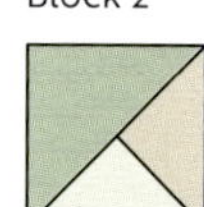
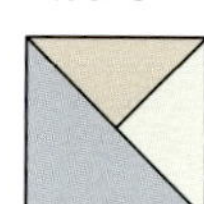
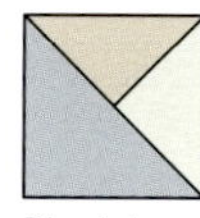
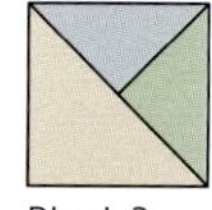
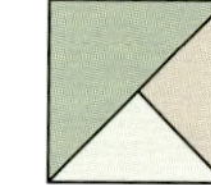
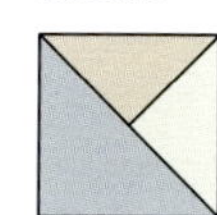
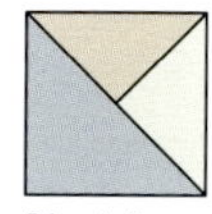
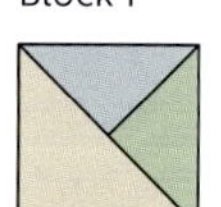
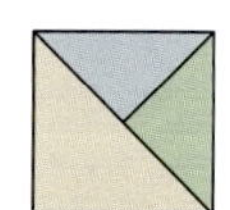
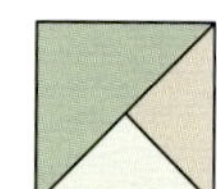
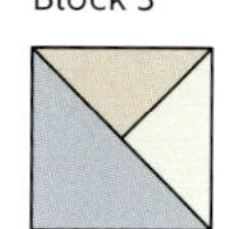
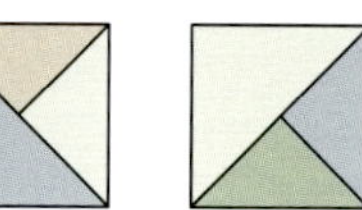
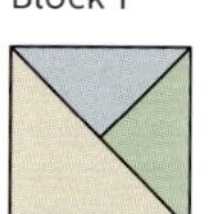
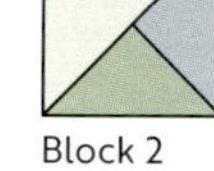
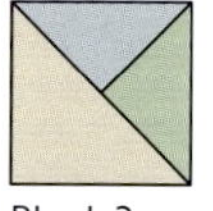
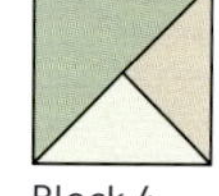
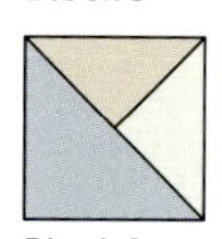
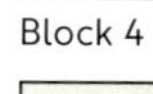
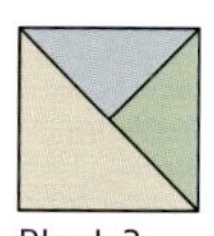
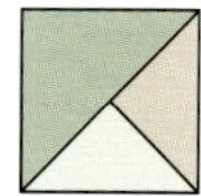
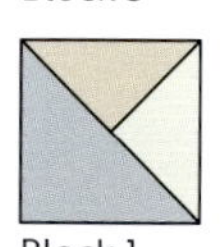

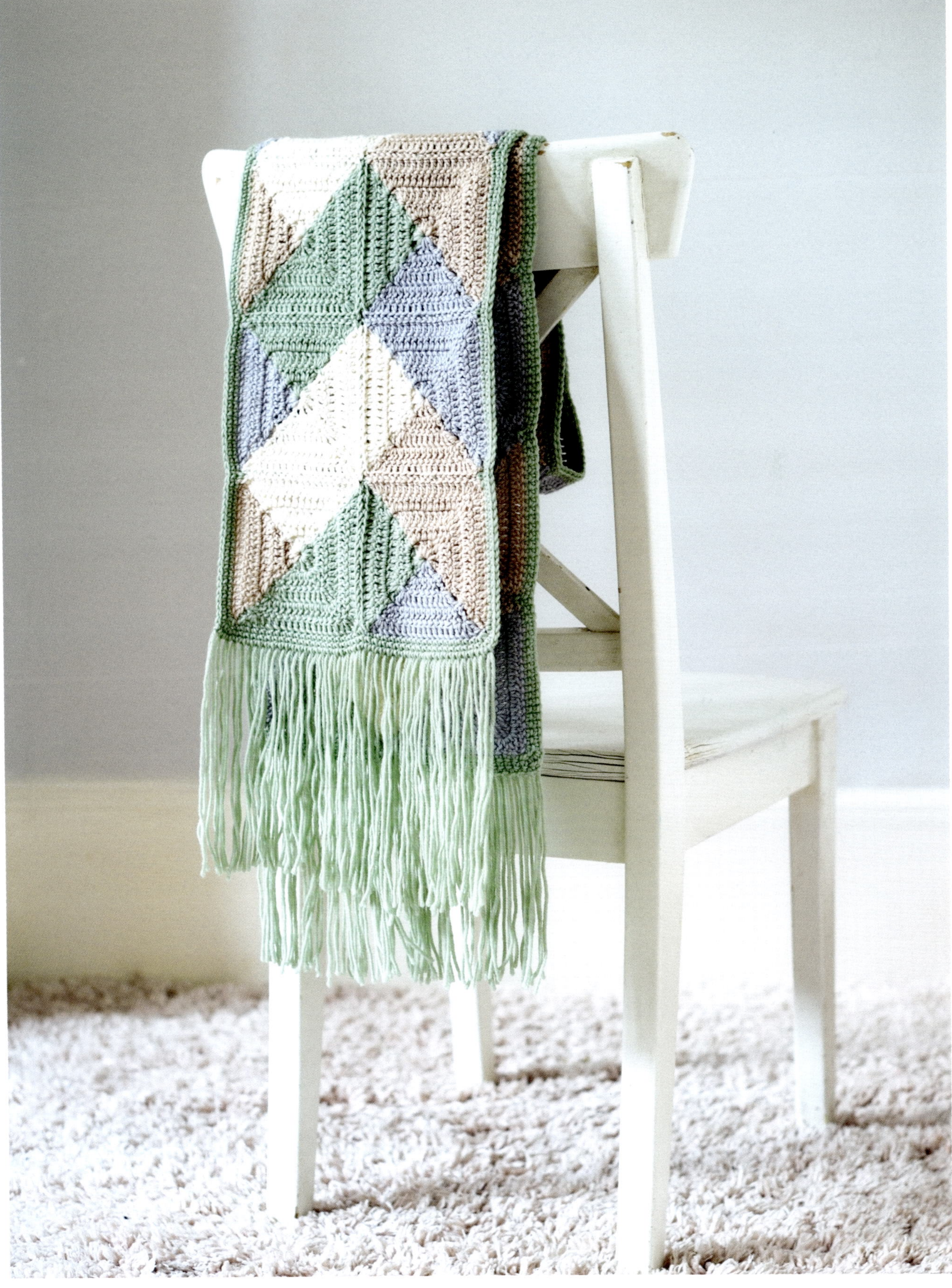

INDEX

ACKNOWLEDGMENTS

For my mum. A gruelling year is complete. Now for many more!

Thank you to Sean, as always—now and forever.
Thanks to Hubble the cat for finding my best crochet hook under the sofa. (You'll see his fur in the photos, no doubt!)

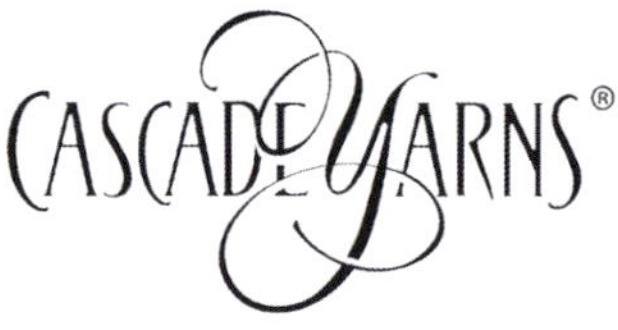

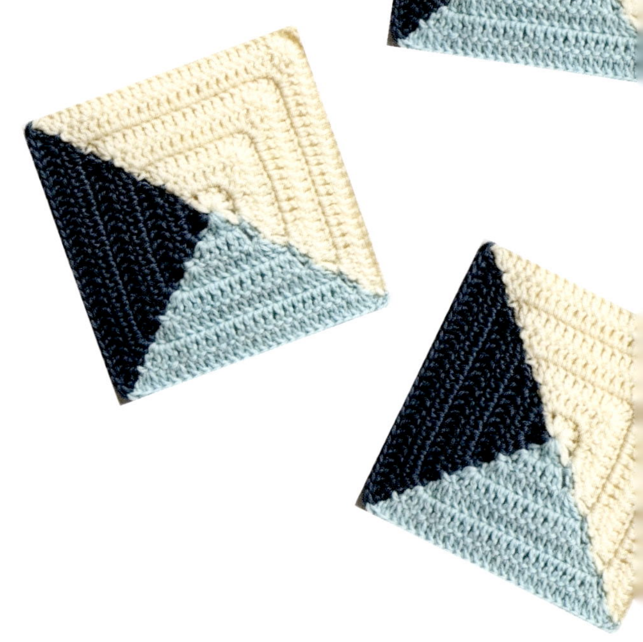

Quarto would like to thank Cascade Yarns® for supplying all the yarn used in this book.

For a full list of yarns available, please visit their website:
www.cascadeyarns.com

You can also find them on Instagram @cascadeyarns

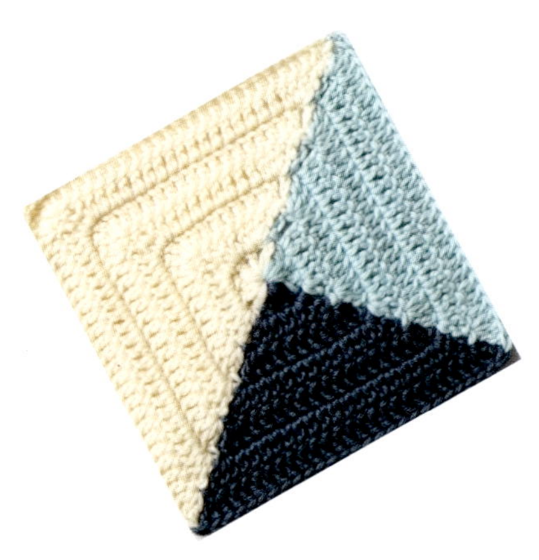

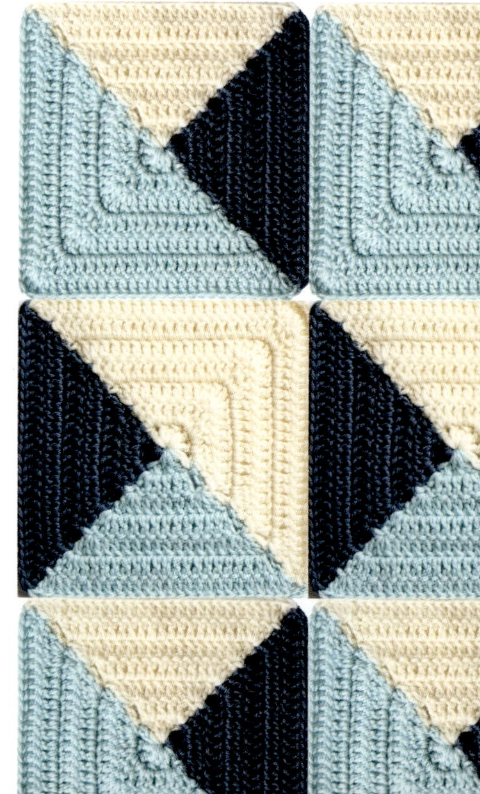